D1576136

Jesus Christ

Before He Became a
Superstar

JAMES K. FITZPATRICK

JESUS CHRIST

BEFORE HE BECAME A
SUPERSTAR

ARLINGTON HOUSE·PUBLISHERS
NEW ROCHELLE, NEW YORK

Manufactured in the United States of America

Library of Congress Cataloging in Publication Data

Fitzpatrick, James K
    Jesus Christ, before he became a superstar.

    1.   Jesus Christ—Person and offices. 2.   Apolo-
getics—20th century. I. Title.
BT202.F59   232   76-8829
ISBN 0-87000-361-5

For Brendan and Eileen

When the Round Table is broken every man must
follow Galahad or Mordred; middle things are gone.

C.S. Lewis

If our religious tenets should ever want a further
elucidation, we shall not call on Atheism to explain them.
We shall not light up our temple from that unholy fire.

Edmund Burke

We are always faced with both the question 'what must be
destroyed?' and with the question 'what must be preserved?'
and neither Liberalism nor Conservatism, which are not philos-
ophies and may be merely habits, is enough to guide us.

T.S. Eliot

The blood-dimmed tide is loosed, and everywhere
The ceremony of innocence is drowned;
The best lack all conviction, while the worst
Are full of passionate intensity.
Surely some revelation is at hand . . .
And what rough beast, its hour come round at last,
Slouches towards Bethlehem to be born?

William Butler Yeats

The philospher might speculate, but the theologian must
submit to learn.

John Henry Newman

Foreword

I AM WRITING in an attempt to rescue the Faith of our Fathers. That must sound pompous coming from someone who is neither theologian nor Scripture scholar. But bear with me for a moment.

First of all, unless I am completely out of touch with the world, many of you will agree that the Faith needs rescuing. I can't be the only one dismayed and bewildered by the enthusiasm with which many modern Christian "updaters" denigrate the beliefs and moral dispositions associated with the good Christian of old. Behavior that not so long ago we were told was pious, is now called square; what was humble, self-restrictive; what was chaste, uptight; what was orthodox, an ethnocentric oddity. We hear these things now from our own clerics, the very things we have heard for centuries from the admitted opponents of the Christian churches.

And these progressive clerics and theologians do not speak as renegades. We have learned to live with that. They do not plead merely for the acceptance of some idiosyncratic theory. On the contrary, they demand that all who accept the label "Christian" join with them in what they insist is the only correct, modern, and adult expression of the Faith. They demand that we grow up out of our "medieval beliefs" and learn to see the faith of St. Augustine, St. Thomas Aquinas, and St. Thomas More as historically conditioned expressions of a human ideal which is expressed best in our time by movements of the political and cultural Left.

An overstatement? In the chapters that follow I propose to demonstrate that such a claim is being made, and quite explicitly by many modern theologians and churchmen. And then answer them.

How will I do it if I am neither theologian nor Scripture scholar? Well, I won't. I'll let Christ. What I propose to do, quite simply, is go to the Gospels, and look directly at Christ's words. And then stand them in the face of the updaters. I think, if you stay with me, you will see why so many of the moderns begin with the premise that the Gospels, as we know them, are more the ramblings of overly zealous early Christians than divine inspiration. You will see that whatever the Biblical Christ was, he* was not a "do your own thing" superstar.

We need not be Scripture scholars or theologians to do what I have done. Christ chose his first followers from the ranks of the artisans and fishermen of ancient Palestine. These rednecks and hardhats were the ones he thought most likely to be open to the fullness of his teachings, and to be able to teach it to the multitudes. The modern theologians of his time, the Scribes and Pharisees, were the ones who had trouble.

Do I have any predispositions that you should take into account before we begin? Well, I am a Roman Catholic. I say that without hesitation or qualification. I do not claim to be a "good" one, as the saying goes. But I do work at it. The Christ I propose to hold in the face of the moderns, though, is the Christ most acceptable to America's Protestants: straight from the King James version of the Bible (though here and there I use other translations as well).

Please do not take that to mean that I am unconcerned about the issues that divide Christians. I am, but I intend to leave them aside for the duration of this book. I will admit, for the record, that I am pleased and proud that it is the Roman Catholic Church that demands that its members believe "more." From where I sit that is a most desirable demand at this moment of ascendant secular humanism in America. I sincerely hope that the day will come when America's Protestants will begin to consider taking the extra steps toward Rome in order to prevent further subjectivist whittling away at the body of the Faith. I do concede that the behavior of Catholic updaters has made that unlikely in the foreseeable future. My Catholic leanings do not hide that from my eyes.

But the essential point to keep in mind is that Catholics and Protestants of a traditional bent have a common ground broader than the breach that divides us.

---

*I will not capitalize all third person pronouns every time I refer to Christ. No symbolism is intended. I felt it would be unwieldy to have too many capitalized pronouns in the text. When I do capitalize it will be for added emphasis.

And a common enemy. We share the belief that Christ is the Son of God, and in a quite literal way, thank you. We share the conviction that the Gospels record Christ's words, accurately; and that those words provide the normative wisdom for living our lives. We stand together against the moderns who tell us that they have found an ''ism'' that offers more.

Christ's words were the wellspring of a way of life that I have come to love. Our people, under their influence, built a society worthy of our respect and loving service. That society's honored emblems—home, hearth, family; Duty, Honor, Country—are expressions of a moral order I want to see preserved, protected and extended for myself, my family, and my fellow Americans. If you want to call it Protestant America I won't balk.

I am convinced, however, that this hallowed social order is now losing ground to a coordinated siege, and that it can be saved only by going back to the well. But we must go openly and proudly, not as correct-thinking secular liberals, afraid of mixing our religion with our public life. That kind of waffling is at the heart of our current troubles. And keep in mind that we might not like what we find. Those of us who consider ourselves Christian in the traditional sense might find that we have been lulled into complacency by the updaters' social-worker Christ. We might not like it when we discover what our fathers meant by the fear of God.

Contents

Introduction

WHAT IS IT EXACTLY that makes so many modern clergymen and theologians so offensive to so many of the Christian people of America? Is it the fact that they bring the faith into the public arena? It can't be that. Billy Graham and Fulton Sheen types have done it for decades now without arousing much anger. Certainly not from those who would call themselves Christians in a traditional and orthodox sense. Is it their style? Can't be. If you think about it, more often than not, the Berrigan and William Sloane Coffin types, and their followers, express their Christian convictions with apparent sincerity and piety. They claim, in fact, to be taking Christ's message *more* seriously than the rest of us. Then what?

At the risk of oversimplifying, let me be blunt. Let me suggest that America's Christians have intuited, and, I would argue, quite perceptively, that their modern social-activist preachers do not . . . well, do not *like* them, or like to be with them.

It is a feeling vastly different from the one we would get when our fire and brimstone preachers scolded and reprimanded us with verbal blasts that almost wilted our starched collars with the threat of hellfire, in a quite literal sense. Those scourges of heaven instilled a sense of shame in us all right, but a shame that came from being too much like the rest of the world, too much like those who have openly denied Christ. We felt guilt because they convinced us that we had been unworthy of our Christian heritage.

What the social activists ask us to feel guilty about nowadays, in contrast, is our refusal to "grow up" out of that Christian heritage. We are being scolded now because we are medieval in outlook, and unwilling to see the light shining from the better people in the better, enlightened circles of our time. And these enlightened circles offer, by and large, exactly those ideologies that have been defined by their supporters as an alternative to the Christian churches' teachings. Our discomfort comes from being given sermons by preachers who quite proudly let us know that they feel more at home in the company of these modern ideologues than in the community of Christians. And I do not mean the way Christ was at home in the company of prostitutes and sinners. Christ went after these lost sheep to bring them back into the fold. For the Christian updaters, traditional Christians are the lost sheep who have to be brought into the fold of certain modern intellectual and cultural movements.

Think about what we have been asked to do in Christ's name during the last ten years or so: develop an appreciation of the legitimate and alternative response to the Spirit by the Chinese and Cuban Communists, but end our immoral willingness to compromise with Spanish and South Korean despots; understand the justifiable violence of the victims of the inner city, but deplore redneck and hardhat bigotry; relinquish our hold over that portion of the world's raw materials that we do not "really need," while at the same time never forgetting the villainy of our ancestors plundering the enormous reaches of the American continents—which *belonged* to widely scattered Indian tribes; experience the mystery Carlos Castaneda found in the peyote-induced awareness preached by Navajo shamans, but spurn the other-worldliness of the medieval Christian liturgy; hate the death stench of the American military in all its forms, but stand in awe of North Vietnam's military vigor and sense of purpose; feel shame when we realize how much better fed are our children than Third World waifs, but disinvite Vietnamese refugees who "would be better off in their own country," to quote ex-divinity student George McGovern.

I think you see what I am getting at. Those Christians who ask us to make our faith "relevant" are not searching through Scripture and the respected books of theology in our heritage to come up with what Christ wants from us in this day and age. They have become convinced that true wisdom lies elsewhere, and that Christ's teachings have worth *only* to the extent that they can be brought into line with that wisdom. Consequently, those parts of the Gospels that meet the test are emphasized and retained as valuable additions to human knowledge. Those that do not are cast aside as accretions, not the words of Christ. C.S. Lewis referred to it as "putting God in the dock," putting the Scriptures on trial and judging them by the secular wisdom of the modern world. His point, obviously, was that it should be vice versa.

16

At least this is what the most genuinely Christian of the updaters do. Their enthusiasm for a school of thought, an ideology, or a learned writer becomes so intense that they cannot imagine that Christ would not agree with them if he were still walking the earth making his wishes known. They "rescue" Christ; try to get him "in good" with the enlightened opinion of the best people at the best schools. Give him the advantage of studying at prestigious graduate schools without the strictures of an *Index* to limit his intellectual development.

This kind of enthusiasm, by the way, is not a strange approach to the world of ideas. The brightest and best educated people on the planet admit to forming their convictions in just this way. They call themselves Marxists, logical positivists, pragmatists, behaviorists, Freudians, relativists, existentialists, humanists, etc., to indicate their choice. Others call themselves Christians. What we are interested in just now are those who are still nominally Christian but who have discovered that they agree more with one of the other groups, and who are determined to teach their fellow Christians exactly why.

Are there others operating in a more sinister way? Perhaps. But it serves no purpose to raise the specter of conspiracy. (Although I must admit that it is no more difficult to imagine a conspiracy to infiltrate the Christian churches than to imagine the successful infiltration of, say, the British Foreign Service by Kim Philby and Donald MacLean. Easier, in fact.) After all, what more could some clandestine cabal do to turn the churches into doubt-ridden parodies of their former selves, mere shells of the institutions the secular Left so feared and hated in the past? What more to turn Christ into a wavering, harmless reed, waiting to be blown about by every wave of change—unworthy of anyone's opposition? What more than the scores of open and proudly proselytizing updaters? "He's just a man, he's just a man," croons the swinging Mary Magdalene in *Jesus Christ Superstar,* the adolescent rock-opera summary of their work. Ludwig Feuerbach, Marx's guide to the identity of Christ, could not have said it better.

No Sure Formulas

Who are these updaters I am talking about? Well, there are so many it is difficult to decide where to begin. But just to pin down the kind of revamping of the Christian message that I am talking about, let me cite just a few. Father Malcolm Boyd is as good a place to begin as any. He is, of course, the Episcopalian priest who became famous in the middle and late sixties for his bestselling books, *"Are You Running with Me, Jesus?"* and *Human Like Me, Jesus.* He offers suggestions in those books to young students in seminaries who have lost faith in the Christian churches because of the churches' failure to join with the forces of social activism. He tells them to stay within the ministry, to "work for change within the existing structures, bringing them closer to the spirit of the humanist revolution.'' And there is more where that came from.

The Rt. Rev. Paul Moore is another case in point. While Episcopal Bishop of our nation's capital in 1968, at the height of violent protest against the war in Vietnam, he told us that the Christian spirit can be seen best in ''small communities'' such as the ''members of the Students for a Democratic Society,'' where the faith lives ''incognito, dressed in strange, secular, even atheistic costumes, but definitely and clearly present.''[1] (One cannot help but wonder what other issue the good Bishop has been able to define ''definitely and clearly'' in the last decade or so.) For, he goes on, ''whenever two or three are gathered together in the name of love [get that—the SDS, in the name of love!], Christ is present through the Spirit, though no one may call him by name.''

And Donald Kirk (not to be confused with Russell Kirk, please). While director of Emmaus, a Protestant-run ecumenical center, he argued that ''not only our society has gone afloat, but Christians have as well. In our consciousness we have become mobile and in exodus. We are continually on the way in our thinking, always questioning, without necessarily seeking a point of rest or terminal point.''[2] Well, almost. He goes on. ''Looking at the past, we have no sure formulas, no tested theories. But we are guided by the radical implications of the gospel. We find its modern application particularly in the New Left.''

Kirk makes the case. His words indicate quite clearly that when a Christian tells us he is seeking to find a modern expression for the Faith, and demands that we respect his right not to be bound by our two-thousand-year heritage, what he is really asking for is the right to be ''something else.'' (In Kirk's case, a devotee of the New Left—but, to still preach *at* us as if he were a member of the fold, as a legitimate participant in the Christian community's self-definition.)

Few men, when you get down to it, can live ''as individuals,'' all the protestations to the contrary notwithstanding. When a Christian no longer wants to be bound by the teachings of his church, it is because other lessons, from other teachers, have taken hold. Why don't they just desert the Faith, then, the way similarly disaffected men have done for centuries? Part of it might be caused by a lingering affection for the Faith, and a conviction, perhaps only subconsciously felt, that Christ's words are not just another existential explanation of man's encounter with the mysteries of life. But I'm afraid, all too often, the main reason many stay within the Church is a sense of duty and missionary zeal for their new belief. They want others to cross over the bridge too. Not an entirely unadmirable approach to life.

But we could call it treason, too. We really could. After all, the dictionary defines treason as a ''betrayal of trust.'' If priests, ministers, and theologians

[1] *The Underground Church*, ed. Malcolm Boyd (New York: Sheed & Ward, 1968), p. 222.
[2] Ibid., p. 138.

18

working to turn the Christian teaching into a carbon copy of "the humanist revolution" is not a betrayal of trust, what is?

How about if we just say that we are dealing with a "level of misrepresentation," to avoid all the unwarranted associations connected with the word "treason?" If you think even that an unfair charge, let me quote Michael Novak to make my point. Novak, as you probably know, no longer writes much as a modern theologian. He was one of the most influential of the group for a while, however. Nowadays he writes mostly of the problems of the white urban ethnics—recently as a paid member of the Rockefeller family's foundation.

While still in his new theologian's garb, he wrote a most interesting little book called *Belief and Unbelief*. In it he recalled the inner turmoil that racked his mind when he found himself, a Catholic, trying to make it as a member of the faculty of a modern American university.

> It is impossible for one who believes in God to work in the intellectual world of the United States without becoming aware that among intellectuals the bias of the age leans in quite the opposite direction. A great many of one's philosophical associates, and certainly the most articulate, are agnostics or atheists.

You have probably heard such a charge before. It is usually followed with a plea to get more Christians onto the faculties at those agnostic institutions. But that is not Novak's goal. What he wants is to bring the wisdom of these agnostic professors to the outdated institutional Christian churches; not vice versa. He admits, quite frankly, that he "feels spiritually closer to men like Albert Camus than to many a bishop and theologian." He even includes in the book an open letter to Jean-Paul Sartre. He asks the then existentialist Sartre (he has since turned to Maoism) to tone down his invective against the established churches. He insists that he can work as a Catholic for the same kind of understanding of human behavior that Sartre works for as an existentialist, and an atheist. Why? Well:

> The true God is no all-seeing eye scrutinizing one's secret conduct, like the projection of an overactive superego. If one believes in God—the true God and no created counterfeit—there is no consolation and no terror to be derived from dreams about a watching, inquiring, waiting authority in a functionary's uniform. No such image manifests the content of the authentic belief in God; no image whatsoever represents the object of such belief.

There is no Father in heaven, you see, who actually cares about His will being done on earth, no "functionary" responding to our pleas for, say, our daily bread; no authority who scrutinizes our trespasses, much less who consoles us by forgiving them. The true God is not like that, and Michael Novak is His prophet. And Jean-Paul Sartre?

I hope that I don't have to go on and on, in what is only an introductory chapter. I hope that I have made my point—that you know what I mean by updaters. But you probably did not need me to finger them for you. We have all seen the *Time* cover story telling us that God is dead; heard of Harvey Cox's Secular and Godless City (a concept so terrifying in its full implications that even Cox has backed off just a bit of late); read of the Passover Plots and Bishop James Pike's Messianic Pretender called Christ; remember nuns laying plans to kidnap Kissinger for Christ, Maryknollers plotting revolution in South America, and Quakers touring American colleges with war horror films made in North Vietnam to weaken our resolve in the late conflict.

We know what the counterculture tells us of Christ. But what does Christ say? Do his words issue a call to a specific and self-disciplined way of life, or are they cultural touchstones, as the updaters would have it, that we can go to for support and corroboration of lessons which we have learned from other sources? Are they like talismans and Tarot cards? Do Christ's words help us to "be ourselves?" Or do they demand that we be more? Can we interpret them to suit ourselves, put them in the dock? Are they propositions or commands?

Well, Christ himself faced the question more than once. Remember his response to Pilate's grilling. He insisted that:

> Thou sayest it; I am a king. This is why I was born, and why I have come into the world, to bear witness to the truth. Everyone who is of the truth hears my voice. (Jn. 18:37)

Pilate, of course, answered with the aplomb of sophisticated relativist: "What is truth?"

The point of this book lies in that exchange. I insist that the Biblical Jesus proclaimed himself to be the Son of God and the teacher of the word of God to man, not just another prophet or wise man whose offerings could be added to the body of human knowledge as one more slant on things. I insist that an honest reading of the Gospels makes that clear. And I insist as well that we Christians have a right and a duty to go on believing that the Biblical accounts that tell us that are accurate. If they are not, then the updaters are right, and we might as well start defining a subjectivist alternative for ourselves. But there just is nothing the world has learned about the Gospels that makes such an admission necessary. There never will be that kind of a discovery. How could there be? Really. The hushed anticipation that greeted the discovery of the Dead Sea Scrolls was due, in part, to the hope that they would provide a bit of de-mythologizing evidence. Some, including Bishop Pike, argued that they did. But the updaters, by and large, have given up on that one. And there are no new finds on the horizon. We are on solid ground if we go on believing as did our fathers that we must take seriously Christ's unyielding insistence that:

I am the light of the world. He who follows me does not walk in darkness, but will have the light of life. (Jn.8:12)

We do not have to await the correct Scripture-scholars' explanation of what he really meant by that. And the next explanation and the next . . .

We can go on approaching the Gospels with trembling awe, seeking the moral guidelines for our lives. They are the Word of God. If the updaters find that a childish notion, fine. That makes it clear that they have placed themselves beyond the beliefs of the rest of the Christian community, and that we should not feel obliged to listen to them any longer. (If only it were that simple . . . I can hear the modern theologians sighing in despair and saying, "But we do agree that Scripture is inspired. But what does *inspired* mean, my good man?" But more of that later.)

If the Gospels are not the Word of God, on the other hand, it might not be such a bad idea to have a full-time parish representative assigned to keep up with what is going on in group therapy, encounter groups, and transcendental meditation circles. It might not be all that bad for us Christians to organize our existential search for undiscoverable truth as efficiently as the rest of America. We could do worse. (Although for the life of me I cannot imagine how.)

But if we do not want to keep up with the Joneses if that means keeping up with modern religious despair, then we must leave "childish things" aside, and go to Christ, and to the Father in heaven he taught us about. Our Father who art in heaven—a much better way of looking at things than the updaters "really real," or "end of our being," wouldn't you agree?

Chapter I

Of Different Drummers and False Prophets

IT IS BECOMING increasingly clear that when future historians look back on our time, their analyses will be constructed in order to explain the nexus between the confident, often arrogantly confident, ascendant West of the 19th and early 20th centuries, and our contracting self-deprecatory era. And I will bet dollars to donuts that the decline in belief in the Christian faith will come up more often than not as the key.

Whether packaged as the White Man's Burden, Mission Civilisatrice, or Manifest Destiny, the interior disposition was the same. Europeans and their American cousins viewed themselves as the inheritors of a worldview that was different from the rest of the planet's—different, and measurably superior. A sense of mission and purpose enlivened and elevated their endeavors and projected them beyond the oceans until it appeared that the globe itself would be united into a network of communities directed from a European and American axis.

Admittedly, adventurers and base-minded exploiters seized the moment as well, and behind the protective cover of their countries' military power and humanitarian and missionary sacrifice, sought to use rather than serve the brown and yellow peoples being brought into the Western orbit. But these exploiters were the exception, not the rule—our modern experts in the academy and the media notwithstanding. Studies by scholars of the Left and the Right have confirmed what our forefathers told us all along, and what those of us unconverted to the spirit of the times intuited for ourselves. The people of the Christian West just did not send their sons and daughters to teach and to heal, to preach the Gospel, to build roads, bridges, hospitals, schools and churches, and to die in steaming jungles and barren deserts, simply to provide a veneer of respectability for commercial plunderers in search of raw materials and markets for their surplus manufactured goods. Colonies usually cost far more than they were worth.

The historical phenomenon the world disdainfully calls imperialism was more the expression of a vigorous and purposeful people, bursting at the seams of their national boundaries because of that vigor, fully confident in the moral and ethical foundations of their way of life. It was nothing like the commercial piracy Lenin described. Only a disgruntled revolutionary, alienated from the finest traditions of the West, could have seen it that way. The social constructs which they intended to teach to others were never viewed as a ruse behind which a naked power grab was to take place. If zeal often clouded judgment about exactly how to apply that wisdom to the rest of the world, that was the failing of all people with vigor. (And far superior, I may add, to our enlightened tendency to crawl away and let the world do with us what it will.)

We tend to laugh at that confidence now; or attack it with ruthlessness. We find it incredible that Hilaire Belloc, one of the most praised minds of the century by anyone's standards, could say in the 1920's that "the Faith is Europe; Europe is the Faith."

Hawaii, the splashy Hollywood spectacular of a few seasons back, was a representative act of penance for the Bellocian presumption. I'm sure you remember the lessons of that movie. Even high school sophomores I was teaching at the time got them quite well. Max von Sydow (the same actor who played Christ in *The Greatest Story Ever Told)* was cast as that pitifully narrowminded New England minister who brought his Puritan misery to the happy and earthy Polynesians romping bare-breasted and carefree in their island paradise. The peaceful natives, spontaneously gentle in their innocence—Rousseau's noble savages—were imposed upon by this wretched Christian acting out the imperialist urge, and taught the Western hangup of guilt. Of course the movie failed to mention the diseases the missionaries helped end, and the ritual murder of infants, and . . .

But that takes us in the wrong direction. The lesson which we were supposed to learn, the outlook which we were to absorb (the outlook of which this movie is only a minor expression) is not one which will be dispelled by a balance-scale test of Western contributions to the Third World against Western-induced

24

problems. We are supposed to learn that the Christians were wrong to come in the hope of making conversions in the first place; that we had no right imposing on the Hawaiians what was, after all, only our version of the search for the meaning in life (called Christianity), and that that version, that mere opinion, that ethnocentric belief, was in no way better than the one which the Hawaiians had developed on their own. H. L. Mencken put the idea in his own inimitable way as early as the 1930's (I hate to admit to how much I enjoy reading the rogue):

> "Go ye into the world, and preach the gospel to every creature"—the most forceful form of the mandate that animates all Christian missionary effort to this day, and has cost, in its time, the lives of millions of poor heathen. It is not hard to believe that the whole passage originated in the enthusiasm of some missionary to the Gauls, eager to have at them gloriously in their sinister forests.[1]

But we expect that from Mencken, the self-proclaimed scourge of what he called the "ancient imbecilities" of the Christian faith. We might even have expected it from the Hollywood movie moguls. We were not ready for the mirror image coming from men who called themselves Christian theologians. Harvey Cox, for example, describes his modern insight into the Christian synthesis of the future:

> The next Summa might consist not of a thousand chapters but of a thousand alternative states of being, held together not by a glued binding but by the fact that all thousand are *equally real*. [My italics.] Imagine what kind of world it would be if instead of merely tolerating or studying them, one could actually *be*, temporarily at least, a Sioux brave seeing an ordeal vision, a neolithic hunter prostrate before the sacred fire, a Krishna lovingly ravishing a woodsful of goat girls, a sixteenth century Carmelite nun caught up in ecstatic prayer, a prophet touched by flame to release a captive people.[2]

It would not be unfair to say—really, Cox would accept it as a compliment from other quarters—that Cox's missionaries would go to foreign lands more to learn than to teach. (And of course Westerners do have much to learn from the Third World. Simplicity, love of and respect for nature, honesty and bravery

---

[1]H. L. Mencken, *Treatise on the Gods*, p. 181.

[2]*Harvey Cox, The Seduction of the Spirit* (New York: Simon & Schuster, 1973), p. 325.

are just a few of the virtues that many so-called primitive peoples seem to have in abundance compared to the modern industrialized West.) Cox would have the Christian and what used to be called the heathen approach each other as possessors of "equally real" religious experiences—as if there were nothing truly unique about Christ's teachings. The contrasting faiths would then be blended and hybridized for the betterment of both—"Go, teach ye all nations" becoming, perhaps, in modern educationese, "Go, experience ye all nations." (The fact that Cox is insulting to the religious beliefs of the Third World in his flippant indifference to truth—his refusal to take their faith any more seriously than he takes Christianity, to be specific—is a topic which we will take up in a later chapter.)

The Enthronement of Doubt

The modern philosophical "isms"—Cox's indifferentism, logical positivism, pragmatism, existentialism, secular humanism, relativism, Marxism, determinism, behaviorism—can accurately be viewed as different expressions of a centuries-old protest against the medieval world's vision of life. The medieval mind was confident that it knew truth; it was formed in the certainty that God's word and will could be discerned in the Scriptures and through the teachings of His not yet divided Church.

That confidence waned under the pressure of Renaissance humanists and 18th-century *philosophes*. But while it lasted it made its mark on history, and in a way Christians should revere. We will never be coherent, or whole, until we learn that the Middle Ages are called "Dark" only by our rationalist enemies. As Cardinal Newman knew so well, our medieval ancestors had their failings, but "even the errors then prevalent, a persecuting spirit, for instance, a fear of religious inquiry, bigotry, these were, after all, but perversions and excesses of *real virtues,* such as zeal and reverence."[3] Sure, there were poverty and injustice. Most of us would have been serfs. But where else on the planet would we have fared better in the 13th century? Blaming that on the religious convictions of the Middle Ages is another secularist con job. All the components of medieval life—art, warfare, commerce, government, play, scholarship—were judged by the degree to which they complied with the codes of conduct taught by Church authorities. And that was to their glory.

All of life was a hymn, a deliberate attempt to create a "Divine Milieu" (to borrow a phrase) which would encourage sinful, avaricious, and concupiscent man to do God's will. Religious values provided the framework of life, and

[3]*The Essential Newman,* ed. Blehl (New York: New American Library, 1963), p. 103.

filled men as in no time before, or since. Chartres was built, not the Twin Towers; Botticelli painted, not Jackson Pollock; St. Thomas Aquinas was the leading intellect, not Sartre; Dante the poet, not Allen Ginsberg. It was hoped that minds and hearts would, in this atmosphere, rise above their intuitive level and reach for divine wisdom and beauty; would be opened to grace. Man's obligation was to discipline himself to obey divine authority, to live a life of duty and service to things higher than himself. The hero was Sir Galahad, not some self-indulgent rock star with expensive and exotic tastes. Religious authorities defined both the human ideals to which men must aspire, and the human transgressions, the evils which should be contained and whose lures must be minimized by the threat of both civil and divine punishment. If that sounds menacing to you, like the medieval threat to human freedom we have all heard about, ponder a bit more of Newman:

> I will not shrink from uttering my firm conviction that it would be a gain to this country were it vastly more superstitious, more bigoted, more gloomy, more fierce in its religion [as we have been told medieval men were] than at present it shows itself to be. Not, of course, that I think the tempers herein implied desirable, which would be an evident absurdity; but I think them infinitely more desirable and more promising than a heathen obduracy, and a cold, self-sufficient, self-wise tranquility.[4]

Can you imagine the additions to that paragraph Newman would have written after a stroll down Sunset Strip or Carnaby Street?

But the Renaissance humanists and the men of the Enlightenment freed us from all that. Our modern world is the result. And—let's be honest—in many ways that is not so bad, not so bad at all. The advances we know in science and medicine, for example, just might never have occurred if all of life had been directed toward medieval ends. Maybe. Maybe the "freeing" was needed for man to develop his full capacities. But the seeds of what we now know as relativism took root as well. What began as an honest challenge to the corrupt intrigues of profligate popes and despotic kings degenerated into a challenge to the very notion of authority itself. Luther's and Galileo's demands that their research and expertise be permitted to add to the body of knowledge upon which genuine authority is based, turned into a solipsistic denial of man's ability to know truth at all. We went from John Calvin to John Dewey; to "Do your own thing, man," the ultimate wisdom of our time. And to "If it feels good, do it"—assertions which Galileo, Luther, and Erasmus would have condemned in the quickest reaction this side of a knee jerk.

[4]*Ibid.*, p. 105.

But what of Christ? A modern Christian might defend his free-wheeling morality by arguing that Harvey Cox is as perceptive a teacher of morals as Luther or Calvin, and he extols the virtues of ravaging a woodsful of goat-girls. Cox is learned, bright, glib. You cannot deny that. Is there anything in the Gospels to indicate that Christ would not agree that truth is a changing, historically determined concept, a process relative to the eye of the beholder? Was Christ a relativist?

Come, Follow Me

Once again, let me repeat a premise already advanced in the introductory chapter, even at the risk of annoying the reader. It might be wise to raise it repeatedly, at the risk of annoying even more. It is the key to my argument. I do not challenge the whole panoply of modern secular intellectuals on my own. I do not have the ammunition. But I hold that Christ does, and that even a backward Catholic-ghetto ethnic like me can see that.

I start from the premise that the Gospels give accurate accounts of Christ's words. The so-called "form critics" can tell me all they want about how certain books of the Old Testament should be seen as "myth expressing religious truth." Maybe Moses did lead the Israelites across a swamp at low tide instead of the Red Sea. Maybe the Tower of Babel was a ziggurat. It is no purpose of mine to quarrel the merits of such a case. But Christ's life is well within the historical period. If we can accept as accurate the stories of Caesar's life and death, why not Christ's? If the Gospel accounts contain deliberate and extreme exaggerations—Christ performing miracles, for example—why were they not exposed by his contemporaries? Why was not the Church's growth stopped before it began? I know that if someone was going around telling the world that Yogi Berra was God and that he proved it by feeding every kid at Yankee Stadium on Batting Helmet Day with only three franks and four Yoo Hoos, and if I were there that day and knew that Yogi did no such thing, I would at least write a letter to the editor of my local paper. Especially if Yogi's new church was threatening to put my own out of business.

If the Gospels are more myth than fact, I refuse to go on. To be quite frank, I know of other myths I would pick for an "equally real" (to use Harvey Cox's term) choice. I would rather find the inspiration for living my life in the fiery Celtic sagas of Cuchulain, or in Odin's journeys. I am willing to contain these pagan lusts, though, because Christ is the Son of the Father. (Those, by the way, who think that this will be a more gentle and introspective world once Christ has been "demythologized" should remember what the people of Europe were like, and what kinds of gods they followed, before they bent their knees to Christ.)

28

In its most current expression, relativism comes wrapped in two robes. One is the demand that we respect the individual's search for truth on an existential level. Just now, the ideas of modern Austrian philosopher Ludwig Wittgenstein seem to be the favored academic and philosophical buttress for the case. He insisted that the human ability to verbalize is inadequate to express fully the complexities of moral knowledge, and that, as a result, it is *literally* impossible for any one individual or institution to put together axioms binding on the moral choices of others. In short, we are simply unable to *say* what really is right or wrong. Only the individual can make such decisions; and he owes us no explanations because he can make none.

The other argument is more political, and most difficult to deal with in a country like ours, so proud of its democratic ideals. The first cliché every American kid learns must be, "It's a free country . . . you're entitled to your opinion." It is an argument that centers on the need for a free people to respect the freedom of choice of its members. To define, say, pornography or homosexuality as immoral, and thus an unacceptable ingredient in our public life, is to deny liberty to those who find such experiences enjoyable and fulfilling. What is porn for you might be meaningful social commentary to me, the argument goes.

William R. Jones, a professor of theology at Yale, makes the point in an article in *The Christian Century* (May 21, 1975). He quotes Elizier Berkovits to demonstrate the legitimacy of what he calls "functional ultimacy." "Man alone," says Berkovits, "can create value. God is value. But if man is the creator of values . . . he must have freedom of choice and freedom of decision. And his freedom must be respected by God himself." Jones adds, "We are already familiar with some of its [functional ultimacy's] essentials as the literal signification of Protagoras dictum: 'Man is the measure of all things.' "

For those who might be puzzled by the prospect of a Christian going back to that pagan wisdom after nearly two thousand years of Christian additions, most especially Christ's insistence that true wisdom lies in working to insure that "Thy will be done," Jones assures good company. "The principle," he says, "is at the core of Sartre's anthropology and also Camus'." Like Novak, Jones lessens the distance between Christians and atheists and agnostics by concession.

But what of Christ? The Biblical Christ. Does he preach functional ultimacy? Does he preach that we should give full approval to those who hear the beat of a different drummer? How about false prophets?

> Beware of false prophets, who come to you in sheep's clothing, but inwardly are ravenous wolves. By their fruit you will know them. (Mt. 7:15)

And remember, know them as *wolves* and as *false* prophets, not as truth-

29

seekers operating with functional ultimacy. The words are unequivocal, the tone commanding, the injunction hard and unyielding. He speaks of man's obligation to do God's will, to seek truth as taught by Him, not to invent it. Of course, the Scribes and Pharisees found such a directive disturbingly out of touch with the intellectual currents of the time. They questioned Christ with the sophisticated disdain of a group leader at a therapy session for updated thinkers. And Christ responded:

> You brood of vipers, how can you speak good things, when you are evil? . . . The good man from his good treasure brings forth good things; and the evil man from his evil treasure brings forth evil things. (Mt. 12:34-35)

No reassuring salve about the worth of the unexamined life. He even expected a more willing and humble response from people who had heard only his Apostles. Remember how he instructed them to treat those towns who refused to heed his warnings?

> But whatever town you enter, and they do not receive you—go out into its streets and say, "Even the dust from your town that cleaves to us we shake off against you; yet know this, that the kingdom of God is at hand." I say to you that it will be more tolerable for Sodom in that day than for that town. (Luke 10:10-12)

For this Christ, then, the moral choices in life are of serious significance. It is not enough to have brooded over your choice in troubled awareness. The right choice, good as opposed to evil, is discernible, and men are to be judged good or evil by their efforts to live by these laws of God. The right choice, not an endless choosing, was the object of Christ's praise. He, unlike many moderns, did find virtue in obedience, humility, and loving service:

> Therefore, everyone who acknowledges me before men, I also will acknowledge him before my Father in heaven. But whoever disowns me before men, I in turn will disown him before my Father in heaven. (Mt. 10:32-33)

And:

> Therefore, whoever does away with one of these least commandments, and so teaches men, shall be called least in the kingdom of heaven. (Mt. 5:19)

There are parishes in America today where the congregation would walk out in indignation before a preacher who delivered a sermon in such unenlightened "code morality" terms. And I am not being cynical.

These choices were not to be easy choices. There would not be a wide variety

30

of "equally valid" possibilities from which we could choose blamelessly and at will. There was a recognizable Way, a Truth, and a Life, and some would choose it. But some would not. And that would make a difference. The choices of even loved ones might have to be condemned and seen as evil, no matter how sincere the motivation for their choice, and even at the cost of great sadness and strife. Everyone was *not* entitled to his own opinion; there were false prophets.

> Do you think that I came to give peace upon the earth? No, I tell you, but division. For henceforth in one house five will be divided, three against two, and two against three. They will be divided, father against his son, and son against his father; mother against daughter and daughter against the mother. (Luke 12:51-53)

And in the same breath, to those in the crowd shocked by this divine arrogance:

> You hypocrites! You know how to judge the face of the sky and of the earth; but how is it that you do not judge this time? (Luke 12:56)

Hardly an Aramaic version of "All you need is love," is it? Even the most convinced of the updaters would have to admit to that. It must be another example of some misguided early zealot running off at the mouth—"the legend-making progress of the early Christians" at work.

As must be that most quoted of all the "later additions": "He who is not with me is against me, and he who does not gather with me scatters." (Mt. 12:30)

How joltingly different from the modern accounts of Christ's message is Christ's! His beloved Apostle, John, understood that message, and anticipated in the first century A.D. the reaction many in our century would have to it: "The light has come into the world, yet men have loved the darkness rather than the light, for their works were evil." (Jn. 3:19) John was not at all reluctant to use those unfashionable terms: "light" . . . "darkness" . . . "evil." But after all, he had studied under and followed a man who knew a whited sepulcher and a brood of vipers when he saw them.

Christ simply—and in all honesty—cannot be pictured as just another in the line of history's great teachers who offered to help men discover the will of God by introspective self-examination. He came to answer and end that confused, agonizing search. He came to save man from it. He told us that "Before Abraham was, I am," and that kind of statement is not made by great teachers. It could only come from a madman, a charlatan, or a liar—or the Son of God. He spoke with a certainty, and a definite tone that was clearly meant to be more than a prophet's verbal matrix for deep thought.

None of the founders of the world's great religions, it must be remembered, made the claim. It is reserved for the kooks of the world, and Christ. Mahomet,

Gautama, Moses, and Confucius were influential because they offered, *as prophets,* to help men see the Word of God. They would have abjured the claim of the Nazarene. A teacher, a rabbi as perceptive and wise as Christ, had to be aware of that, even if he was not the Son of God. A man who inspired thousands of followers in his lifetime, and millions after his death, a leader with a presence and a power sufficient for his followers to go to their deaths as martyrs rather than deny him, had to be able to grasp the dazzlingly unique nature of his claim. He had to know exactly what he was saying, whether he was God or not, and those who call themselves Christian have to face up to that, and to the subsequent responsibility to heed his words without *any* equivocation, or functional ultimacy, at all.

Evolving Truths

An interesting way around the demands Christ's words place upon our actions has, however, turned up in recent years in Catholic updater circles. It is called process theology.

Catholic relativists had a problem, as one might guess. The Catholic Church has demanded and received from its members through the centuries an assent not only to the truths contained in Scripture, but also to a teaching authority headed by the pope (the so-called magisterium) which defined and developed those truths for the faithful. A Catholic trying to argue that truth can be seen as changing, varying from person to person, society to society, and time to time, would come up against that wall at every bend of the road. But on the other hand, if he stayed loyal to the Church's authority, he would fail every course that he took in his evening studies at Michael Novak's atheistic and agnostic American universities. (Okay, there is a trace of snideness here. I know. *Mea culpa.* But one can never forget Novak's revealing admission about the atmosphere in the American intellectual world that we are sending our children—and our clergymen—into these days. All those ministers, priests, brothers, and nuns studying at the feet of academicians who have nothing but contempt for the Christian mind; trying to "make it," to prove that they too can be modern and sophisticated. They want to be intellectuals and seem willing to pay the price—the Faith of our Fathers. I have been at many social gatherings where liberated clerics poke fun at the old-fashioned notions they have thrown off in the last five or so academic years. Makes you see why Catholics had an *Index* for so long. If a man's faith cannot take two night courses at Hunter or Berkeley, then he does need protection.)

The Catholic relativist answer? The Holy Ghost made me do it—and in that many words. Since the "Spirit" has been sent to the World, as Christ promised, the claim is made that a divine inspiration can be discovered in the world's "process." An "ongoing revelation" can be seen in the lives and words of our contemporaries. Truth is not known, in other words; it is becoming. Religion books used in Catholic schools and religious training classes under the influence of this process insight, as a result, make use of the words of modern poets, philosophers, politicians, social activists, and members of "exploited" groups more than they do the words of Christ. Speeches by John F. Kennedy, Martin Luther King, Cesar Chavez, Saul Alinsky, poems by Leroi Jones, essays by Norman Mailer become the source of developing insights into God's will for man. How is the Spirit talking to us *today,* becomes the question; and, as might be expected, he is coming in loud and clear from the Left.

The fact that papal pronouncements have branded as false the claim that there is such a thing as ongoing revelation, and have insisted that revelation as such ended with the death of the last Apostle, inhibits the process theologians little since papal pronouncements too, they insist (those who think papal pronouncements worthy of a reasoned response, at any rate), are part of the ongoing process and have to be understood in their historical context. What might have been relevant for 14th-century minds often is irrelevant for those of the 20th. Besides, they tell us, with a Wittgenstein-like shrug, how are we to know what the word revelation really means anyway?

"There are no absolutes," said one Catholic process theologian at a meeting of American Catholic bishops in the spring of 1975. "All is in process. Our perception is absolute only for the here and now." There are no false prophets, only slow learners.

Chapter II

That Even the Winds Obey Him

THIS RELATIVIST denial of objective religious truth comes in a variety of packages. Before looking at them in the light of the Gospels, one point must be made: They all depend upon a successful casting of doubt upon the Evangelists' accounts—obviously. You just cannot question or treat as myth events which everyone knows to be factual—not if you want anyone to listen. Members of the Flat Earth Society have to keep their tongues in cheek when they try to explain away the television accounts of the moon landing. Oh, there are a few interesting and money-making theories about how Hitler might still be alive in Argentina, or of how Audubon might have been Louis XVII, or of the possibility that Napoleon might have escaped from St. Helena and had a loyal stand-in live out his life there for him. But even in these fanciful revisions, plausibility depends on some incongruity or fuzziness in the accepted story. Without such an insertion of doubt to suspend our disbelief, they would not even make it as successful rainy day diversions.

The key, then, for any theological updating of the Christian message is the premise that what the Bible tells us about Christ is unreliable. You might be able to impugn the attitudes and convictions of the Christians of old, but it would be difficult to argue that, after nearly two thousand years of reading the Bible, they had not grasped what was in its pages. As one typically disdainful cleric put it to

35

me one evening, ''Sure the Bible says that Christ said that, but you don't really believe that those stories are factual, do you?'' His eyes rolled superciliously, then descended condescendingly. ''My Lord, most of them were written hundreds of years after Christ's death. Anything could be in there.''

Most Catholics, because of the clear lines of authority in the Church, have not felt troubled by such challenges until recently. It was not until the atmosphere that followed upon Vatican II that Catholic theologians in appreciable numbers felt free to express such heterodox opinions, often in the face of papal condemnations. Perhaps this explains the strangely zealot-like enthusiasm with which Catholic demythologizers work. It is a flattering and heady new brew for them. But the basic claim is an old one, as Protestants know. From the early 1900's at least, Protestants have had to deal with a position which was developed most fully in the middle years of our century by the German theologian, Rudolf Bultmann (although nowadays there is a school of thinkers who call themselves post-Bultmannian to indicate that they would like to move further even than Bultmann in reinterpreting the identity of Christ). It will probably be Catholics, though, who will fight out most fiercely the differences, since the Protestant tradition leaves more room for the experience of switching sects or congregations in search of an outlook compatible with one's own.

Bultmann's basic position?

> The whole conception of the world which is presupposed in the preaching of Jesus as in the New Testament generally is mythological; i.e., the conception of the world as being structured in three stories . . . the conception of the intervention of supernatural powers . . . the conception of miracles, especially the conception of the intervention of supernatural powers in the inner life of the soul, the conception that men can be tempted and corrupted by the devil and possessed by evil spirits.

The Gospel narratives must be wrong when they tell of such things since, as we know:

> . . . it is different from the conception of the world which has been formed and developed by science since its inception in ancient Greece and which has been accepted by all modern men.[1]

We must resolve this conflict between our modern understanding of how the world turns and the Gospel's repeated depiction of miraculous events that do not fit into that understanding, not by any claim that the Son of God could suspend the laws of physics and biochemistry through divine power. That

---

[1]*Contemporary Religious Thinkers,* ed. Macquarrie (New York: Harper & Row, 1968), p. 274.

would be a retreat into the medieval view of the world, unworthy of modern men. We must instead deny the accuracy of the Bible. If the Bible tells us that Christ had powers beyond those of the modern physicist or even theologian, that he could heal lepers, make the blind see, and raise himself from the dead, it must of necessity be inaccurate.

We must not fly in the face of "the modern conception of the world [where] the cause and effect nexus is fundamental."

Consequently, the Scriptures must be approached with a highly selective gleaning hand. We should feel free to leave behind the "mythical" elements and focus instead on those portions which can be pressed into the service of human needs:

> For modern man the mythological conception of the world, the conceptions of eschatology, of redeemer and redemption, are over and done with. Is it possible to expect that we shall make a sacrifice of understanding, *sacrificium intellectus,* in order to accept what we cannot sincerely consider true—merely because such conceptions are suggested by the Bible? Or ought we to pass over those sayings of the New Testament which contain such mythological conceptions and to select other sayings which are not stumbling blocks to modern man?

To the second question he of course answers yes.

For fairness' sake, it must be said that Bultmann and most of his followers argue that we should "abandon the mythological conceptions precisely because we want to retain their deeper meaning." But for accuracy's sake we must add that all this means is that we are to look upon the Gospels, and judge them, from the transitory viewpoints of modern psychology and anthropology, as if our age had a unique source of wisdom.

"This method of interpretation of the New Testament," he goes on, "which tries to recover the deeper meanings behind the mythological conceptions I call de-mythologizing." (How about "Doubting Thomistic?") The Rev. Dr. Norman Perrin, a professor of the New Testament at the University of Chicago Divinity School, shows us how it is done. *The Denver Post* (January 10, 1975) covered a lecture of his in which he spoke of the miracle stories as a "conventional form of propaganda in the ancient world," and argued that the "question is not whether the stories are true but whether the belief they express is valid or invalid." When asked for an example of a New Testament miracle account that might be literally untrue, the paper reports that Perrin "nearly exploded." "That," he responded, "is like asking a returned astronaut to discuss whether the earth is flat or round." The New Testament miracle stories were "nothing special, just a conventional means of expressing belief in Jesus," he said. "One of the problems religious people face is acceptance of the proposition that literal language is real and nonliteral (or figurative) language is unreal."

37

Older Heretics

Pope Leo XIII as early as the late 19th century was forced to deal with arguments very much like Bultmann's. The demythologizers in the Catholic Church at that time, the Modernists as they were called, were approaching the Gospels with comparable skepticism. (Non-Christians have been doing it since the beginning of the Church. It is not really an original or brilliant insight. It is, in fact, quite logical once you refuse to accept that Christ was what the Bible tells us he told us he was.) Not that Catholics confronted by demythologizers will be able to use Leo as an authority, since the power of the pope has to be demythologized, too, say the updaters. I quote from Leo's encyclical on Sacred Scripture only to make clear the traditional view—and my view—of the accuracy of the Scriptures, and to indicate how similar to the modern updaters were the condemned Modernists of his time. It is a perennial heresy. (Traditional Protestants, of course, do not have to accept papal teaching authority here to grant the accuracy of the Pope's words.) Leo first deals with the enemies of the Faith:

> Now we have to meet the Rationalists, true children and inheritors of the older heretics, who, trusting in their turn to their own way of thinking, have rejected even the scraps and remnants of Christian belief which have been handed down to them. They deny that there is any such thing as revelation or inspiration, or Holy Scripture at all; they see, instead, only the forgeries and the falsehoods of men; they set down the Scripture narratives as stupid fables and lying stories; the prophecies and the oracles of God are to them either predictions made after the events or forecasts formed by the light of nature; the miracles and the wonders of God's powers are not what they are said to be, but the startling effects of natural law, or else mere tricks and myths; and the Apostolic Gospels and writings are not the work of the Apostles at all.

Sound as if he were talking about someone you know? Someone who runs adult education groups at your church maybe?

He then restates the traditional Christian view in the face of the challenge:

> . . . it is absolutely wrong and forbidden either to narrow inspiration to certain parts only of Holy Scripture, or to admit that the sacred writer has erred.

Why? Because all of the books of the New Testament especially are:

> . . . written wholly and entirely, with all their parts, at the dictation of the Holy Ghost; and so far is it from being possible that any error can co-exist with

38

inspiration, that inspiration not only is essentially incompatible with error, but excludes and rejects it as absolutely and necessarily as it is impossible that God Himself, the supreme Truth, can utter that which is not true.

He, of course, does concede the legitimate areas of question and interpretation—i.e., the fact that chronology varies from Gospel to Gospel, that certain incidents appear in one Gospel and not in others (which does much to certify the overall accuracy of the New Testament. If it were a con job by con men clever enough to establish a two-thousand-year-old faith, why did they not get together to "get their facts straight" before they wrote?). But Leo insists that when dealing with Christ's words and actions there is no room for interpretation or qualification. As St. Augustine put it so well (he, too, had to deal with demythologizers, as early as the fourth century), our Faith:

> . . . forbids us to think that any of the evangelists could speak untruly even when the same event is narrated by different individuals and in different words. Thus the evangelists may change the order of events; they may prefer one mode of expression to another (provided they have the same meaning); they may, while clearly recalling the event itself, not succeed, despite their efforts to do so, in preserving the exact words which were spoken on the occasion.

But the stories are true in all their essentials. That has always been the Christian belief . . . even if the incidents do not satisfy Bultmann's standards of scientific process.

In the Name of My Father

It is on this point that the updaters balk. Indeed, it could be said that all their other objections to the traditional interpretation of Christ's moral directives depend upon this logical-positivist refusal. Why? Well, if a modern man, say one of the Indian gurus who comes floating out of the East every few years to fleece American college kids out of their fathers' money, began healing lepers, curing the blind, making the lame walk, and raising people, including himself, from the dead, our tendency would be to accept his teachings even if they centered on walking around on our hands with cigars clenched between our toes. I shouldn't be flippant here, or appear to be, because I am quite serious. The Biblical accounts of Christ's life contain incident after incident so descriptive of divine power that it is difficult to imagine modern men, who have panicked over rumors of flying saucers and made a millionaire of the author of *Chariots of the Gods,* not accepting his words without question, if they believed the stories to be true. Perhaps the modern theologians themselves would still

39

equivocate. Pride, even in the face of divine authority, did not die with Adam. But few of the rest of us would listen to their doubts.

I can remember hearing a theologian arguing, and quite persuasively I must admit, that Christ's raising himself from the dead was not as important as the overpoweringly divine force evident in his words. Okay. But the miraculous occurrences found in the Bible provide inescapable evidence that Christ was *more* than just a great teacher. We do not have to be sensitive and perceptive to grasp the beauty of his words and to know that we must follow Him. Christ came to save all men, not just drama critics and poets.

To keep their audience, then, and to convince us that there is room within the Christian community for situation ethics, secular humanism, Marxism, existentialism, or whatever other secular worldviews our local updater favors, it became *necessary* to demythologize. The miraculous and supernatural ingredients in the Gospel accounts had to be made part of the "myth-making process of the early Christians," as the phrase goes, inserted to make the case that Christ was the Messiah. Those myths, in updater parlance, include the Virgin Birth, the exorcism of devils, angels, hell and heaven and life after death in general, the Transfiguration, healings, even the Resurrection and the Ascension. I am not exaggerating for emphasis. For the theological moderns the anti-Christian denigrations of Christ found in Hugh Schonfeld's *The Passover Plot* came closer to their understanding of Christ than does Leo XIII's or Billy Graham's.

How to begin, then? If the updaters deny that the Gospels accurately record Christ's life, we will gain little headway with them if we make the case that Christ time and time again stresses his cures, his miracles, and his suspension of the physical laws of the universe. But for the rest of us, it is of extreme importance. The miracles were our Lord's proof to us that his words, too, transcend this world. If we ignore that, we leave ourselves open to the whole panoply of updater doubts.

Few updaters, you see, make explicit or public their denial of the accuracy of the Gospels—for the time being and for the most part, anyway. Especially if they work in parishes or schools attended by traditional-minded Christians or their children. It is only in the tone and slant of their lectures and sermons, or in the books they choose for religious education classes, that we see reflections of a Bultmannian or post-Bultmannian Christ.

I do not charge malevolence. The updaters would argue that they are working in their congregation's best interests, preparing us to be "eased" into a sophisticated, adult understanding of the coming secular age. Father Gregory Baum[2] tells us that modern theologians must move cautiously lest they "dis-

[2]*New Horizon: Theological Essays* (New York: The Paulist Press, 1972), pp. 22, 64–65.

turb'' the faithful who might not be ready to hear that "we no longer hold that the words attributed to Jesus were necessarily spoken by him or that the recorded incidents of his life were necessarily actual occurrences," much less that "God does not exist" but is actually "man's never-to-be-caught-up-with future" and the "divine presence by which man becomes more truly human." (Which, in case you haven't caught on yet, is what the moderns mean by the "immanent" God. Make no mistake about it, whether it sounds sensationalist or not, the modern theologians of Baum's bent are self-appointed missionaries from the modern world, working to bring us out of our Christian past. They are experts in the Christian faith, all right, the way missionaries who studied Chinese culture for years before going to the Orient were experts on Confucius. It is that expertise, not a living faith, that they refer to when they call themselves theologians.)

In their scheme, they assure us, Christ will not be forgotten. After all, as Bishop Pike used to say, Christ did experience a "breakthrough" of human love which enabled him to come dazzlingly close to a full and mature understanding of what it means to be a man. Pike even conceded that Christ's might have been one of the best such breakthroughs in history. Father Baum accepts that in Christ we have "God's self-communication made explicit." Christ knew more about that "never-to-be-caught-up-with future" than your average man (although I don't understand how he knows that if we can't trust the Gospels).

The updaters don't ask us to turn against Christ. They *use* him to prepare us for the next step toward wisdom—the direction of which varies according to the pet ideology of the updater.

This is the pivot point. A Marxist will then talk about Christ's warnings to the rich; a secular humanist about his call for love of our fellow man (*agape,* in the current fashion); determinists of his stress on forgiveness; situation ethicians on the warnings to the holier-than-thou Scribes and Pharisees. They will magnify those portions of the Scripture that reinforce their ideological predispositions. And, as Bultmann suggests, ask us to forget the rest.

The New Testament can be trusted in their favorite passages, you see. There it is accurate (or is it that it is worthwhile and effective to pretend that it is accurate?). But when their positions are countered by the numerous passages that indicate that Christ's words mandate something else? Then the hands go up, the grimaces start, and the deep sighs roll. "Christ could not have really said *that!* Devils, angels, hell! Come now."

The miracles are important, then, for those of us who are determined to preserve the ancient beliefs. If we are resolved to immunize ourselves and our children from the demythologizers and their intrusions into our parish life, and to insist upon retaining the impact of Christ's words in their fullness, we cannot flirt with the idea of giving in a little here for the sake of good will and understanding within the Church. An admission that the miracles are more likely to be representations of the *effect* of the experience of Christ upon the imaginations of the Evangelists than fact, is a *most* serious concession indeed.

A supernatural element is necessary and absolutely required. How else are we to explain what we call inspiration and Biblical inerrancy? If Christ could not walk on water, it just might be that he could not guarantee that Luke would not let poetic license get the best of him. *But,* and correlatively, if Christ could tame the seas and raise himself from the dead, and if he really was going to be "this day in Paradise" with the good thief, sitting at "the right hand of the Father" for whom "all things are possible," then it is not a childlike faith to believe that the Evangelists were inspired in their narration.

Even if it were, a childlike faith is exactly what Christ demands; a *sacrificium intellectus,* if you like. "Amen I say to you, unless you turn and become like little children, you will not enter into the kingdom of heaven. Whoever, therefore, humbles himself as this little child, he is the greatest in the kingdom of heaven" (Mt. 18:2-4).

A Christ operating without *some* manifestation of his divinity would have been a Christ without authority. The Biblical Christ did not deliver religious and philosophical propositions, and leave it at that. He proclaimed himself to be the Son of God, and proceeded to demonstrate it to the multitudes with a display of power those crowds could see were not of this world—demonstrated it so clearly, in fact, that he insisted that those who denied him after such proof would be worthy of eternal damnation. Sorry, brother, these are His words, not mine:

> And if anyone hears my words, and does not keep them, it is not I who judge him; for I have not come to judge the world, but to save the world. He who rejects me, and does not accept my words, has one to condemn him. The word that I have spoken will condemn him on the last day. For I have not spoken on my own authority, but he who sent me, the Father, has commanded me what I should say, and what I should declare. (Jn. 12:47-49).

Christ heals, and exorcizes devils, and *then* preaches. It is part of a package. It is true that Christ would not put on a show with a miracle at the demand of the Pharisees whenever they wanted one. But in general, he provides proof of his claim with some kind of sign. Check it yourself. If he did not, you know, you might have to agree with the updaters who insist that the Gospels would be more persuasive as myths. Christ would come across as a most unattractive figure if he demanded the kind of total dedication that he did demand—even sometimes to leaving wife, family, and home, and taking up the cross and following him—on the strength of a particularly effective sermon. He knows that. It was the miracles that made his offer the one you couldn't refuse. (Come to think of it, if you take away the miracles, this Christ of ours is a pompous, petty despot—telling a disciple to come and follow him without even taking time to bury his own father: "Let the dead bury their dead." What kind of man would say that kind of thing? Especially when he is also on record as demanding that we must "visit the sick and bury the dead." Obviously, only a man who knew that he was more than a man, and that joining in his earthly mission was not in the category of ordinary earthly affairs.)

The Record

In the early days of his ministry, Christ instructs the disciples of John the Baptist to tell John that his public ministry has begun. How was John to know that it really was the Christ, the Messiah?

> Go and report to John what you have heard and seen: the blind see, the lame walk, the lepers are cleansed, the deaf hear, the dead rise, the poor have the gospel preached to them. And blessed is he who is not scandalized in me. (Mt. 11:4-6)

For the Scribes and Pharisees too (before they became determined to eliminate his growing influence, at any rate), he relies on a manifestation of divine power. After curing a leper, Christ charged him to:

> . . . go show thyself to the priest, and offer the gift that Moses commanded, for a witness to them. (Mt. 8:4)

For the cured themselves there was little doubt about what had happened. Remember the words of the cured blind man, when he was questioned by the Pharisees about the possible diabolical source of Jesus' healing power. (Note that the Pharisees did not dismiss the miracles as folk tales being spread by Christ's overenthusiastic followers. They knew them to be fact; they feared their effect, and tried to attribute them to the devil.) The cured blind man denied the Pharisees' insinuation, of course, and added:

> Why, herein is the marvel, that you do not know where he is from, and yet he opened my eyes. Now we know that God does not hear sinners; but if anyone is a worshipper of God, and does his will, him he hears. *Not from the beginning of the world has it been heard that anyone opened the eyes of a man born blind.* * If this man were not from God, he could do nothing. (Jn. 9:30-33)

*The emphasis is mine—here, and in all future Scriptural quotations.

43

The first moment of the Apostles' full understanding of Christ's nature also comes as a consequence of a display of supernatural power. It came on the night when

> . . . the boat was in the midst of the sea, buffeted by the waves, for the wind was against them. But in the fourth watch of the night he came to them, walking upon the sea.

The Apostles, as one might expect, were terrified at the sight. Jesus calmed them by assuring that "It is I; do not be afraid." We all remember Peter's request for proof, and Christ's invitation to Peter to also walk on the water. Peter began to sink when he became frightened by the strong winds. "Lord, save me!" he cried. Jesus extended his hand and took hold of Peter and asked, "O thou of little faith, why didst thou doubt?" The winds died then and they returned to the boat. The awe-inspired Apostles worshipped him, saying, "Truly thou art the Son of God." (Mt. 14:24-33)

Those words cannot be overemphasized. They do not follow a rap session. This experience of divine authority, not the evocative power of Christ's words in and of themselves, was the *mysterium tremendum* in the Biblical accounts. (Which in no way, I repeat, derogates the power of the words. It is just that Christ is making sure that those of us who cannot grasp the wonder of them will not be left in doubt either.) Their willingness to follow Christ flowed from the only possible answer to their question: "What manner of man is this, that even the wind and the sea obey him?" (Mt. 8:27)

In the oft-discussed cure of the paralytic, the words were chosen to underline the divine nature of the cure. "Take courage, son; thy sins are forgiven thee." When the Scribes questioned that apparent blasphemy, Christ assured them that he meant exactly what he said:

> Why do you harbor evil thoughts in your hearts? For which is easier, to say, "Thy sins are forgiven thee," or to say, "Arise and walk?" But that you may know that the Son of Man has power on earth to forgive sins . . . Arise, take up thy pallet, and go unto thine house. (Mt. 9:5-6)

The power to cure the lame is used to shed light on the nature of the God-man who possesses such healing graces. He can heal souls too.

At times Christ displays the traces of exasperation and disappointment we might expect when hardened hearts prevent men from seeing that. When he walked in Solomon's portico in the Temple at Jerusalem during the feast of the Dedication, the Scribes attempted to trap him into an indictable statement. They demanded that "If thou are the Christ, tell us openly." Jesus answered:

I tell you and you do not believe. The works that I do in the name of my Father, these bear witness concerning me. But you do not believe because you are not of my sheep. My sheep hear my voice, and I know them and they follow me. And I give them everlasting life. [He does not add, "But that's okay, fellows. I'm okay, you're okay. We got to dance to our own music."]

The Jews understood. They rose in anger and took up stones to punish him for his "blasphemy." Before they could, though, Christ probed their anger. Is it, he asked

. . . because I said I am the Son of God? If I do not perform the works of my Father, do not believe me. But if I do perform them, and if you are not willing to believe me, *believe the works,* that you may know and believe that the Father is in me and I in the Father. (Jn. 10:25-38)

Christ presents himself, then, as someone unique and momentous in history. The rules have been suspended. He is conceding to the Pharisees and the Scribes, in fact, that he has made a statement that *would* be blasphemous if it came from anyone else. He does not give an anti-capital punishment lecture about taking up stones in the first place. He pleads with them to *look* at what he has done. He asks them to consider the power of the Father evident in him. He will later raise himself from the dead for the same reason; and, if we can judge from the doubts of our updaters, meet with as much skepticism.

Depart from Me

The miracles are not occasional vignettes. They are highly visible strands woven into a bright and central part of the Scriptural fabric. If the Evangelists cannot be trusted here, so much of the Bible has to be dismissed that we cannot help but treat the entire narration with great reserve. Which is what the updaters want. How else can they open us to things like their latest addition to the faith: the "real" meaning of the Resurrection? The one where Christ's teachings become so much a part of the psyche of the disciples that his Spirit was "with them" again even though his body was still in the tomb, or wherever it was that the Passover Plot body snatchers had stashed the corpse.

In the words of the recently published *The Common Catechism: A Book of Christian Faith,* the latest updater epic: "God identified with Jesus and his cause." It was not anything "materialistic" since "Jesus did not just come back to life as we know life." They do not mean by that anything "higher." They mean something less real.

45

Christ's words demand that we accept the presence in the world of the Son of God. Even Peter could not accept that at first, and not only when Christ asked him to walk on the water. When Christ promised him a catch of fish after he had toiled all night in vain, Peter hesitated. But he obeyed. When the huge catch that followed was boated, he repented, and begged forgiveness. "Depart from me," he pleaded, "for I am a sinful man, O Lord." (Luke 5:8)

Matthew reacted to the miracles in a like manner. For him they were the signs of God's presence—no equivocation. Christ's reputation grew on these miracles more than on anything else:

> And great crowds came to him, bringing with them the dumb, the blind, the lame, the maimed, and many others; and they set them down at his feet, and he cured them; so that the crowds marvelled to see the dumb speak, the lame walk, and the blind see. And they glorified the God of Israel. (Mt. 15:30-31)

When the woman who had been suffering from hemorrhage responded to that reputation by reaching furtively from the crowd, saying to herself, "If I touch but his cloak I shall be saved," Christ warmed to her and rewarded her faith. "Take courage, daughter; thy faith has saved thee." (Mt. 9:21-22)

Christ repeatedly welcomed such shows of awe, and those who seek to remove the miraculous incidents to make it *easier* for modern man to accept the Faith should keep that in mind. How will those who refuse to accept the possibility of a miracle, warm to the teachings of a leader who reacted as Christ did to that woman, and to the blind man, Bartimeus, on the wayside near Jericho?

> And as they were leaving Jericho, a great crowd followed him. And behold, two blind men sitting by the wayside heard that Jesus was passing by, and cried out, saying, "Lord, Son of David, have mercy on us!" And the crowd angrily tried to silence them. But they cried out all the louder, saying, "Lord, have mercy on us, Son of David." Then Jesus stopped and called them, and said, "What will you have me do for you?" They said to him, "Lord, that our eyes be opened." And Jesus, moved with compassion for them, touched their eyes; and at once they received their sight and followed him. (Mt. 20:29-34)

He rewarded Jairus, the ruler of the synagogue, similarly when he pleaded with Christ to save his daughter. "Do not be afraid," said Jesus. "only have faith." He then took the girl by the hand and said to her, "Girl, I say to thee arise." "And the girl rose up immediately and began to walk; she was twelve years old. And they were utterly amazed." (Mk. 5:34-42)

John, who by all accounts was the Apostle closest to our Lord, and a prime witness to his everyday life during the ministry, understood the purpose and context of the miracles. After Jesus fed the five thousand with the five loaves and two fishes, with enough left over to fill twelve baskets, John wrote, "When the people, therefore, had seen the sign which Jesus had worked, they said, 'This is indeed the Prophet who is to come into the world.' " (Jn. 6:14)

Even the Fig Tree

Lepers, blind men, the lame, the man with the withered hand, exorcized devils . . . a refusal to accept such a prominent part of the Gospels tells us much about those who do the refusing; perhaps more than they would have us know. It is no secret that, for the past two hundred years anyway, the atmosphere of the secular world has placed great stress on the fully autonomous intellect. We are taught by existentialists, situation ethicians, and most of those who accept the umbrella term "liberal," that a man cannot be fully human until he lives by inner moral imperatives. John Stuart Mill told us that if there is a God, He will judge more favorably those who do evil, after having weighed their actions, than those who do good out of obedience and loyalty to church or tradition. More recently Paul Tillich argued that religions should lead men to freedom from the moral law by helping us grow in the Spirit that knows no law. Daniel Callahan proclaims that he would "repudiate" a God who punished men for their individual moral choices—in spite of Christ's repeated mention of hell.[3] (He mentions hell more than he does heaven, you know.) In many modern colleges, most noticeably in those run by religious organizations, the philosophy and theology departments seem to have been set up for the purpose of freeing students from the "code morality" of their parents that hinders the process of genuine moral growth.

The message has filtered down to the rest of us, too. It can be seen in the slang clichés of doctors and cab drivers, engineers and housewives. "I gotta be me." "I'm entitled to my own opinions." "It's my life, let me live it." "If I do it because I have to, what good is it?" "I must be true to myself." "Be good to yourself, there's only one you." "Do your thing." "I did it my way," sings Frank Sinatra at every concert, with a demeanor people used to reserve for hymns. "Different strokes for different folks." "Make your own kind of music."

Let's be frank: you just don't say these things to someone who can calm the seas and raise himself from the dead. You bend your knee in awe to such a

[3]*Spectrum of Catholic Attitudes,* ed. Campbell (Milwaukee: Bruce Publishing Co., 1969), p. 46.

being, even though that kind of self-abnegation is what the modern world tells us is a sign of the slave.

But Christians must not shirk from challenging the respected opinion of their age. Even on intellectual—but not only on intellectual—grounds. As G.K. Chesterton put it so well:

> A piece of peculiarly bad advice is constantly given to modern writers, especially to modern theologians: that they should adapt themselves to the spirit of the age. If there is one thing that has made shipwreck of mankind from the beginning, it has been the spirit of the age, which is always exaggerating still further something that is exaggerated already.[4]

There are theological updaters who would rather stoke a Pittsburgh blast furnace with a padlock key than be out of step with respectable academic opinion. Sheep mentality is as pronounced among aspirant intellectuals as anywhere. But that is their problem; and ours only if we insist on allowing their vanity to enter our lives too. It might be backward and childish to accept worldly authority without question. For Christians, it is imperative to obey divine.

The updaters, in all honesty, treat the Gospels as if they were a newly discovered caveful of intricately carved Inca amulets. Just as archaeologists and anthropologists would be more interested in *why* the Indians drew flying dragons and two-headed jackals than in whether or not there were such creatures, they tell us we should be interested in *why* the early Christians told the stories about Christ's cures and Resurrection and Ascension. Perhaps we can be comparably inspired. But in a constructive and enlightened way. No martyrs, please. Our updaters stoutly refuse any *sacrificium intellectus*. (Could it not be said that for updaters "theologian" has come to mean one who skillfully explains away a literal reading of the Gospels?)

I can remember hearing, but I can't remember where, an interesting analysis of Christ's miracles. It must have been on one of those late-night talk shows, since almost all the details are blurred in my memory. I probably was half asleep. But there was one line from a minister involved in the discussion that sticks with me. "You know," he said, "I'd trade away all of the socially relevant beatitudes if we could just get rid of that fig-tree story. It's such an embarrassment with educated groups."

It is no one's favorite story. There are others people don't like. Mary Magdalene bathing Christ's feet with expensive oils and drying them with her hair bothers some libbers—not to mention the "socially conscious" (whose

---

[4]G. K. Chesterton, *Lunacy and Letters*.

views were first expressed by Judas). Christ's harsh reprimands to Peter bother others, his violent outburst against the money changers in the Temple still others. A few of my aunts used to complain at family picnics about Christ being more complimentary to Mary, who sat and listened to him talk, than to Martha, who was toiling away in the kitchen to make his stay pleasant.

But all these stories have their defenders too. Valid points about the importance of Christ, spiritual values, and righteous anger can be drawn from them. But that fig tree . . . no champions.

You might not even remember the incident. It came about, Matthew tells us, as Christ was returning to Jerusalem from Bethany:

> Now in the morning, on his way back to the city, he felt hungry. And seeing a fig tree by the wayside, he came up to it, and found nothing on it but leaves; and he said to it, "May no fruit ever come from thee henceforth forever!" And immediately the fig tree withered up. (Mt. 21:18-19)

Some have tried to dismiss the event as a parable. A similar story in parable form does appear in Luke. But it is a difficult row to hoe: whenever Christ speaks in parables it is plainly noted. Others have called it an error in transcription. But it appears in Mark as well. Moreover, Matthew was an eyewitness (Mark may have been, too)—a primary source, as the history professors say.

Clearly, if you or I pounded a ring of long, ungalvanized nails through the trunk of a local apple tree because we could not get a winesap when we wanted one, people would not see anything divine in our actions. Although they might be interested enough in our behavior to lock us up for a while to study it.

But Christ's actions are not bound by our standards. He should *not* be acceptable to us if he can fit into a sensitivity-session concept of what is normal and "well-adjusted." The Christ of Christians is the Light of the World. And, as Martin Buber put it so perceptively, an eclipse of the sun is caused by an obstruction between our eyes and the sun, not by some failure in the heavenly body.

Could Christ have found a better way to display his divine power, and the stakes inherent in a refusal to serve him? By killing the tree he shows us a hard and demanding, seemingly vindictive, side of himself. But is that inappropriate? For sure? Might not it be better for us to be shocked by that withered tree than by the doors of hell?

I do not pretend to have fathomed the deepest meaning of this mysterious passage. It has puzzled Scripture scholars, even the most orthodox, for centuries now. But I do insist that it is far better to approach it with piety and wonder than to laugh it off as a folk tale that has crept in while someone's guard was down. Once we start playing that game, we just might end up talking about

49

Christ being "really" divine—as the so-called "idealist" updaters do—the way the tree in Bishop Berkeley's courtyard was "really" a tree.

Of course, if Scripture scholars can demonstrate an error in transcription somewhere along the line, perhaps by uncovering ancient scrolls that treat the account in parable form, as it appears in Luke, that is another story. (I hope that no one takes what I have said so far as a denial of the legitimacy of serious Scripture scholarship. There is a difference between working to expand our knowledge of the Bible in its most authentic and accurate form, and treating it as religious folklore, as an Aramaic version of the Upanishads.)

The Antagonist of Faith

John Henry Newman has much to say on these matters, as on most modern heterodoxy. It is astounding to see how clearly he understood and answered the challenges that so bedevil us today, as early as the second quarter of the 19th century. And fascinating to see how the challenge never dies, no matter how deeply men like Newman, Belloc, Chesterton, and C.S. Lewis seem to drive it back into the ground. Apparently updaters, like the poor, will always be with us. I quote Newman at some length in order to capture the fullness of his highly reasoned approach:

> To rationalize in matters of Revelation is to make our reason the standard and measure of the doctrines revealed; to stipulate that those doctrines should be such as to carry with them their own justification; to reject them, if they come in collision with our existing opinions or habits of thought, or are with difficulty harmonized with our existing opinions or habits of thought, or with difficulty harmonized with our existing stock of knowledge. And thus a rationalistic spirit is the antagonist of faith; for faith is, in its very nature, the acceptance of what our reason cannot reach, simply and absolutely upon testimony.

And remember, please, that Newman is not a backwoods preacher. (Not that anything is wrong with them, especially in comparison to some of the modern seminarians I have met.) No matter how the updaters pose as the only thinkers in town, a living and open faith does not make you a yahoo. Even by purely worldly standards, the one who trusts the accumulated wisdom of the centuries rather than the intellectual fads of a season is the party of the intellect at its best.

Newman knew and accepted what modernist theologians refuse: that we are not to strut and posture proudly as unyielding men of reason in our dealings with Scripture. He was willing to approach the Gospels as a man of faith, not as a rationalist; not as one who would

. . . accept the Revelation, and then explain it away; to speak of it as the word of God, and treat it as the word of man; to refuse to let it speak for itself; to claim to be told the *why* and *how* of God's dealings with us, as therein described, and to assign to Him a motive and a scope of our own; to stumble at the partial knowledge which He may give us of them; to put aside what is obscure, as if it had not been said at all, to accept one half of what has been told us, and not the other half . . . to garble, twist them, in order to bring them into conformity with the idea to which we have subjected them.[5]

Newman puts his finger on the central prejudice of the rationalists and his kin, the modern updater: "The rationalist makes himself his own centre, not his Maker; he does not go to God, but he implies that God must come to him."

If it were not so serious an issue we could make great fun of updater attempts to keep up with the times. They are always two steps behind. They have been telling us for years now that we must be willing to rid the Gospels of the otherworldly element in order to make them "relevant" to modern man. And where has the world gone in the meantime? In the opposite direction. Flying saucer cults, witchcraft, astronauts from other planets building Inca temples, ESP, Uri Geller, *The Exorcist,* Tarot cards, I Ching, yogas, Rev. Moon, Carlos Castenada's shamans, athletes turning Muslim, the revival of dowsing, Zen, Krishna chanters, and resurgent Pentecostals have all, it seems, become as American as apple pie to a generation that has seen, through a distorting prism, that man needs more than electric hair dryers, stretch pants and subsidized rents at a swinging singles' apartment on New York's East Side. But here come our progressive Christian updaters telling us that we had better tone down all that stuff about walking on water and healing lepers. Not only, as Chesterton warned, did they end up exaggerating what had already been exaggerated beyond reason, but they did it at the wrong time for the wrong people and in the wrong country.

The kids, whether Krishna chanters or Hell's Angels, are right—to the extent that life does have to be more than it seems. We need miracles. If Christ is not what the Gospels tell us, then the brooding, lonely emptiness found in Sartre's plays might be an accurate description of life. It is no accident that the "brightest and the best" of the atheists of our century have been drawn like lemmings to such solipsistic gloominess. It is no coincidence either that the attractions of suicide take up so much space in their most thoughtfully worked-out prose.

The sense of wonder that fills a believer's life—the miracle of birth, the joys of parenthood, the warm glow of Christmas mornings around the family

[5]*The Essential Newman,* p. 99.

51

Nativity scene, love, sacrifice, honor, bravery, glory—depend in large measure on the existence of a personal and loving God who provides the measure, the rhyme and the reason, for all these experiences. Without Him, life does become filled with all the atheists' burdens: child-bearing a bloody nuisance, a figure distorting accident; marriage a self-limiting trap; love a biochemical carnal appetite; bravery a *macho* attempt to conjure up self-esteem where there should be none. We end up, like them, pondering whether to throw ourselves into the river, rather than marvelling in Christian fashion at its life-giving rush to the sea.

Chapter III

The Narrow Gate

ONE NEED NOT have studied thoroughly the works of Sartre, Genet, Camus, or Heidegger, or the linguistic analysts whose suggested approach to the moral questions of life ends up being near to identical to them, to have been affected by the philosophical attitude the world calls existentialist. Like Marxism, we have all absorbed it simply by being alive and sensate in our time. Movies, paperback books, television shows, pop records, to say nothing of classroom sessions in Europe and America for the last twenty or thirty years, have elevated existentialism's central tenets to the position of near orthodoxy. All those hardbitten Hollywood heroes—from Bogie to Clint Eastwood—living proudly by their own rules; lonely housewives oppressed by their roles in marriage and motherhood; despondent business executives trying to find out "what it's all about" with a bottle and a broad; alienated, sad-eyed but idealistic (of course) students; Bergman's and Bunuel's lost souls, were just part of the presentation.

It has gotten to the point where even Christians appear reluctant to challenge the creed: that there is no personal, loving, judging God who punishes and rewards, that life is empty, meaningless and absurd, and that happiness comes only from a successful conjuring up for ourselves of the best "role" and "self-identity" that we can contrive in the great charade called life. At times the Christian best-shot seems only to be the assertion that as "Christ follower" we can find meaning in life as well as with any other identity; maybe even a successful encounter with our fellow men, maybe even love. Act "as if" life is worthwhile by Christian standards, we seem to say to the world, and maybe you'll be able to find worth; and maybe the expectation of Christ's promise of everlasting life with him in Paradise will even allow you to keep it going right up to the moment of death.

Not that such an approach is all that bad, as long as it is made as a first pitch instead of a faithless sellout. There is nothing wrong with showing that the Christian commitment offers at least as much as the richest promises of another way of life. Missionaries have known how to maneuver similarly for centuries. And, there are *some* Christian preachers who have been effective of late in showing the lost and lonely children of the godless age that it really is more satisfying to "be yourself" by following the old catechism maxim of knowing, loving, and serving God in this life in anticipation of being happy with Him forever in the next, than in a drug-charged search for sensual pleasure. Unfortunately, they all too often have been of the faddish and suspicious Jesus-freak sort. One cannot help but brood sadly, and boil angrily, over these poor confused young people who might have been brought into the Christian churches if the established churches, infatuated with the dream of being progressive, had not come across as such weak and pallid imitators of the secular world they found so empty in the first place.

Christians are acting shamefully, however, if they limit their missionary efforts to a first-pitch demonstration of the emotional rewards of being a good Christian. Christianity is the Way even for those who find it a cross—as some do. Golgotha comes before Easter.

Existentialism, by the existentialists' testimony, only becomes attractive at that point in life when the fullness of the Christian promise leaves, and the Christian disciplines, as a result, fail to make sense. It is a rival system. (With only a few notable exceptions. I won't try to probe the conscience of those like Nicolai Berdyaev or Soren Kierkegaard, who speak of an existential encounter with Christ, except to note that their prose, steeped in mystery as it is, still militates against the idea of a teaching Christian Church.) The existentialists offer an alternative to Christianity, not a parallel glimpse at the mystery of life. The existentialists know that. The confusion lies with Christians who refuse to take them at their word. Or Christ at his, and retool his teachings so that he can make it over black coffee and cigarettes with Jean-Paul Sartre and Simone de Beauvoir. (Or is it that they—the aspirant Christian intellectuals—hope they can worm their way into those circles?)

Signed Masterpieces

We are all familiar with the existentialist premise, *"L'existence précéde l'essence,"* in Sartre's famous epigram. There are no natural or divine laws by which human behavior can be judged. We live in a "homocentric" world, says Karl Jaspers, where "man is everything." Alternative views, including the Christian, with stress on duty and obedience to ideals higher than oneself, limit man, make him less free, and less human. Which explains why, for Sartre, the "saint" for our time is the thief, pederast, and jailbird Jean Genet, a man unafraid to live life on his own terms. (Sartre does not intend to shock with this admission. He revels in it.)

It is, of course, the sin of Adam—to be as God. Dostoevsky knew the temptation. As he writes in *The Brothers Karamozov,* "If there were no God, everything would be possible." Conversely, if there is a God—the God described by Jesus, to be specific—the demand for moral autonomy is arrogant beyond measure. It is no coincidence that Sartre is an atheist. And it is no coincidence that Christian theologians such as Gregory Baum, who became infected with a Sartre-like stress on the importance of freedom from Church authority and dogma, take the next step with him as well: Theologians have discovered, Baum tell us, that "divine transcendence" does not refer . . . to God's independent existence in a supernatural world . . . does not refer to a "supreme being" . . . but to the deepest dimension of "history (and the cosmos)."[1] Would it not be fair to say that for the moderns, "theologian" is to God the way "allergist" is to hay fever?

Throughout Sartre's career, he has hammered out the message with exasperating persistence. Only in a free and unrestricted encounter with life can one find worth. The old virtues, obedience and loyalty to God, king, country or Church, are childlike refusals to meet life. It is the *way* that we choose, not the choice, that matters; not whether you win or lose, kid, but how you play the game.

In Sartre's *Les Chemins de la Liberté*, one of the characters imaginatively fondles a knife, contemplating the freedom that will be his in a violent lashing out at the world's injunctions against murder and suicide. "For there would be neither Good nor Evil unless he invented them," the "hero" realizes in agony. In *La Morte dans l'Ame,* Mathieu, the partisan guerrilla in the French resistance, fights to his death not because it is honorable to fight for God or country, but for the experience of the last minutes before death, the ultimate, perfect moment for creating and testing self-worth. In *La Nausée,* Sartre's admittedly

[1]*New Horizon: Theological Essays,* pp. 65–70.

autiobiographical character asserts that "I write, I shall keep on writing books. They are necessary." But not necessary because they serve the cause of justice, or elevate the human sensibilities, or testify to the truth. For "culture does not save anything or anybody; it does not justify. But it is a product of man; he projects himself into it and recognizes himself in it." Genet projects himself in his way; Sartre in his. But it is qualitatively the same thing for the existentialist.

Sartre has come to see of late, however, something most French peasants could have told him if he had asked: that this vision into the emptiness and despair of life does not satisfy for long; not beyond the momentary sense of superiority one feels when he places himself above and beyond the ways of his people. La Nausée soon comes over us. "Other people" become "hell," as he says in No Exit. Their lives touch ours and there is no existential way out. Our choices become limited, by becoming important. Thoughts of duty, sacrifice, and responsibility begin to haunt us. "God would have got me out of my difficulties," he sighs in Les Mots. "I would have been a signed masterpiece, sure of playing my part in the concert of the universe, I would have waited patiently for Him to reveal to me His designs and my necessity."

We could interrupt the gloomy ruminations of this self-admittedly wretched old man and simply say that He did—in Christ. But we must never forget that faith is dependent upon grace. We can turn away from our Lord, but he has to have beckoned first. It is not a failure of intelligence or a refusal to read at length and think deeply that prevents Sartre from embracing Christian joy. How much of his refusal is due to a perverse and culpable hardness of heart? We will never know in this life. Surely he has read most of whatever it was that led Jacques Maritain to live out a life, by all visible signs and by his own testimony, filled with a sense of well-being and purpose, and to die in serenity as the Peasant of the Garonne. "Judge not . . ."

But this reservation must not hold us back from condemning openly and without qualification the moral and philosophical squalor—La Nausée—Sartre and his followers would have us adopt in one suidical stroke. It is a bromide, I know, but we can hate the sin without hating the sinner. Christ freed us from Sartre's emptiness, and it would be condescension (to Sartre) and faithlessness (to Christ) to pretend that we can "see his point."

From Doubt to Treason

Sartre's intellectual odyssey would make a poignant and revealing morality play for our age. (As a matter of fact, the Huns of the future, after they ride through our Rome, just might take home copies of The Balcony as justification to their children for why they had to put their victims to the sword.) His

56

existential premises have taken him down a syllogistic path that is ominously sound, and one which many others appear likely to follow, once you grant those premises. From brooding Left Bank philosopher to shameless shill for the European Maoist Left. Nowadays, say Parisians, wherever there is a demonstration or strike, at the universities or the Renault plants, you'll find the slouched and stiff, wattled and bespectacled figure of Sartre shouting out encouragement for student rioters or handing out pamphlets to the, alternately, bemused and disdainful workers. He has issued statements in praise of the career of Stalin, of the murderous Baader-Meinhof gang in Germany, of Frantz Fanon's paeans to the murder of whites, of Castro's dictatorship, of Lumumba in the Congo, and of Mao's continued use of terror to prevent the bourgeoisification of China. In the name of his free and limitless choice, he has become an unembarrassed tout for the most brutal totalitarian enemies of the Christian West.

A paradox? On the contrary, it is consistent, which is why it is so serious an issue. Especially when Christians like Michael Novak and Harvey Cox acknowledge the appeal of such a devolution of thought to Christians of their temperament.

Edmund Burke once wrote that "Society cannot exist unless a controlling power upon will and appetite be placed somewhere; and the less of it there is from within the more of it there must be from without." Existentialists fly in the face of that wisdom.

But not Sartre—not recently, anyway. In a roundabout way he has come to agree with Burke. But permit me to proceed slowly. It is an important development. One should not challenge such a prominent part of our *Zeitgeist* in an offhand way.

The starting point for the existentialist is his demand for *subjective* truth. Truth must develop from within a man, as a result of his life experience—his existence. No tradition, heritage, or long-standing moral code can be allowed a philosophically legitimate binding force on his mind. *But,* once one comes to accept this premise, for whatever reason, it is only a short step over to the point where his people, his country and its religious foundations and traditional wisdom, become enemies; a barrier to be overcome on his road to mature wisdom; shackles that limit his hoped-for intellectual and moral autonomy. In other words, as Sartre tells us quite frankly, it becomes a healthy and natural thing for a free man to "hate" and "to try to escape" the ways of the social order in which he was raised—as he admits to hating bourgeois, Christian France.

Once the aspirant existentialist succeeds in this, however, a bedeviling paradox begins to torment him. Few men, as we know now, can live as aliens, as Kafkaesque insects, with no way of identfying themselves as part of a community in pursuit of something honorable. Few, if any, can endure being existentialists, choosing endlessly from meaningless choices in a charade of life. That is why suicide has always been the burning question in existentialist circles. It is one way off the treadmill.

Some, like Albert Camus, sought their way out of the paradox by groping determinedly toward a sense of commitment and a loving relationship with their fellow men. (Some admiring Christians have even suggested, perhaps in a bout of wishful thinking, that if Camus had lived ten years longer his search would have led him to the Mystical Body of Christ, the perfect community.)

But those are the choices: a) suicide, or b) the traditional social and moral order of the West, or c) one of the challenging "isms," such as Marxism. There has to be some way for those who want to go on living to be freed from the absurdity of living life as an absurdity. Either the ways of their people which have become habitual and require minimal imposition by force; or a new and revolutionary order which will have to be imposed by an armed elite.

Obviously, for those as alienated from the West as Sartre and his coterie, this choice is not one that requires long and arduous thought. If you actively hate the ways of your people, *on high principle,* you are not likely to go back to them. You might commit suicide. But if not, the external disciplines and overall regimen that you crave to give meaning to your life (and to save you from *really* having to live with the Saint Genets of the world, as Thomas Molnar notes) are likely to come from the enemies of your people. Hate can do a lot for a man. Or as Sartre himself explains when discussing the reasons for his support of the Communist regime in Russia, even after the invasion of Hungary: "In the name of the principles my class had inculcated in me, in the name of its humanism and humanities, in the name of liberty, equality and fraternity, I dedicated to the bourgeoisie a hatred which will end only with myself." And even if that means ideological alliance with Stalin and his heirs.

Simone de Beauvoir has written of the days that she and Sartre spent as high school teachers in the 1930's arguing and discussing issues endlessly in coffee houses. "We were re-inventing man," she said.[2] Well, so are the Marxists. And for someone interested in remaking Christian man, they are the only game in town just now.

Perhaps the bigger question is why Sartre's views prove to be attractive to so many. It is not difficult to imagine a few individuals with a hate for our civilization intense enough for them to go over to the enemy, or a Charles Manson. Alienation, leading to an exisentialist despair from which we are rescued by a new and Communist-defined sense of mission in life—an easily understood journey. Once Christ is denied, at any rate. But why so many? I would suggest for starters that most of those who desert Christ for such

[2]Quoted by Germaine Bree, *Camus and Sartre* (New York: Delacorte Press, 1972), p. 92.

emptiness and sorrowful treason had never known Him in the first place.

But even if there were no Communist presence in the world offering itself as an alternative, another danger would remain. By denying the existence of a discernible moral code, the existentialists drain of all plausibility the idea of a higher level of behavior to which we *ought* to aspire over and against our petty stock of moral knowledge. Without such a capacity, what we know as civilization cannot survive. A society can rot away from within so totally that it will fall without a push from beyond its borders.

What is even more frightening, though, is that the existentialists are removing this element of the "ought and ought not" from our lives at the very moment when others of comparable influence are stressing the residual animal impulses in man that often lead to violent anti-social behavior. I am thinking of the Desmond Morris (*The Naked Ape*) and Konrad Lorenz (*On Aggression*) breed of anthropologist. At the same time, people like British psychiatrist Ronald D. Laing are insisting that it is wrong for us to keep under detention those we think insane, since insane behavior is a quite logical way to deal with the absurdities of life in modern Europe and America. In fact, he argues, those of us who do not act crazily in protest against our society are the ones with the real problem. Think about it: three of the leading influences in our modern culture are leading us to the conclusion that our instincts are basically animal; that the insane are the ones who have the clearest insights into truth; and that there are no moral codes to which we should aspire even if we are not animals or insane. Maybe Johnny would be better off if he could read with even less ability when we pack him off to college.

Two of the most discussed plays of the last few Broadway seasons, Peter Schaffer's *Equus* and Edward Albee's *Seascape,* offer cutting artistic expression of this "enlightened," downgrading view of man. Both authors are progressive thinkers more intent upon increasing our inability to see man as a being made in the image and likeness of God than in shocking us out of it. Artists are, after all, those of us with the more sensitive antennae. The death wish of liberal America is more alive in them than in the rest of us, just as the religious glory of Christendom was more alive in Michelangelo and Botticelli than in the local coopers.

In *Equus,* the young hero loves horses. Not like Jody in *The Red Pony* or Elizabeth Taylor in *National Velvet.* He loves them in a sensual way, and reacts to his neighbors wagging their fingers by gouging out horses' eyes. The moral clash of the play, however, centers on the narrowminded family and the parochial neighbors who precipitate such an acting out on the boy's part. Who, pray tell, are they to define his actions as insane or evil? By what standard? As Laing reminds us, our entire Western world is insane. How can we force others, especially our young, to share in its lunacy? Maybe the insane are really better off. (And the deracinated, thoroughly liberalized New York critics and theatergoers are nodding in agreement at the thought. The play is doing quite well. "Yes, yes," they are saying as they leave the theater, "who are we with all our hangups and therapy bills to condemn such behavior? Remember the party last week, darling. The boy wasn't really that different from us, you know.")

In *Seascape,* Albee chastises us, again, this time for trying to make life seem more than it is by imposing upon our true selves false society-made notions of honor, piety, heroism, and all that rot. Such self glorification leads to the horrors of the modern world—Vietnam, McCarthyism, scorn for gays. Better we be like the play's heroes: lizards, who have none of these hangups. If we only could be like them, living out our life in the eternal swamp, happily eating away, breathing and rutting, without the Western compulsion to judge right from wrong, sin from virtue. As Malachi Martin notes in criticism (*National Review,* June 6, 1975), for Albee, men

> . . . have two alternatives. Either: imitate the lizards and other well-behaved animals, and like them trust the self-fulfilling purpose of life—which is living. Or be worse than lizards, and self destruct. If anyone were to suggest a third alternative in a Pulitzer Prize candidate play (say: Seek the Kingdom of God, and all else will be accomplished in you), this would not merely be unsophisticated (which is not why Albee doesn't include it), but irrelevant and subjective.
>
> There is, summarily, no escape hatch upward for us humans, no high ground from which to view our bodies, our minds, and our lives. You can delve into the murky instincts within us. You can consult the animals we were, and, in some ways, still are. You can get insights about the primeval ooze. All we need and all we can have is "inside here" and "back there." And to hold this view to the exclusion of properly religious issues is to be objective and truly human. To see and discuss marriage or hippomania within a paradigm of moral obligations, of God's will and of God's healing grace, that is to be "subjective."

Yes, we've come a long way, baby. The existential philosophers have told us that life is an absurd dung heap, and our playwrights are giving the message artistic life.

The Desires of Your Father

Then there's women's lib—which comes to mind thanks to those "long way, baby," cigarette ads. (Which are very perceptive, by the way. That does seem to be what women's lib is all about—sharing in the mistakes and the worst features of the world of men.) Let us not start off on the wrong foot. Let us concede for the moment the demand for equal pay for equal work. But only for the moment. Even that minimal demand, when pushed by the lib leaders who know where they want to go, is loaded with an anti-Christian animus that cannot go unchallenged. It is *not* progress to make the job market attractive to women at the expense of the image of motherhood. And don't think that that is not being done. *The Phyllis Schafly Report* in December, 1974 made a study of the full intentions of those organizations most committed to achieving the Equal Rights Amendment. The U.S. Commission on Population Growth and the American Future, established in 1970 by the Rockefeller family, states for example that the ERA should work "to neutralize the legal, social and institutional pressures that historically have encouraged childbearing." Lester Brown in the widely read *Saturday Review/World* (July 27, 1974) argues: "Given the need to reduce fertility and birthrates, it is now imperative for every society to create employment opportunities for women sufficiently attractive to induce many of them to opt for these rather than for childbearing." In *The Futurist,* Jeanne Binstock writes that we need "to demand that the ancient and honorable occupation of motherhood fall into disrepute, and that women commit themselves to other occupations. Women must be *liberated* to enjoy the fruits of other occupations, *whether they want to or not"* (emphasis in the original). Congresswoman Patsy Mink in a *New York Times* article argued that if we "encourage policies which will permit women to choose other roles, many will leave the home and thus decide to have fewer children. We should encourage this movement into the work force."

A Christian social order, in contrast, would do all within its power to give legal protection and elevate to its deserved place of honor woman's role as wife and mother. It is one of the deepest and most troubling signs of our loss of confidence in the worth of our Christian civilization, and of our self-hate, that American women are proving susceptible to this well financed campaign that tells them that meaning in life can be found more by working in an insurance office or selling cosmetics or writing "swinging lifestyle" articles for a women's magazine than by raising new life in Christ.

But fortunately the women's lib movement admits that it is about far more than equal pay. The battle against the libbers does not have to be fought out on that bumpy ground. The movement is more concerned with "rescuing" women from the traditional role of "mere" wife and mother. Motherhood is their existential trap. Anyone who has been around a few libbers for a half hour or so knows that there is the deepest of scorn in their circles for the American woman of the past—our mothers, to be exact. Their conversations are filled with snide references to "stupid housewives," and "breeding machines," and "silly little things" who find meaning in life "cleaning and dusting and watching a brood of brats all day," and "waiting hand and foot on some oaf." (Come on now, libbers and friends . . . fess up. Right? These are near-to-exact quotes from conversations I hear almost daily in the academic circles in which I am forced to move.)

Inherent in this libber disdain for woman's role in the family is a blatant challenge to the idea that there is a divine order in which women have a part to play, whether it is exactly to their liking or not. (I imply in no way, I hope it unnecessary to say, that there is anything "wrong" with career women. If the libbers were interested only in protecting those women who are not wives and mothers, they would get no quarrel from me. But they have moved so far beyond that plea that it is hardly worth dwelling on the issue.)

The libbers reject what George Gilder has seen so clearly, although from a different angle, in *Sexual Suicide*: that it is no mere coincidence that a woman's body both carries and nourishes new life. It is an indication of the role assigned to her in the natural order of things. Women are to be the source and sustenance—physical and moral—of new life, a responsibility subordinate to no other in life where God's will matters. But the libbers insist on treating this solemn responsibility as an *unnatural* burden! As some freakish flaw in nature from which they demand release! They demand that their sexual identity carry *no* unique responsibilities, up to and including the sex of the partner they choose in the "relationship" called sex. (Not the "reproductive act," of course. Gross, how kids keep on threatening to come from a practice so pleasurable . . . damn nuisance! Whose idea was that, anyway?)

Let's be blunt: blunt and honest. The libber demand for a "lifestyle of their own choosing" is a demand to which *no one*–no Christian especially—is entitled. It is not what is meant by taking up your cross in life. It is not the attitude taught by the God-man who knelt, sweating blood while contemplating his death, and lifted his eyes to heaven and said, "But not my will but thine be done." The God of the Gospels *is* a chauvinist pig—by Ti-Grace Atkinson's standards. The libbers know that. That is why some of their noisiest demonstrations take place outside churches. They know that Christ's words demand something far different from the kind of life extolled in the pages of *Ms.* and *Cosmopolitan*.

If you keep your ears to the ground, however, you will hear rumblings that just might bode well for us. Not just that the Equal Rights Amendment is having a harder time getting passed than anyone expected. The libbers are still pushing for that. I am thinking more of the libber revolt against the ongoing prospect of plugging more and more dangerous drugs and gadgets into their bodies in order to stop those bothersome "accidents" that keep threatening to disturb their freedom. They are complaining of the wrong things, of course, and finding a shocking and ugly way out by way of Lesbianism and masturbation, but if one can judge anything from the reviews of certain women's lib novels, there is a growing recognition, too, of the horrible irony of women almost killing themselves in their attempt to prevent or kill their children.

Obviously, and emphatically, men have much to do with this sordid state of affairs. Women should not be fooled by the open-minded friendship of *Playboy* and that ilk; the women's lib movement is right up their alley. A separation of sex, love, and new life is what they have been preaching all along. It doesn't bother them a fig if their sex-objects think themselves "liberated" rather than oppressed the morning after a "meaningful encounter." It is difficult to be a Beatrice or a Rowena in a world filled with would-be Lenny Bruces—I would imagine. But it is as difficult to be a Galahad to would-be Bella Abzugs or Gloria Steinems, too. Women's lib will only make permanent and institutionalize such lowered expectations.

Those of us who know Christ know that life—including sex, marriage, and love—has meaning, and that there are moral choices that will give us dignity and worth, if we can only discipline ourselves to meet them. That is why Christians dance, sing, and feast their way through holydays instead of brooding away their days off over coffee and cigarettes. Think of Swiss farmers kneeling for the Angelus, or the faces of the Spaniards who carry the statue of Christ through their villages; and then of the sad-eyed photograph of Sartre on every dust cover of every gloomily titled book he has ever written, and you will get the picture.

You can get the same message by listening to people who find life empty and their selves "not whole"—when they tell of how they envy those simpler souls with a faith. Of course, they say that with the superior and condescending air of a ten-year-old looking back on how much more fun Christmas was when he believed in Santa Claus. There are circles now in America—perhaps you should consider yourself fortunate if you don't know it first-hand—where the Laing vision has been so internalized that you are thought *abnormal* if you are not receiving psychiatric care. The idea is that you display a callous and boorish lack of sensitivity if the absurdity of life has not depressed you to the point where you can't go on without "help." All the truly beautiful souls, you see, are overcome with the poetic emptiness they have been taught by Sartre and Simone de Beauvoir.

But, as we should know, they are not the only teachers:

> If you abide in my word, you shall be my disciples. Indeed, you shall know the truth and the truth shall set you free. (Jn. 8:31-32)

For Christians, those words present, first and foremost, a challenge and a course of duty. But they offer hope, as well. Life will not be a Sartrean pigsty with no exit other than suicide or Mao to free us from the hell-like experience of others.

But that Christian solace comes only with a successful handling of the challenge. It is a package deal. The cross sets you free. A refusal condemns. (And I can think of few more excruciating hells than a Sartre-like life, even if that were the only consequence of rejecting Christ.)

> Why do you not understand my speech? Because you cannot listen to my word. The father from whom you are, is the devil, and the desires of your father, it is your will to do. He was a murderer from the beginning, and has not stood in the truth because there is no truth in him. (Jn. 8:43-44)

And in an explicit summary:

> He who is of God hears the words of God. The reason why you do not hear is that you are not of God. (Jn. 8:47)

There is no latitudinarian concession here. Christ does *not* excuse the Pharisees because "they are not of God." They are to blame because they have not opened their hearts to the light *when they should have*. "If I speak the truth why do you not believe me?" (The modern answer, I am afraid, would be to suggest a course in behavioral psychology at N.Y.U. to get at the *real* answer.)

Christ promised that the correct choice would bring a heavenly reward which would make our most severe earthly trials seem trifling inconveniences. But we would have to choose.

> Not everyone who says to me, "Lord, Lord," shall enter the kingdom of heaven; but *he who does the will* of my Father in heaven . . . Many will say to me in that day, "Lord, Lord, did we not prophesy in thy name, and cast out devils in thy name, and work many miracles in thy name?" (Mt. 7:21-22)

Christ's next words could have been written yesterday, in specific answer to those who belittle the need for adhering faithfully to a moral code above and beyond our will:

> And then I will declare to them, "I never knew you. Depart from me, you workers of iniquity!" Everyone who hears these my words, *and acts upon them,* shall be likened to a wise man who built his house on rock. (Mt. 7:23-24)

It was *not* upon an inner disposition to handle each situation in our life with existential "awareness" that we are to be judged:

> By their *fruits* ye shall know then. Do men gather grapes from thorns, or figs from thistles? Even so, every good tree bears good fruit, but the bad tree bears bad fruit. A good tree cannot bear bad fruit, nor can a bad tree bear good fruit. (Mt. 7:16-18)

Notice the explicitness, the black-and-white nature of the words. "Good" . . . "bad"—used repeatedly.
We can tell one from the other, and are expected to do just that—or else.

> Every tree that does not bear good fruit is cut down and *thrown into the fire.* Therefore by their fruits you will know them. (Mt. 7:19-20)

> Enter by the narrow gate. For wide is the gate and broad is the way that leads to destruction, and many there are who enter that way. How narrow the gate and close the way that leads to life! And few there are who find it. (Mt. 7:13-14)

> And he who does not take up his cross and follow me, is not worthy of me. He who finds his life will lose it, and he who loses his life for my sake, will find it. (Mt. 10:38-39)

There is no department store of equally valid because equally ambiguous moral and religious choices:

> Amen, amen, I say to you, he who enters not by the door into the sheepfold, but climbs up another way, is a thief and a robber. But he who enters by the door is shepherd of the sheep. To this man the gatekeeper opens, and the sheep hear his voice, and he calls his own sheep by name and leads them forth. And when he has let out his own sheep, he goes before them; and the sheep follow him because they know his voice. But a stranger they will not follow, but will flee from him, because they do not know the voice of strangers.

You might think the thrust of that parable clear enough. Perhaps Christ was anticipating the sophistry of our times as well as answering puzzled faces in his audience when he went on:

> Amen, amen, I say to you. I am the door of the sheep. All whoever have come before me are thieves and robbers; but the sheep have not heard them. I am the door. If anyone enter by me he shall be safe, and shall go in and out, and shall find pastures. The thief comes to steal, and slay, and destroy. I am come that they might have life, and that they might have it more abundantly. (Jn. 10:1-10)

Later, just after his triumphal entry into Jerusalem, Christ warns the Apostles that they will not always have palms waved before them; that they will suffer persecution for his sake. But even that will not lessen their responsibility. They must even be willing to suffer death, for:

> If anyone serves me, let him follow me; and where I am there also shall my servant be. If anyone serves me, my Father will honor him. (Jn. 12:26)

There is no lessening of that requirement in our time, whether we learn our doubts on the Left Bank of Paris, or in theology classes in our church basement. It is the mission of Christians to work against such despair:

> What I tell you in darkness, speak it in the light; and what you hear whispered, preach it on the housetops. And do not be afraid of those who kill the body but cannot kill the soul. (Mt. 10: 27-28)

Obviously, if it need be said, he does not think that anyone will risk death for going around the Roman Empire telling people to "do their own thing."

"But rather be afraid of him who is able to destroy both soul and body in hell." (Mt. 10:28) Just in case you have doubts about the one who will judge us—thinking perhaps that Christ is referring to "the deepest dimension of human history and the cosmos," he adds:

> Therefore, everyone who acknowledges me before men, I also will acknowledge him before my Father in heaven. But whoever disowns me before men, I in turn will disown him before my Father in heaven. (Mt. 10:32-33)

No praise of coffee-house indecision about the meaning of life. Such doubts saddened Christ:

> And Jesus was going about all the towns and villages, teaching in their synagogues, and preaching the gospel of the kingdom, and curing every kind of disease and infirmity. But seeing the crowds, he was moved with a compassion for them, because they were bewildered and dejected, like sheep without a shepherd. Then he said to his disciples, "The harvest indeed is great, but the laborers are few. Pray therefore the Lord of the harvest to send forth laborers into his harvest." (Mt. 9:35-38)

Notice that Christ conveys the image of what Gabriel Moran in his high school textbook for religious studies sneeringly calls the "Santa Claus God." Christ did preach the existence of a Father who answered our prayers.

In the Face of the World

Admittedly, those of us who like to consider ourselves well educated and scholarly might find ourselves in an uncomfortable position if we accept Christ's words. For we cannot *really* be intellectuals—at least by the modern world's standards—if we do accept his words. Accepting Christ means that we must deal with much of modern psychology and sociology, for example, exactly the way those disciplines suggest that the world approach Christianity—not too seriously. I hope you do not harbor lingering doubts about the nature of the "beneficial interplay" between religion and the behavioral and social sciences we hear being discussed. If you do, ponder for a moment the words of Freud, who, in this instance, is a master challenged by few in the field. Only updaters can feel at home in the company of these behavioral scientists, and only because they too see religion as a "crutch" man will some day be able to do without. (How about modern theologions = the ecclesiastical wing of the social sciences?) Religion, says Freud,

> . . . is an attempt to master the sensory world in which we are situated by means of the wishful world which we have developed within us as a result of biological and psychological necessities.

Consequently,

> If we attempt to assign the place of religion in the evolution of mankind, it appears not as a permanent acquisition but as a counterpart to the neurosis which individual civilized men have to go through in their passage from childhood to maturity.[3]

You can see why the psychologists and sociologists are so willing to work within the framework of the Christian churches. We *really* need help, from the perspective of their training. And from the Christian perspective . . . well, they are modern Eves offering a new apple. If we are serious about Christianity we have to take their search for "normalcy" and "interpersonal integrity" as an affront. We must regard Freud and his followers (broadly defined) the way we would Indian rain dancers or Mayan cargo cults.

We can concede that studies such as theirs offer a fascinating insight into human intellectual ingenuity; that they can achieve some limited good; that it is worthwhile for man to know himself in all his forms of development, including mistaken ones; and that the human skills—literary and analytic—refined and developed even in pursuit of chimeras, can be worthy of high praise. But we can never pretend that those who deny Christ really are closing in on truth. For etiquette's sake, and to make sure that our "subjects" will allow us to see them operate without pretense or self-consciousness, we might allow our skepticism to go unspoken. We could not observe rain dancers for long if we laughed at them or treated their confidence with scorn.

[3]*Contemporary Religious Thinkers*, pp. 124–125.

This pose can be maintained successfully. Christians can, as we have all heard, be *in* but not *of* the world. There is nothing wrong with a fascination for Freudian psychology or Skinnerian determinism or Tom Sawyer's use of dead cats. I can remember studying under that sadly vanishing breed of Jesuits who knew as much about Heidegger, or Nietzsche, or Beckett's plays, as anyone, but who never let their appreciation for worldly achievements prevent them from making clear to their students that the refusal to accept Christ limits even intellectual achievements of this caliber to mere approximations of truth. They knew—and acted as if they knew—that Christ was the Way, and never pretended that maybe there was more to offer in the pages of last semester's most read paperback in Columbia's campus bookstore.

There is a difficulty in such an approach, however. The academicians whose work excludes Christ know the pose. And all those clerics and nuns who have asked, and been granted, permission to shed their collars and veils have figured that out. That was why they complained when their professors treated them differently from the rest of the class, and prefixed their classroom remarks with disclaimers such as: "Now, Sister, I know you might not buy what Kate Millett says about sexual experience, but most experts now agree that . . ." Or, "Of course, Father, you might not agree, and certainly I do not blame you for it, but the Church has been on the wrong side of human liberation all down through history and that explains . . ."

Sadly, when our religious shed their collars and veils to meet the world, they succumbed to it instead of converting it, or even making a try. Which was the reason for the collars and the veils in the first place. Our fathers knew the scars of original sin, and would have known in an instant that anyone who tried to tell us that his vocation would be able to stand up to such pressure, if it were a valid one, was someone who was talking through his Pelagian hat. (Some of the defecters from the clergy who have turned out the looniest, made damn good religious while the external disiplines were there to give them the support most humans need in life—from my experience anyway.)

Chapter IV

In the Days
of Noah

THERE ARE NUMEROUS examples of the Christian surrender to the existential mood in our disordered world. The most obvious, perhaps, are evident in the way motivation and responsibility for human action are weighed in updater circles. Like Freud, the updaters seek to unseat the Christian understanding of man's personal struggle against a concupiscent nature—to give us the real reasons why people behave the way they do, as opposed to all the medieval tripe about surrendering to or overcoming temptation.

Our central concern, though, just now, is not so much with proving Freud and his behaviorist descendants wrong, as it is showing that Christ taught a different spirit and message. I do not propose to take on Freud. I am not—all the saints be praised—a psychologist or a psychoanalyst. But I know enough about his contribution to intellectual history to know that he was a challenger to Christ's teachings; that, in fact, it could be said that his mission in life was to free mankind from the notions of free will and personal guilt—sin—taught by the Christian churches, and the social institutions of the West formed under their influence.

What kinds of things am I talking about? Well, it is not easy to argue vigorously against many of the interpretations. They almost always parade under a banner inscribed with Christ's words to the men about to stone the woman taken in adultery: "Let him who is without sin cast the first stone."

I am talking, of course, of the demands made on us by progressive theologians that we should not be in favor of stern and expeditious punishment for violent criminals because of their culturally deprived childhoods, for unruly students because of their problems at home, for political terrorists because of the history of discrimination faced by their people; that we should not be too critical of homosexuals, sex criminals, dope users and others who seem prone to "anti-social acting out" in general, since society is the real villain for not having set up the proper atmosphere in which these poor unfortunates, liberalism's naturally good men, could develop to mature and responsible adulthood. It is a mood similar to that which leads Martin Marty, a Lutheran theologian, to, first of all, write for *Playboy*, and then to concede in his article that there just might be something to the underlying premise of Hugh Hefner's ethics, and that "adultery and premarital sex just might not be as wrong as we thought because of certain conditions those involved might face."

Beyond Freedom and Dignity

It makes little sense to argue—and I, certainly, am not inclined to try—that the behaviorists have demonstrated nothing of worth. I accept the idea that our moral dispositions can be scarred or buffed to a brighter sheen by the atmosphere in which we grow. I have seen happy and open adults desiccated into carping misanthropes by five years of a bad marriage. I can imagine what fifteen years of childhood in such an environment can do to wound a person's character. We *do* have to take a man's background into account before we distribute praise and blame. No quarrel. If that plea for greater forgiveness and compassion were the primary objective of the behaviorists, they would deserve praise. But it is not. Their premise is something very different, and decidedly anti-Christian—i.e., that we are not really responsible for our actions; that we are closer to a lump of clay that can be molded and shaped by social pressures than we are to a free moral agent made in the image and likeness of God—the definition of man traditionally accepted by Christians. The behaviorists deny, to be direct, that there can be guilt; that a man is truly in control of the welter of environmental forces that surround his life, and therefore is to be blamed or praised for his reaction. B.F. Skinner, as we know, takes the premise to its logical end, arguing that behavior can be so totally controlled and directed that man some day will be seen as a creature "beyond freedom and dignity." That phrase was chosen as the title for his book to indicate the extent of the external control of our actions that behaviorists like Skinner think possible, and to shock the reader into an immediate recognition of exactly what kind of "sentimentality" he must be willing to shed in the name of progressive thought about human nature. Christians would do well to dwell on the words. The updater pitch—so far, anyway—has stressed only the greater love and understanding and Christian forgiveness which will be encouraged once we learn to understand the reasons why people behave in the way old-fashioned Christians call sinful. Much of their writing, in fact, seems to indicate that we would do well to stop talking of sin altogether.

Unfortunately the next round, whether the updaters like it or not, is Skinner's. Without the capacity to sin—to be *evil*—man deserves neither credit nor praise, neither freedom nor dignity. Praise requires responsibility. If our actions are environmentally controlled, the soldier who fights his way through a drumbeat of machine-gun fire to rescue a wounded comrade deserves no more praise than one who deserts at the first radio report of hightening tensions; the faithful and self-sacrificing wife and mother no more respect than the happy hooker; a KKK hangman no less than Harriet Tubman. If you take this behaviorist step (and it is a logical and necessary one, isn't it?), all the updater talk of *agape* and commitment to our fellow man becomes verbal fudge. Our fellow Pavlovian creatures might deserve pity and some self-serving applications of the golden rule, but not love. (Perhaps that is why so much of what progressive theologians call love comes across in a mawkish and insincere way—the easy love "for mankind" that requires only the figurative display of a bleeding heart, as opposed to the love of those near to us, which requires that we come home nights to duty, sacrifice, and often pain.)

Go and Sin No More

A quick glance through the textbooks of religious training being sold of late, or at the religious activities organized by progressive clerics, or at the essays being written by the Modernist champions, shows the behaviorist bias at work. Religion books which work at helping the student understand *why* he behaves the way he does rather than at changing his immoral behavior are becoming increasingly common, and near-to-indistinguishable from the texts used in psychology classes in secular high schools and colleges. (Which would make the authors proud, since it would tell them they have learned well the lessons of their graduate-school professors who wrote the psychology books used in the secular schools.) Retreats and rap sessions in teenage centers, and encounter groups organized to help troubled Christians deal with their "inability to cope with life" and their "communicative failures," are directed nowadays toward examining the "life factors" which cause alienation rather than purging us of our sins. Father Andrew Greeley writes that Christ so understood the problems of human behavior that in the Gospels "the woman taken in sin is not required to express her sorrow or promise amendment. Before she can say anything Jesus sends her away with forgiveness."[1]

It would be difficult to find a better example of updater gleaning of the Scriptural text than this statement. Whether it is a result of remarkable disingenuousness, naivete, or a bad memory, I'll leave aside. (I would like to think that Greeley's memory failed. I like much of what he writes elsewhere, especially when he leaves theological questions to others.) Whatever, it is an example of the updater determination to make the Scriptures work for them; in this case, for Greeley's sociology lectures. Since modern sociologists "understand" the temptations of the flesh to the point of explaining them away, and never think it proper to criticize those who "live in sin," Christ must be made to agree with them. No matter what the Gospels say.

But the fact of the matter is that the message of the story of the woman taken in sin is not at all what Greeley thinks—or would have us believe. There is no doubt that Christ interceded on behalf of the woman. (I think that I loved Christ for that story before any other as a boy.) But the final cymbal clash of the story, the solar-plexus uppercut, the exclamation point, is the unmistakable warning that she must:

"Go and sin no more."

"Sin no more" . . . not "try to minimize your exploitative sexual encounters," not "be true to yourself." Not, as a Father Finian of Topeka tells his congregation, try to "get all your shit together when it comes to your own sexuality." Here are a few more words of wisdom for teenagers from this Topeka priest: "Once a teenager can, you know, really, be able to accept the fact and be able to tell his chick, 'Yes, you turn me on, I'm horny as heck tonight. What are we going to do with it?' " then we are making moral progress. He, like Greeley, tells us that Christ was explicitly non-condemnatory of the woman-taken-in-sin's failure to "integrate sex and love." He tells us "we have no place recorded where he bitched her out at all."[2] "Go and sin no more"?—those early Christians again, I guess.

To deal intelligently with these pop-psychology claims, Christians ought to face up—head on—to that much used term: hangups. In the determinist scheme, as we know, our behavior is caused by one or more of them. The only healthy and natural way for us to behave, as a result, is to purge ourselves of these inhibiting factors in our lives, these scars inflicted upon our psyches by society. Morality is best understood as a search for the true, the genuine, the

[1]Andrew Greeley, *The Jesus Myth* (New York: Doubleday, 1971), p. 44.
[2]*The Wanderer*, March 20, 1975.

72

spontaneous, the natural "inner me." Virtue, of a sort, arrives when we have successfully peeled back the layers of our life like an avocado until we no longer fear "letting it all hang out." Harvey Cox, for example, talks of how bathing nude at Esalen, the Big Sur retreat house for enlightened thinkers seeking religious insight into their lives through group-sensitivity encounters, helps people do just that.[3] Sixteen of his fellow retreatants disrobed, he tells us, near a pool surrounded by candles whose "yellow glow softened the epidermal colors." At first there were some bourgeois hangups in evidence. "We gawked and blinked for a second or two." But after getting into the pool, things improved. "We had transgressed the outside world's arbitrary borderline, demarcated by briefs and bikinis that mask but do not hide the essentials. . . . That alone gave us all a little lift." Later, once society's barriers had been thoroughly washed away, there was a "group long-stroke massage"—"one person rubbing another's back while he/she kneads someone else's toes and simultaneously has his/her neck tenderized by the fingers of a third or fourth person. In the semi-darkness it is hard to know whose limb is whose." Soon Cox was his true self. "The combination of water, chanting, body dissociation and massage was moving me beyond a pleasantly sensuous swoon into something closer to what I could only imagine was either a fanciful reverie or a mystical trance." Perhaps, he thought, he had reached "what Norman Brown calls 'polymorphous perversity' "—the state "that children seem capable of but adults have lost." This, you see, was what Christ meant by "becoming as little children," Cox surmises. Polymorphous perversity!

Bishop Pike was the one who introduced Cox to Esalen. After the long-stroke massage, both he and Cox sat around the pool listening to Allen Ginsberg, who "sat cross-legged in a robe, the candlelight glistening in his glasses, and told us of how the future of religion was entwined with the future of LSD" and "about masturbation and screwing as religious experiences" while "several of the young girls and fellows who had come to Esalen with him sat on the floor near his feet with their eyes half-closed, nodding and smiling and occasionally snapping their fingers or groaning appreciatively."

Cox, in his enthusiasm to get Christians into his latest view of how life is to be lived in a godless world, has, of course, confused Rousseau's noble savages with Christ's little children, innocence with sensual abandon. But I guess we should be used to such distortions by now.

What he and updaters of a similar stamp call hangups are, when you think of it, pretty close to the Christian notion of learned virtue and a correctly formed conscience. We are *supposed* to have hangups about our behavior; it is hardly enlightened to try to drown them out. Indeed, the modern world could use a

---

[3]*The Seduction of the Spirit,* pp. 198-208.

massive dose of hangups. Times Square and Sunset Strip are worlds without hangups of the Christian sort; and, as anyone with eyes can see, all that means is a substitution of the sickest of pagan hangups for the Christian.

Man, in fact, is at his most glorious when resplendent in his hangups. Enlightened people used to pray for them (grace) rather than try to dispel them in the name of a group-grope. Hangups are what lead to purity of heart, bravery, a spirit of self-sacrifice—what a younger and healthier world called chivalry. Through such "psychic imbalances" the people of Christendom proved able to rise above their concupiscent nature and become more than noble savages living for the instant and irresponsible satisfaction of various lusts. Cox's hangups were once a good man's most prized possession. They made him capable of courtesy, honor, and love. And they are the moral armor which we can, and must, develop in our time if we are to overcome temptation and live our life by Christ's words. What the world needs now—are hangups.

There is a wonderfully amusing, and typically trenchant, passage in C.S. Lewis' *Pilgrim's Regress* that makes the point. Two characters in that allegory stumble into a cave where sits a transparent man with blood gurgling through visible veins encased in a Halloween-like skeleton, gastric juices bubbling, bowels moving, lungs bleating, heart bumping. The character who represents our behaviorist and determinist moderns becomes excited and overjoyed. At last he has found what man is *really* like, stripped of all the trappings. The traditional man of the West, on the other hand, is cautious. He tries to cool his companion's ardor. He knows that real men come with what their Christian culture has given them, the "embellishments" of bravery, purity, poetry, dignity, and song. He knows that a "real man" is more likely to come dressed in the bright livery of a knight, carrying a delicately carved shield upon which is a motto that serves as constant reminder that he ought to be *more* than he wants to be, including willing to die in combat for honor or for Christ.

For Christians know that they can be more than Pavlovian mice. They can be Galahads and Lohengrins. And more importantly, they know that Christ expects us to work towards that goal. Daniel Callahan might tell us that: "The male and female . . . whose passions are simply too strong for them, or whose circumstances make physical involvement all but inescapable, deserve no condemnation at all" and that we, in fact, "must remove sexual 'sins' other than the obviously exploitative kind, from the category of important transgressions."[4] But Jesus commands, "Go and sin no more."

Christ spent much of his time on earth with sinners, helping them rise to just

[4]*Spectrum of Catholic Attitudes*, p. 115.

74

this task. So much so, in fact, that he was scolded for it by the Pharisees. "Why," they asked of the Apostles, "eateth your master with publicans and sinners?"

> But when Jesus heard that, he said unto them, They that be whole need not a physician, but they that are sick. But go ye and learn what that meaneth, I will have mercy, and not sacrifice: for I am not come to call the righteous but sinners to repentance. (Mt. 9:12-13)

This passage, it is true, is a favorite of the revisionists. They often use it to shock middle-class congregations and to explain why they favor the company of political radicals, drug users, and swinging singles' bar habitues. "Christ moved mostly with the outsiders of respectable society. He was not liked by the solid citizens either," was the way I heard it.

There is something to that. But, as we have already noted, Christ went among them as a *physician* striving to heal their moral sickness, not as a co-reveler seeking to learn "where it's at" in order to be "with it" enough to preach "relevant" sermons back home on Sunday. He is willing to work with the sinners, to preach to them, to help them *change* their evil ways. But he is also willing to speak harshly when they fail to respond. He understands the lures of sin and the environmental forces that work against man in his search for virtue. He knows of temptation. He told his Apostles of his own temptations by the devil during his fast in the desert. But he overcame those temptations, and he tells us that he expects us to work against ours as well. He didn't turn the stones to bread and then explain how hunger can do strange things to a man—which would have been a pretty good way to stress the importance of allowing an Esalen-like surrender to our primal selves.

When we fail to ward off temptation? When we equivocate?

> But whereunto shall I liken this generation? It is like unto children sitting in the markets, and calling unto their fellows, And saying, We have piped unto you, and ye have not danced; we have mourned unto you, and ye have not lamented. For John came neither eating nor drinking, and they say, He hath a devil. The Son of Man came eating and drinking, and they say, Behold a man gluttonous and a winebibber, a friend of publicans and sinners. But wisdom is justified of her children. (Mt. 11:16-19)

The updater cloud has so enveloped our society that even those of us who work to dispel the smog might have trouble with Christ's words here if we have not thought about them for a while. Especially about Matthew's next sentence:

75

"Then he began to upbraid the cities wherein most of his mighty works were done, because they repented not." (Mt. 11:20)

After all, we might say to ourselves, there could be very good reasons why John might not have appeared a wise and virtuous teacher to his contemporaries. Perhaps his coarse ways reminded some of a demented and cruel father, or perhaps some in his audience had been mugged by an itinerant preacher when they were young. And Christ was drinking with sinners. What if a few of the folks who failed to appreciate the compelling nature of his words had grown up in homes with mothers who were not only winebibbing, but honkytonk angels to boot? Would not an "associational transference of value-judgement syndrome" make it unlikely that they would follow Christ, and free them from any responsibility for that failure? Nope. "Woe unto thee," says Christ. If those with advanced degrees find such a condemnation deplorably out of line with the best and most progressive thinking in the social sciences, he adds for clarification: "I thank thee, O Father, Lord of heaven and earth, because thou hast hid these things from the wise and prudent, and hast revealed them unto babes." (Mt. 11:25)

This childlike willingness to obey Christ is, of course, actually only a willingness to rise to the truth, above our inclinations, predispositions, and temptations. Christ does not ask us not to think; just not to think of ourselves as an equal to him, or to think that for some reason we are not the ones he means when he calls for obedience. It is one of the most quoted of Christ's parables —the good seed—but we are foolhardy if we let ourselves think it untypical. It must be read alongside all the other of Christ's often harshly delivered warnings. Everyone knows the parable; it should not be necessary to repeat it in its entirety. But Christ's summing up must be emphasized:

> Hear ye therefore the parable of the sower. When anyone heareth the word of the kingdom, and understandeth it not, then cometh the wicked one, and catcheth away that which was sown in his heart. This is he which received seed by the wayside. But he that received the seed into stony places, the same is he that heareth the word, and anon with joy receiveth it; Yet hath he not root in himself, but dureth for a while: for when tribulation or persecution ariseth because of the word, by and by he is offended. He also that received seed among the thorns is he that heareth the word; and the cares of this world, and the deceitfulness of riches, choke the word, and he becometh unfruithful. But he that received seed into the good ground is he that heareth the word, and understandeth it; which also beareth fruit, and bringeth forth, some a hundredfold, some sixty, some thirty. (Mt. 13:18-23)

Read that again—especially those of you who are flirting with the idea that we moderns have complex thoughts to keep in mind ever since Freud put pen to page—thoughts that Christ was unaware of. Read it again. Christ covers *all* the bases (which should not surprise us; after all, He is God). He explicitly provides for any and every objection our behaviorist/determinist moderns could raise to challenge the traditional notion of responsibility for behavior; provides for and dismisses. Read it again.

Some of us just might be, Christ assures us, the seeds by the wayside, and unable to hear his words because of environmental or psychological impairments. The insane and retarded, to take the most obvious and extreme cases, are not culpable for their actions, as the Christian churches have always taught. Some of us, on the other hand, might lack perseverance. We are the seed on the stony ground who live in the Faith only briefly. Others prove unwilling to fight off the temptations of the world. The thorns of worldly pleasure crowd out our convictions, *after* we hear them and know them to be true.

Christ is distinguishing between those who *cannot* understand his words through no fault of their own, and those who hear his words but then surrender to the temptation to ignore them, for a variety of reasons, and who *are* deserving of blame and punishment for that failure. He is not demanding perfection. He speaks of degrees of goodness—"some a hundredfold, some sixty, some thirty." We all do not have to be Damiens working with the lepers or Maria Gorettis dying to preserve our purity. But we *can* be evil. We can hear the word, know it for what it is, and then ignore or abuse it and let it die. Those who surrender to the evil one *can* be worthy of damnation. Remember the wheat and the tares, especially when the so-called "Good News" the updaters like to talk about makes us feel too confident (the sin of *presumption,* they used to call it) that we have it made with that breezy clown-like Jesus in the Superman shirt in *Godspell*:

> He that soweth the good seed is the Son of man;
> The field is the world; the good seed are the children of the kingdom; but the tares are the children of the wicked one;
> The enemy that sowed them is the devil; the harvest is the end of the world; and the reapers are the angels.
> As therefore the tares are *gathered and burned* in the fire; so shall it be in the end of the world.
> The Son of man shall send forth his angels, and they shall gather out of his kingdom all things that offend, and them which do iniquity;
> And shall cast them into a furnace of fire; [did you ever wonder where those silly old Christians dreamed up such a horrific metaphor as hell fire? You thought Dante was to blame?] there shall be wailing and gnashing of teeth. Then shall the righteous shine forth as the sun in the kingdom of their Father. Who has ears to hear, let him hear. (Mt. 13:37-43)

Andrew Greeley might think that "Jesus compelled no one to follow him." Weelll, maybe, if you can convince me that a "furnace of fire" and "wailing and gnashing of teeth" are not threats, or a degree of compulsion.

God Will Mind

Am I saying that souls are falling into hell, as St. Theresa tells us of her vision, like the leaves from the trees? No. I leave the numbers to Christ. I insist only that Christ's teachings are replete with the warning that, at the very least, we are to live our lives with the thought that we are responsible for the wickedness we perpetrate; that most men, in fact, *are* responsible; and that we just cannot be faithful to Christ's words if we assume that *everyone* is one of the seeds by the wayside, unable to respond to Christ in the first place. Why would Christ have had to be crucified if that were the case?

It is likely that America will have to face up to this issue in the near future—if we still have the inner resolve to meet such challenges. We will have to think long and hard about what we mean by responsibility and guilt, concepts which have served as the framework of our common-law development, whether the secularists like to admit them or not. We are moving, it is true, into an era when illegality is being defined only by the extent to which an action can be seen to do measureable damage to another; and away from the older idea that certain forms of behavior are to be prescribed simply because they are wrong, and that those who commit them are worthy of punishment. Punishment and prescription in this time-honored view were meant to serve an educative function, especially for our young, to show them what virtue and vice "look like." There still are laws on the books which reflect the older attitude, most especially in the area of what constitutes pornography—much to the chagrin, and in the face of the protests, of the moral levellers. And, of course, there still are the societal pressures against homosexuality.

To be honest, I find the prospect of having to linger on such an issue depressing. To concede that we are finding it difficult to summon the will to keep even this ancient and abjured perversion out of the ranks of "acceptable alternative lifestyles" is to imply that it might be too late to hope for a return to a Christian consciousness in America. The churches themselves seem fettered with doubts, and open to the gay advance. A Lutheran minister, for example, writes in *The Gay Lutheran,* a journal published in cooperation with an organization called Lutherans Concerned for Gay People, that "I am a child of God, a man, a homosexual, a Christian, a Lutheran—in that order—and I am a husband committed to my wife, who knows I am gay." He also states proudly that "I am a pastor." These Lutherans Concerned for Gay People have drawn up a statement which has been submitted to Lutheran authorities. It asserts in part that "as gay Lutherans we affirm with joy the goodness of human sexuality which God has given us," and that we "call upon our church to further a greater understanding of human sexuality in all its manifestations. We ask our church to seek to remove discrimination against gay women and men wherever it exists." Also, "we ask our church to receive and welcome us as it receives and welcomes others."

Where are Christians to turn in the face of such an affront? Well, we cannot, it is true, discern the degree of guilt for sin, even for this sin. Our attack should not focus on those who take such blatantly anti-Christian positions. Some gays just might be seeds by the wayside, unable to help themselves overcome their lust. But conceding that is a long way from conceding that such moral blindness transforms pederasty into a *virtue* for those so afflicted, any more than genocide was a virtuous act for Nazi true-believers disturbed enough to imagine Auschwitz an entirely fitting and proper remedy for the "Jewish problem" in Europe.

We can and must continue to condemn actions defined by Christ and his Church as sinful—even while making our concession (if that is the right word) that an individual's problems *might* make him unable to bear full responsibility for a transgression.

Yes, certain homosexuals might not be fully guilty for their perversion because of physical and psychological problems that impair their ability to act morally.

Of course, such an admission from the Christian churches will hardly satisfy the leaders of the gay rights movement, who insist that they are *not* in the position of knowing not what they do. One recently stated in a television interview that he will not be happy until American mothers look forward to the prospect of their sons or daughters walking down the aisle in a gay "marriage" with as much warmth as they anticipate a marriage to a member of the opposite sex.

The acts themselves, however, remain evil—in and of themselves. Our "problems" cannot make evil acts good. If a homosexual act is not a sin, then it must originate in a frightening, devastating sickness of the soul. But the gay spokesmen insist they are not sick! Well, they can't have it both ways. If they are not sick, homosexuals are to struggle against their temptations with as much resolve as anyone else in life; and never allow themselves to succumb to the blandishments of an updater like Douglas Rhymes, who tells them that Christians in the future will have to "look more realistically at the question 'How is he [a homosexual] to express his sexuality to the greatest degree of wholeness for himself and others?' rather than just go on with the dreary and often totally unrealistic counsel of enforced celibacy."

Only ten years or so ago you could have written a hilarious comedy skit—Sid Caesar or Peter Sellers would have done wonders with it—of a homosexual marching in the streets with his "lover," demanding the right to be married in a church, to serve as a prison guard, to teach in our schools, to organize dances for gays on college campuses, and even to adopt children. Who would have thought ten years ago that in America we would find our teenaged children listening to "glitter" rock records that extol the bisexual activities of the singer, or find network television rewriting their scripts to placate homosexual demands for equal time? We have all that now. We have gotten to the point—we really have—where in the public debate on this issue, the so-called straights are pictured as the ones with the problem. "Who says that your opinion about sex is more perceptive than the homosexuals'?" we are asked. "Prove it." "What is truth?" Bella Abzug has contributed her wisdom, too. "Gays should be entitled to all the fruits of our society," the lovely but humorless lady tells us.

Straight America seems to have learned well its relativist and behaviorist lessons. We seem unable to deal with the issue in a persuasive way. Our church leaders cannot summon up the will to say that homosexual activity cannot be tolerated in public life, nor treated as a mere preference, even if some people really do find such activity pleasurable, because it is evil and sinful; that our people have a right and a duty to create a social atmosphere in which such evil is met with the full opprobrium it deserves. "If people find pleasure in such acts, by what standard can we condemn them? How can they be blamed for the social and psychological pressures that make them act as they do?" We hear such things now from our pastors, not only from Allen Ginsberg.

Having a tendency to sin—whatever the sin—is not a sin. True. It is the scar of original sin. It is what we *do* with our tendencies that counts. A homosexual who works successfully to control his carnal appetites—just as unmarried heterosexuals must, by the way—is blameless and guiltless by all Christian standards. There just might be Christian saints who fit into this category. Those who stumble and fall but are contrite, deserve our understanding; they get God's forgiveness, as do all repentant sinners who are resolved to sin no more (even if that resolve does not last a lifetime). This trespass, too, will be forgiven, if contrition is sincere. What is being demanded of Christian society by the gay rights movement, however, is the elevation of the sin into a position of respectability, not protection for the sinner. There is a vast difference between a school refusing to hire individuals, or a landlord refusing to rent an apartment to individuals, because they "look a little gay," and those same people refusing to deal with the gay lib advocate who proudly professes his behavior to be normal, and demands that we behave as if we think so too. A closet queen, as the phrase goes, has no difficulty getting jobs or housing until he loses his shame and leaves the closet. In the former case, we have an inexcusable and unwarranted condemnation based on mere supposition; in the other, a simple and commendable display of Christian opposition to immoral behavior which has already been admitted to by the perpetrator, a perpetrator who glories in it and asserts that he has no intention of mending his ways. One is an uncharitable and perhaps rash judgment, the other a legitimate refusal to concede that the behavior in question is anything less than offensive. The Old Testament God unleashed fire and brimstone upon the cities of Sodom and Gomorrah after their inhabitants became openminded enough to refuse to make those condemnations. Christ did not take it upon himself to add any qualifiers to that story. As a matter of fact, he threatened with comparable wrath the cities of his time who refused to follow his teachings. It was not the social worker Superstar who said angrily:

> And thou Capharnum, shalt thou be exalted to heaven? Thou shalt be thrust down to hell! For if the miracles had been worked in Sodom that have been worked in thee, it would have remained to this day. But I tell you it will be more tolerable for the land of Sodom on the day of judgement than for thee. (Mt. 11:23-24)

Before some gay rights activist turned Biblical revisionist (and there are creatures vile enough to suggest that Christ's love for John was of the Times Square variety) begins to use this passage to tell us that Christ was toning down the condemnation of Sodom's sin, let us state the obvious. Christ was using the punishment of Sodom—a paradigm of divine wrath—as a warning to those who would reject him in Capharnum. He threatens them with comparable punishment to make clear the nature of Capharnum's failure. He compares it to an evil so base that his audience would immediately recognize the seriousness of rejecting his offer to follow him. The point is that Sodom got what it deserved—and that Capharnum would get worse.

Woe unto You

If I tried my hardest to uncover Scriptural passages that indicate anything other than the traditional Christian view of guilt, I could think only of Christ's repeated demands that we be as willing to forgive our fellow men as He was. But this forgiveness, *of necessity,* implies responsibility and guilt. We cannot forgive sins for which our fellow men cannot be made responsible in the first place. Moreover, Christ's forgiveness requires a willingness to repent, and such determination cannot be extended to actions beyond our control.

Updaters might argue that Christ's insistence that we must love our neighbors as ourselves for the love of God is incompatible with the traditional understand-

81

ing of guilt, but they would have to take Christ's words out of context to do that. The greatest conmandment was to love God above all things—which means to follow His law. And they would have to ignore almost everything else Christ said in the New Testament, or insinuate that Christ was just as likely to be in error as any other first-century preacher, which is exactly what certain theologians are beginning to suggest—as we will see in a later chapter. Updater theology feeds its own fires. The more they say and get away with, the more they dare.

Think of Christ's repeated dealings with the Pharisees (who, although the updaters continue to associate them with the institutional churches, resemble most the holier-than-thou updaters who strut out their confidence that they have interpreted the Spirit in a way the masses cannot grasp). Christ understood that the social and intellectual atmosphere of the first century A.D. would make it difficult for these men to accept the idea that a Nazarene carpenter was the Son of God, hard for them to dispel at will the learned wisdom of their heritage. But he nonetheless requires them to do just that.

"Woe unto you scribes and Pharisees, hypocrites! for ye are graves which appear not, and the men that walk over them are not aware of them." (Luke 11:43)

And to the lawyers of the Temple:

"Woe unto you also, ye lawyers! for ye lade men with burdens grievous to be borne, and ye yourselves touch not the burdens with one of your fingers." (Luke 11:46) (In our time, of course, some of the greatest burdens—say, busing, or lowering America's standard of living to help the Third World countries, or increased welfare payments—are being called for by updaters whose clerical life does not require of them the full sacrifice resulting from these actions.)

He was not as condemnatory of the Samaritan woman who had been married five times, it is true. As we have noted, Christ did understand the degrees of guilt. But neither did he tell her that she should continue in her choice of a lifestyle as long as she found it "meaningful" and "personally satisfying."

> Jesus saith unto her, 'Go, call thy husband.' The woman answered and said, I have no husband. Jesus said unto her, 'Thou hast well said, I have no husband. For thou hast had five husbands; and he whom thou now hast is not thy husband; in that saidst thou truly.' (Jn. 4:16-18)

No call to rap over the complexities—"he whom thou has is *not* thy husband." *Finis*.

In the same vein:

"If ye keep my commandments, ye shall abide in my love; even as I have kept my Father's commandments, and abide in his love." (Jn. 15:10)

And: "Ye are my friends if ye do whatsoever I command you." (Jn. 15:14)

If we refuse that friendship: the "furnace of fire." But it is not just that. We have a world to gain:

> And as it was in the days of Noe, so shall it be also in the days of the Son of man . . .
> But the same day that Lot went out of Sodom it rained fire and brimstone from heaven, and destroyed them all. Even thus shall it be in the day when the Son of man is revealed.
> In that day, he which shall be upon the housetop, and his stuff in the house, let him not come down to take it away: and he that is in the field, let him likewise not return back.
> Remember Lot's wife.
> Whosoever shall seek to save his life shall lose it; and whosoever shall lose his life shall preserve it.
> I tell you, in that night there shall be two men in one bed; and one shall be taken, and the other shall be left.
> Two women shall be grinding together; the one shall be taken, and the other left.
> Two men shall be in the field; the one shall be taken, and the other left. (Luke 17:26-36)

One called . . . "the other left." I will concede that some of those who will be taken to paradise might be the ones we would least expect. I will concede that Christ will dazzle us with his mercy, as soon as the updaters tell me who will be left behind. (Perhaps just traditional Christians—have you noticed that the updaters are capable of quite a bit of condemnatory wrath when they speak of us?)

Chapter V

Better the Millstone

SITUATION ETHICS—should the subject be dealt with in a chapter of its own? After all, it is true that the claims of the situationists, or contextualists as they are sometimes called, are for all practical purposes simply conclusions drawn from existentialist and determinist-raised doubts about man's capacity to judge or set standards for human choice. It is also true that the words of Christ that stand against those doubts serve as more than adequate answers to the positions championed by Joseph Fletcher and his followers.

There are, however, so many more biblical passages to add to this case that it might be justified to write a chapter for no other reason than to list them. The weight of the Scriptural evidence in support of the traditional Christian understanding of responsibility and guilt is overwhelming, and that point has to be made. The most desirable reader response just might be an exasperated, "Okay, okay—enough; He wasn't a first-century Harvey Cox."

But there are elements in the situation-ethics debate that do have to be weighed carefully and in a separate context. In many ways the situationists present a far more serious challenge than the existentialists and behaviorists, and one more difficult to handle. The situationists work from within the Christian body of knowledge. (Fletcher, for example, insists repeatedly in his work that he is not an existentialist.) They do not, with Sartre and Marx, veto

85

Christ. Instead, they isolate and exaggerate portions of Christ's words to reach their conclusions. (An error I could very well make, too, I know. My case rests on the clear voice of twenty centuries of Christian tradition. Could *everyone* have been wrong?)

It is an often heard complaint of pastors all over America and Europe that the generation of young adults between 18 and 30 has drifted from parish life and "the institutional Church"; it is a complaint confirmed by a quick glance around church on Sunday.

It would be difficult to uncover more conclusive evidence of the impact of the situationists, except perhaps the preached positions of our updater clerics, which are likely to increase the already scandalous rate of defections. I am thinking especially of the advice they give to the young: that they should not consider the "church experience" (or anything, for that matter) mandatory, if they do not find it "meaningful." (Do not Modernist theologians and preachers measure success by the extent to which they enable people to get by without the "crutch" of church attendance?)

The price we pay—the sad-eyed parents, for example, who tell of how difficult it has become for them to keep their children practicing their faith after a year or two studying at the feet of the updaters—is enough to drive one to rage. We Christians have been victims of a betrayal of trust of the basest sort—if I may say so. I await the exposé of the priest or minister who will tell us of how he participated in the grand plan to take our children from our faith without getting us riled up in the process, so that we can get a firsthand account of this deliberate and calculated deception perpetrated right under our noses. It will make a grim—but true—story. In fact, I could have written it myself if I hadn't boiled over in anger during the years I taught religion at a Catholic high school, and allowed the updaters there a peek into my unliberated medieval soul. Before they found me out, I used to hear regularly all the snide derogations of the idea of a personal God, original sin, the Virgin Birth, the Resurrection and Ascension, middle-class Christian attitudes about sex, and the rest of the updaters' grocery list of backward beliefs.

Agape

Everyone has heard the situationist case in one form or another, perhaps without knowing that it was called situationism. For a while in the sixties the air reeked with it. We have all heard that right does not exist independently and prior to our actions, but is actually a predicate of them; that there are no intrinsic standards of behavior to which we must conform; that instead, in every instance when a moral decision is to be made, the only consideration is, in Fletcher's words, "What does God's love demand of men in this particular situation?" For example, wouldn't even "a transient sex liaision, if it has the element of caring and tenderness, and selfless concern" be a virtuous act? he asks rhetorically. "Jesus taught this situationist kind of freedom from moral law. He held that morals were made for man, not man for morals."[1] (As you can see, although Fletcher insists he is not an existentialist, he does, like them, argue that we create moral good for ourselves. We do not reach for and attain virtue; we determine it in our life-experience.)

If you have read this far you know that Jesus taught no such freedom from the law (except perhaps from the obligation to wash up before dinner), and you know that it will be more than possible to demonstrate that with his words.

Before doing that, however, there are a few preliminary points that have to be made.

For one thing, it is no accident that the situation-ethics debate arose just shortly after the "God is dead" school of theologians made their mark. It is a quite logical and almost necessary coupling of events. Even though some philosophers have argued that there is a natural law accessible to the human intellect whether or not there is a personal God, it has always been easier to argue the case for objective right and wrong with God's will as the measuring rod. Without question, it has been easier to end long discussions of moral issues by making reference to a divine command, especially when the objective was a teachable and enforceable standard for behavior to set the stage for saving souls, rather than a full understanding of the complexity of the human mind. A Paul Goodman or a Gore Vidal, we always understood, might be able to argue persuasively for their lifestyles for weeks and books on end, and in a way more attractive to the young than, say, Billy Graham in opposition, but when the time came to write texts for Sunday school we would just refer to the Ten Commandments or the words of Christ, and brand the challenge as immoral—or so we used to think.

Without a personal God, this brand of decisiveness has become, in practice anyway, near to impossible. If Americans couldn't agree on *Deep Throat,* where can we agree?

But let us not get lost in these waters. The point is that we obviously feel freer to question and ignore traditional norms after the fear of an all-powerful and judging God has been dismissed from our minds. Once we lose that fear, it is not long before our major concern becomes situation ethics—whether we call it that or not.

When Fletcher insists, then, that he does not deny the validity of Christ's

---

[1]Joseph Fletcher, *The Situation Ethics Debate* (Philadelphia: Westminster Press, 1968), p. 249.

words, or the interpretive view of them taught by the Church for nearly two thousand years, and that he wants us to bring that heritage to bear upon the evaluation of our actions, there is a trailer. We are *not* to worry about offending God in that evaluation. Instead, we are to ask, does the contemplated action encourage and promote the Christian love—*agape*—which Christ came on earth to promote? We must remember, he says, that "sins are offenses against love (i.e., against God), but if love in any situation calls for violation of a moral law, no sin is committed that needs excuse or remission. If an act is loving, it is good and therefore right. If it is loving, it is right and therefore good."[2]

Certainly there is another issue raised here, one which we shall deal with in detail in a later chapter, i.e., what does Fletcher mean when he tells us that "God is love?" Does he mean what Christians from antiquity have meant—that God, the personal God, is perfect love in addition to perfect justice, and perfect everything else? Or that Love is God? That luv is God? Updaters have become expert at walking the tightrope on issues as fundamental as this, never slipping into openly heretical statements, but conveying their message with a shop talk that drips with implications other updaters grasp with no difficulty at all. However, as the recent, widely publicized split in the Missouri Synod of the Lutheran Church between the traditionalists and the new Evangelical Lutherans in Mission (ELIM) and their Seminary in Exile (Seminex) indicates, in all likelihood it won't be long before we reach the point of no return in many Christian communities. Things have drifted too far for reconciliation. Christians are unlikely to adjust themselves to a scenario which includes individuals with open scorn for the most fundamental beliefs in the Christian dispensation teaching that scorn to young Christians. It is not as if the feud were over whether Christ was born in a stable or a cave, or whether the nails went through his wrists instead of his palms. The updaters are aware of the breach, too. They do not want stodgy fundamentalists inhibiting their children's free pursuit of truth. Only their confidence that they will soon dominate the educational process in the established churches (a confidence their current success seems to assure) keeps them within the establishment, not a tolerance for traditional views. A measurable drift in the direction of orthodoxy would flush them from their roosts, and lead them to push the idea of "cleaning house." Once the leaders of the Missouri Synod began to demand a profession of orthodoxy, the ELIM break came like a knee-jerk, and ministers like the Rev. Wayne Saffen, one of the liberal clerics most responsible for bringing on the confrontation, began to say things like (when speaking of his fellow Lutherans of a traditional bent) "I no longer regard them as fellow Christians or as fellow human beings." And, in

[2]*Ibid.*, p. 256.

a spasm of *agape,* no doubt, "To hell with them. Let them be lords of the dungheap."[3] Nice and loving there, Reverend.

Lead Us into Temptation

It must also be noted that the situationists have openly abandoned one of the oldest of Christian beliefs—the effects of original sin. Their understanding of human nature is now identical to that of the Rousseauean Left. They too are confident that man can live best and most virtuously without prohibitive commandments or the fear of God haunting his mind. Indeed, it is this confidence that underlies their every effort. They have bought liberalism's presumption about the "naturally good man" hook, bobber, and bait. It is what leads them to muse about how much better man will be with only the guideline of "love." The Christian churches, in their scheme, ought not saddle us with the burden of threatened guilt to help us overcome our temptations, but free us to make the loving choice most of us will make when confronted with a moral decision. "All you need is love," as the song says. If in our actions—whether they appear adulterous, cowardly, or profane on the surface—we have proceeded with a selfless concern for our fellow man, *as we see it,* there is no sin, no need for remorse. People can be trusted with that degree of freedom.

There is some truth in that. Some people can be given that loose general framework—I guess. But the only ones I can think of right off the bat are those we call saints. And they are saints because a combination of God's grace and self-discipline has enabled them to overcome their temptations, not because they have learned to "come to grips with their psychic needs."

But we all are not saints, and most of us know it. (I do at any rate. I always marvel at the situationist confidence when I think of what a few beers and a sleazy bar can do to my understanding of the requirements of Christian love. Sometimes the threat of hell is barely enough.)

Hundreds of country-and-western songs proclaim the American understanding of these issues on radios and juke boxes all over the country. Instead of "Make your own kind of music," housewives and truck drivers hum along to calls for God to "Please help me, I'm fallin', and that would be sin," and to admissions that "There's a devil in the bottle," and that "It wasn't God who made honkytonk angels." It makes you wonder if the situationists live in a world without temptation; or if things have gotten so free-wheeling in academic circles these days that they cannot picture people doing anything other than

[3]*The Christian News,* May 19, 1975.

89

giving in to the lures of sin. It must be one or the other, since the situationists are unable to face up to the fact that there *are* people who do say no to sin; that it is quite possible to do so; and that people up until recently expected it of members of our social order—period, plain out.

But what of Christ? Fletcher tells us that "like Abelard in the twelfth century, the situationist says sturdily that those who crucified Christ were according to their own consciences guilty of no sin."[4] Would Christ agree?

This quote provides a near-perfect starting gate for our survey of Christ's words, because Christ *would* agree with the essence of the statement. Fletcher's position here has been part of the Christian understanding from at least the time of St. Thomas Aquinas, who argued that we must follow even an erring conscience. *But*—and this is a big "but," the "but" the situationists ignore—Christians have always understood, as well, that Christ taught an obligation to form a correct conscience so that we will *not* continue in error. Fletcher appears to say this too. He wants us to approach life with our Christian principles in mind and to use them as a general framework for our choices. But where Christians have been willing to concede that we might not be *guilty* of our sins because of an improperly formed conscience, for Fletcher that is not enough. He makes our interior disposition superior to and corrective of the Christian moral norms, and the sole arbiter of the nature of the act itself. If we act with what we think is a concern for love, our behavior is not only permissible, *it is good*. Our actions are not measured by any standard beyond our minds—not by God's mind, for example.

Why aren't the norms for determining guilt, once so familiar to grade school children—grievous offense, sufficient reflection, full consent of the will—or some other version of them, adequate in situationist eyes? Especially when you think of all the room for deep self-examination the words "sufficient" and "full" leave open. It raises the grave question of whether the situationists harbor an unsatisfiable animus against the churches and the Christian tradition itself, more important to them than their oft-stressed concern for the individual. It is obvious. In the situationist scheme, the churches cannot continue as we know them—as teaching bodies, preservers and protectors of the body of the Faith. They would become something closer to therapeutic centers, where the counselors would be Christian clerics (or ex-clerics) well suited to the job because of their familiarity with the Christian experience and temperament, and well equipped, therefore, to help Christians overcome those "hangups" and to see the wisdom the clerics have learned in their graduate courses in social and behavioral science. That would, of course, be a change of major proportions: the cooption of the Church by the world, nothing less.

[4]*The Situation Ethics Debate*, p. 257.

If this is not the situationists' long-range objective, why doesn't the much maligned "casuistry" of the past satisfy them, when the worst examples of it are so much like the best of the situationist wisdom? People used to say—some half jokingly, some quite seriously—that Jesuits could talk themselves out of guilt for any act imaginable. Why isn't a similar possibility for a suspension of personal responsibility enough to satisfy the situationists? Apparently because it leaves intact the teaching authority of the churches, a teaching authority that cannot be tolerated by a mind imbued with the secular spirit of the age. Why else? Think of all those stock moral dilemmas we went through as schoolchildren. They were all situationist. Is it all right for a starving man to steal a loaf of bread? A soldier to kill himself by falling on top of a grenade that is about to explode and kill his comrades? A husband to kill a rapist about to attack his wife? If a drunk driver kills a pedestrian, is he responsible for murder, or just for being drunk?

Why aren't such probes acceptable? Because they center on *guilt*. Such questions presuppose that an evil act can exist, irrespective of our responsibility for it. Such an approach does not deny the existence of a moral law. The situationists do. In so doing, they move against the Christ found in the Bible.

Let us underscore that point by trying to picture Christ as a situationist.

Let us concede, once again for the sake of emphasis, that after "loving God above all things," Christ did say that the greatest commandment was to "love your neighbor as yourself for the love of God." There should be no quibbling on this point. Christ was preaching the need for a total and unreserved willingness to love one another as he loved us far more than the need for staying away from wine, women, and song. Perhaps there has been a stodginess parading under the name of respectability that has become too prominent in the churches—maybe. Let us concede it for the moment. To show that Christ's words stand square and plumb against the situationist case, we do not have to show that he did *not* stress our need to love our neighbor as much as the situationists would have it. Christ did teach us to love our neighbor; but he taught many other things as well, including an obligation to live by the moral code he accepted and superadded to—the Ten Commandments.

If Christ were a situationist, we can assume that he would have approached his audience as Joseph Fletcher and Bishop Robinson approach theirs. Fair enough? They have set out the standards for situationism, and a situationist Christ must adhere to them. Right? (I hesitate, of course, since such a thought is as ludicrous to me as I assume it is to you.) But it is what a Christian situationist has to accept. If:

a) a person claims to follow Christ, and
b) he is a situationist too, then
c) there must be a causal relationship between a) and b).

91

What else could it mean when you say that you are a Christian situationist? (But, my good man, the situationist would say, "I have already told you that the Bible is in error in its depiction of a wheat-and-tares Christ.")

Let us admit, too, and also once again, that Christ did differentiate between those who should have been able to respond to his word and those who would be unable to (the seed by the wayside). Such an admission must be stressed in order to take the steam out of the inevitable updater attack against those who defend our fathers' notion about moral guilt; i.e., that we are behaving like the men about to stone the adulterous woman when we refuse to grant the legitimacy of situationist subjectivity.

Let us admit that we humans do not have knowledge of guilt, and certainly not of who is going to be condemned to hell. Let us even admit to the possibility that God can somehow balance His infinite justice with His infinite mercy so that fewer than Torquemada thought will actually suffer that judgement. (Just for the record—Christ does speak of *few* choosing the narrow path.) But if we are to entertain such a thought, why should it lead us to the conclusion that we are incapable of acts *worthy* of eternal punishment? Or that a loving God would be doing anything other than *not* punishing us for trespasses both heinous and worthy of hell? We can be evil. Christ assures us of that. And his words must be our main interest as Christians.

Who goes to hell? Let's leave something for God, if the modern theologians do not mind. The questions we must ask ourselves are: Did Christ want us to approach life with the fear of God's righteous punishment in our minds? Did he want us to adhere to moral codes over and against our personal preferences? Or did he want us to work with the malleable guidelines of the situationists?

Well, let me put it this way—if there are few of us worthy of hell, if the subjectivists are right, they are right *in opposition to the Christ of the Gospels*. If we are all without sin, Christ didn't want to let us in on the good news.

But for curiosity's sake, how would a situationist Christ have got his message across? Say, when he talked of the behavior and words of John the Baptist? John, if you remember, had spoken harshly to the Pharisees who came to his baptisms in the river Jordan:

> But when he saw many of the Pharisees and Sadducees come to his baptism, he said unto them, O generation of vipers, who hath warned you to flee from the wrath to come?
> Bring forth therefore fruits meet for repentance:
> And think not to say within yourselves, We have Abraham to our Father: for I say unto you, that God is able of these stones to raise up children unto Abraham. And now also the axe is laid unto the root of the trees: therefore every tree which bringeth not forth good fruit is hewn down, and cast into the fire. (Mt. 3:7-10)

92

Would not our situationist Christ do something to tone down the rhetoric of this closed-minded firebrand? Especially since John was tying his message so closely to Christ's; saying that Christ was the one who:

> shall baptize you with the Holy Spirit, and with fire: Whose fan is in his hand, and he will thoroughly purge his floor, and gather his wheat into the garner; but he will burn up the chaff with unquenchable fire. (Mt. 3:11-12)

Would not our situationist Christ reprimand such a preacher, tell him of the "good news," and demand that he stop talking of a condemnation to come, since, in truth, interior dispositions are likely to make us all "good fruit?" Yet Christ says of John:

> Verily I say unto you, Among them that are born of women there hath not risen a greater than John the Baptist: notwithstanding, he that is least in the kingdom of heaven is greater than he. (Mt. 11:11)

But let us go on, since the updaters might argue that John was not comparable to the least in the kingdom of heaven because he had not seen, as those of the kingdom of heaven have, that we must approach the question of guilt with situationist insights. What would Christ have said on the occasion when he talked specifically of temptations? Would not our situationist Christ have tried to diminish the guilt complexes of those who have broken his commandments and assure them that breaking the law is not as important as why we do it?

> Whosoever therefore shall break one of these least commandments, and shall teach men so, he shall be called least in the kingdom of heaven: but whosoever shall do and teach them, the same shall be called great in the kingdom of heaven. (Mt. 5:19)

Christ goes on, not to loosen up the requirements of the law or to qualify what he has just said by giving leeway for personal evaluation of the consequences of our actions, but to tighten up our responsibilities, to demand that we be willing to strive for even greater adherence to the rightful codes of human conduct. I quote at length even though it is one of the best known sections of the Bible. You have heard it before, I am sure, but read it now not just for the words, but to catch the tone and attitude toward the law that Christ demands, and to see if these are any Fletcher-like reservations:

> You have heard that it was said by them of old time, Thou shalt not kill; and whosoever shall kill shall be in danger of judgement:

> But I say unto you, That whosoever is angry with his brother without a cause shall be in danger of the judgement: and whosoever shall say to his brother, Raca, shall be in danger of the council: but whosoever shall say, Thou fool, shall be in danger of hell fire.
>
> Therefore if thou bring thy gift to the altar, and there rememberest that thy brother hath aught against thee; Leave there thy gift before the altar, and go thy way; first be reconciled to thy brother, and then come and offer thy gift. (Mt. 5:21-24)

No, Christ does not say, "He will be condemned." He says, "shall be in danger of judgement." He knew at least as much about the possibility of mitigating circumstances as the folks at Big Sur. But we are—unmistakably—*liable* to judgement. His message is thus the opposite of the situationist code. To quote further from Matthew 5.

> Ye have heard that it was said by them of old time, Thou shalt not commit adultery.
>
> But I say unto you, That whosoever looketh on a woman to lust after her hath committed adultery with her already in his heart. [Come on now, updaters, can you really picture anything like Cox's favorite quote from Norman Brown— "polymorphous perversity"—coming from the lips of this teacher in any but a condemnatory way?]
>
> And if thy right eye offend thee, pluck it out, and cast it from thee: for it is profitable for thee that one of thy members should perish, and not that thy whole body should be cast into hell.
>
> And if thy right hand offend thee, cut it off, and cast it from thee: for it is profitable for thee that one of thy members should perish, and not that thy whole body should be cast into hell. (Mt. 5:27-30)

Remove the notions of guilt, remorse, repentance, and penance from our moral considerations? How?

In case anyone fancies that the evils Christ was warning about were the failure to get out of Vietnam sooner or to comply with busing orders more willingly (not that evil might not be involved here), Christ warns that "out of the heart proceed evil thoughts, murders, adulteries, fornications, thefts, false witnesses, blasphemies: These are the things which defile a man." (Mt. 15:18-10)

He really does sound more like Elmer Gantry than Harvey Cox. I am not being facetious. At least the preachers caricatured by Sinclair Lewis are exaggerations of Christ—frightful exaggerations, but of Christ. They are trying, whether sincerely or not is another question, to imitate Him; not, in updater fashion, some worldly guru who denies Christianity lock, stock and barrel.

When our Lord assured us that "All manner of sin and blasphemy shall be forgiven unto men," he does seem to indicate divine leniency. True. But not the leniency of the situationist, which rests on the denial of moral norms that command our adherence. If the situationist assertion stands, Christ's offer of forgiveness is redundant, since "*so-called* sins" bring no shame. Situationists who like to quote this promise that "all manner of sin and blasphemy shall be forgiven," conveniently forget to mention the words of Christ that come *immediately* on the heels of this assurance of mercy: "Either make the tree good, and his fruit good; or else make the tree corrupt, and his fruit corrupt: for the tree is known by his fruit."

And: "O generation of vipers, how can ye, being evil, speak good things . . . an evil man out of the evil treasure bringeth forth evil things."

And: "But I say to you, That every idle word that men shall speak, they shall give account thereof in the day of judgement."

And: "For by thy words thou shalt be justified, and by thy words thou shalt be condemned." (Mt. 12:31-37)

Too harsh, you say? They would laugh at you *where* if you tried to defend such thoughts?

> And ye shall be hated of all men for my name's sake: but he that endureth to the end shall be saved.
> But when they persecute you in this city, flee ye into another: for verily I say unto you, Ye shall not have gone over the cities of Israel, till the Son of man be come.
> The disciple is not above his master, nor the servant above his lord.
> It is enough for the disciple that he be as his master, and the servant as his lord. If they have called the master of the house Beelzebub, how much more shall they call them of his household. (Mt. 10:22-25)

There will be the righteous "who hath ears to hear" and there will be the rest:

> Then shall the righteous shine forth as the sun in the kingdom of their Father. Who hath ears to hear, let him hear.
> Again, the kingdom of heaven is like unto a net, that was cast into the sea, and gathered of every kind: Which, when it was full, they drew to shore, and sat down, and gathered the good into vessels, but cast the bad away.
> So shall it be at the end of the world: the angels shall come forth, and sever the wicked from among the just, And shall cast them into the furnace of fire: there shall be wailing and gnashing of teeth. (Mt. 13:43-50)

"To thine own self be true?" A far cry from "furnace of fire" . . . "sever the wicked from the just" . . . "cast the bad away" . . . "wailing and gnashing of teeth."

(I do not want to give the impression that I am having great fun listing these passages, tweaking the updater nose with just a little too much verve. I am gloating a bit, I admit. They are *so* wrong in their picture of Christ. But it is a nervous gloating, I assure you. The thought of a furnace of fire and gnashing teeth does not make me feel comfortable. It was not meant to.)

> When the Son of man shall come in his glory, and all the holy angels with him, then shall he sit upon the throne of his glory:
> And before him shall be gathered all nations: and he shall separate them one from another, as a shepherd divideth his sheep from the goats:
> And he shall set the sheep on his right hand, but the goats on his left.
> Then shall the king say unto them on his right hand, Come, ye blessed of my Father, inherit the kingdom prepared for you from the foundation of the world. (Mt. 25:31-34)

Christ goes on to list the virtues which will be most rewarded at this final judgement, and they are the acts of charity the updaters favor most in their flirtation with humanism. Great reward will be given to those who clothe the naked, give drink to the thirsty, feed the hungry, visit the sick and imprisoned. I would not quarrel a bit with the idea (it was Dante's as well) that avarice and cruelty will lead to a more serious judgement than the sins of the flesh. But those other evils Christ excoriated—"evil thoughts, adulteries, fornications, thefts, covetousness, wickedness, deceit, lasciviousness, evil eye, blasphemy, pride, foolishness"—are part of the scenario too. I will accept, in fact, a situationist assertion that for Christ an unrepentant Ebenezer Scrooge would be liable to severe punishment—as long as they accept in turn that the characters Warren Beatty plays will get a piece of that action, too; and that those who champion the values of the editors of *Screw* and *Oui* will not come out smelling like roses; as long as the updaters don't try to tell me that on Judgement Day Christ will wink at these free thinkers (to put it mildly) and nod in agreement that they were the ones who understood his words most accurately, and paraphrased them best when they told us, "If it feels good, man, do it."

Indeed, it cannot be said that Christ was any milder than John the Baptist in his dealings with Herod. Herod's sin was right up the alley of the situationists. He had married his brother Philip's wife. Think of the room for situationist debate, or of how a similar situation would be analyzed at Big Sur—or at your local seminary, I'm afraid. "Who was hurt? Was the relationship a loving and giving one? Was it exploitative? Was Philip's wife being used as a sex object? Was their sex and loving all together?"

John's approach, if you remember, was quite different. "For John had said unto Herod, It is not lawful for thee to have thy brother's wife." (Mt. 14:4) And he stood by this code-morality pronouncement, unenlightenedly, right up until he was beheaded for saying it.

Christ echoes John's words in his treatment of the question of adultery and divorce. After conceding that Moses permitted divorce, he went on to make clear that only:

> For the hardness of your heart he wrote you this precept.
> But from the beginning of the creation God made them male and female.
> For this cause shall a man leave his father and mother, and cleave to his wife;
> And they twain shall be one flesh; so then they are no more twain, but one flesh.
> What therefore God hath joined together, let not man put asunder.

And further:

> Whosoever shall put away his wife, and marry another, committeth adultery against her.
> And if a woman shall put away her husband, and be married to another, she committeth adultery. (Mk. 10:5-12)

Now we know that among the Christian congregations that call themselves traditional, there is a difference of opinion about exactly when and whether divorce can be acceptable. In Matthew's treatment of Christ's words, mention is made of adultery as a qualifier to Christ's demand for permanence. But if we grant that, it must be admitted that Christ's words do not treat marriage as a contract of convenience that we can dissolve at will. (One New England updater pastor performs a ceremony now where the marriage vow reads: ''Till love do us part.'') It cannot be said—it would be a parody to try—that Christ's approach is in any way parallel to the situationist claim that the demands of love might even *require* the dissolution of a marriage, or that the marriage vows are to be treated as lightly as does Father John Milhaven when he argues that:

> for many people it is wrong to have sex relations outside marriage because experience has shown that they would thus hurt themselves, their partners, or others. But it is quite possible that for other people, in certain circumstances, extramarital sex relations hurt no one, further love, and therefore ought to be had. Only love is right, just as hate and indifference are always bad and wrong.[5]

Christ's contrasting tone is evident when he warns of what is in store for those who work to lessen the faith of those who believe in his teaching, especially the faith of the young: ''And whosoever shall offend one of these little ones that believe in me, it is better for him that a millstone were hanged about his neck, and he were cast into the sea.'' (Mk. 9:42)

''Better the millstone''—could Christ have been so inflexible and demand-

[5]*Theological Studies*, September 1966, p. 485.

ing? Must not that line be unique and/or of suspicious origin? The lines directly beneath the millstone quote should clear up any confusion. Christ speaks of the punishment of a "fire that never shall be quenched: where the worm dieth not." (Mark 9:43-44) Cotton Mather did not learn his rhetorical flourish at the local pub, you know. (Whether they are literal flames or not is beside the point. Christ is telling us that the pain will be real. It will hurt like hell.) We are not to risk such punishment by deluding ourselves with the wisdom of "false teachers" even if the false teachers are ourselves. Christ came to teach us to avoid temptations, not learn to learn to adjust to them. "Can the blind lead the blind? shall they not both fall into the ditch?" (Luke 6:39) Yes, Virginia, there is a ditch. But we can avoid it:

> Whosoever cometh to me, and heareth my sayings, *and doeth them,* I will show you to whom he is like.
> He is like a man which built a house, and digged deep, and laid the foundation on a rock: and when the flood arose, the stream beat vehemently upon that house, and could not shake it: for it was founded upon a rock.
> But he that heareth, *and doeth not,* is like a man that without a foundation built a house upon the earth; against which the stream did beat vehemently, and immediately it fell; and *the ruin of that house was great.* (Luke 6:47-49)

If You Love Me

When speaking to the woman anointing his feet with oil and her tears and drying them with her hair, Christ shows his mercy and forgiveness first and foremost. "Thy sins are forgiven thee; thy faith has saved thee; go in peace." "Her sins, *which are many,* are forgiven." Then he adds (I can see the updaters about to spring from their seats—aha!) "for she has loved much." (Luke 7:47-50) Okay. But again, *she has sinned.* She is *forgiven* because of love and repentance, not assured that her behavior was really "good." Christ treats her acts as evil. She is another of the lost sheep of which the Good Shepherd is so patiently solicitous—another prey of the Hound of Heaven. But she *was lost.* She has returned in sorrow from her wicked ways, and Christ is, as he promised, always ready to receive those who return expressing sorrow. The prodigal son, we must never forget, was prodigal. He has to come home from that distant city before he receives the outpouring of fatherly love that has so captured the imagination of Biblical illustrators down through the centuries.

Incongruous, this talk of love and punishment so evenly balanced by the same teacher? Not when you remember the way we were to demonstrate love for Christ:

If ye love me, keep my commandments.

And I will pray the Father, and he shall give you another Comforter, that he may abide with you forever;

Even the Spirit of truth; whom the world cannot receive, because it seeth him not, neither knoweth him: but ye know him; for he dwelleth with you, and shall be in you.

Notice again the anti-relativist thrust. The Apostles have been given truth by Christ. And the world that cannot see that is in error. Christ goes on:

I will not leave you comfortless: I will come to you. Yet a little while, and the world seeth me no more; but ye see me: because I live, ye shall live also.

And that day ye shall know that I am in my Father, and ye in me, and I in you.

He that hath my commandments, and keepeth them, he it is that loveth me; and he that loveth me shall be loved of my Father, and I will love him, and will manifest myself to him. (Jn. 14:15-21)

At this point an Apostle asks Christ to clarify, and Christ underscores his stress on living by God's law:

If a man love me, he will keep my words: and my Father will love him, and we will come unto him, and make our abode with him.

He that loveth me not keepeth not my sayings: and the word which ye hear is not mine, but the Father's which sent me. (Jn. 14:23-24)

It does not take much to see the connection between the broken families and rising divorce rates of our times and the declining American understanding of what love *really* means—as taught by Christ, that is. Christ knew that love involves pain as well as joy. His Father so loved the world that He sent His only begotten Son to die for its sins. That, it is true, is not the kind of love preached to us by the latest sex manuals, and by Hollywood. But it is a thought essential to upholding the worth and dignity of sacrifice and self-denial, and without these virtues marriage and the family, and civilization itself, cannot survive. It is no accident that the glossy weekly newsmagazines regularly devote space to the end of the family. Whether they are acting as advocates for that cause is important, but not as important as the fact that they have been perceptive in noting the likelihood of such a devolution.

I don't want to take off on an anti-young folks tirade, but we are in the midst of a social phenomenon that welds our eyes to its excesses. A significant portion of an entire generation is just now reaching adulthood, having been reared in a social environment which has taught, and continues to teach, that love is better expressed by an electric vibrator than by a cross. I mean to be shocking, because the situation is shocking, and deplorable. The movie ads in the major metropolitan newspapers (the suburbs are only slightly better) make one wonder how a young person growing up in America will ever be able to develop a sane and balanced understanding of the meaning of sex in his life. We have reached the bottom of the sewer. All that is left is the assault on us through television, and that, as we are beginning to realize, has begun, most especially on the Public Broadcasting System—in the name of meaningful social commentary, of course. Whether our young people can succeed at marriage or parenthood is a question that has to be asked. The figures so far indicate that they probably can't. The divorce rate for new marriages is closing in on 50 percent these days. How our country can survive with this sort of citizenry is another question. Sometimes it is difficult not to think that we shouldn't. The sight of these pseudo-sophisticated (it is commonplace! To act as if you know it all, without having read *anything*!), self-centered, bejewelled, alternately preening and sloppy—sometimes preening about their sloppiness—ostentatiously obscene young adults, is a depressing experience for those who grew up in the America of just twenty or thirty years ago. It isn't the boisterousness. Raising hell is as American as cherry pie. They are not really that boisterous anyway. That word implies some *gaieté de coeur*, as they say in Brooklyn. It is more the way their vices are carried openly, as a taunting sign of their rejection of the inner disciplines that have made the Christian people of America what we are. It is an undisguised affront. They are telling us that our ways, our beliefs are not worthy of sacrifice. Instant gratification is the rubric of life, the only guideline that can be followed in confidence, once you know "where it's at." The slouching, bedraggled countenance is no accident. Men walk straight and tall only when there is reason. There is nothing in America worth that purposeful and proud demeanor, they are telling us. Life is a search for what "gets you through the night."

Of course, history instructs us that societies so lacking in purpose fall. Marcus Aurelius, watching his Rome becoming comparably dissolute, insisted that his people must "stand straight or be made to stand straight." But that doesn't always work. (It didn't for Marcus Aurelius, if you remember.) Often the armies of the conquering barbarians are the only ones with sufficient vigor to restore health to a corrupt people. Often it is too late for any internal rehabilitation. Without an elevating vision of life to inspire the reconstruction—a religious vision—a society has nowhere to turn.

Admittedly, the drift of America into the permissiveness of today has multiple causes. But it is fair to suggest that Christians would not have joined the lines at the porn movies and the abortion mills, and slid into the despair of the drug culture, with so little resistance if they had known the Christ that St. Peter knew. Perhaps the older generation is more to blame for not teaching that

Christ to the young. The Christ who reacted to Peter's lack of perseverance with a harsh "Get behind me, Satan!" would have given them second thoughts before they jumped down the chute.

So would the Christ who said that:

> I am the true vine, and my Father is the husbandman.
> Every branch in me that beareth not fruit, he taketh away.

For what?

> If a man abide not in me, he is cast forth as a branch, and is withered; and men gather them, and cast them into the fire; and they are burned. (Jn. 15:1-6)

Of course our swingers do not hear such words from their favorite updater cleric. They might be scolded if they eat lettuce that wasn't picked by the right union, but not for involvement in a way of life that would have been condemned by any Christian just twenty years ago. It is easy to become numbed by the enormity of the social decay we have experienced during the last decade. Things that we accept as everyday occurrences now would have been condemned even by the World Council of Churches twenty years ago.

> He that rejecteth me, and receiveth not my words, hath one that judgeth him: the word that I have spoken, the same shall judge him in the last day.
> For I have not spoken of myself; but the Father which sent me, he gave me a commandment, what I should say, and what I should speak.
> And I know that his commandment is life everlasting; whatsoever I speak therefore, even as the Father said unto me, so I speak. (Jn. 12:48-50)

And in the same vein to the doubting Pharisees:

> Verily, verily, I say unto you, Whosoever committeth sin is the servant of sin.
> And the servant abideth not in the house for ever: but the Son abideth ever.
> If the Son therefore shall make you free, ye shall be free indeed.
> I know that ye are Abraham's seed; but ye seek to kill me, because my word hath no place in you. I speak that which I have seen with my Father: and ye do that which ye have seen with your Father. (Jn. 8:34-38)

Christ speaks of the devil, of course, when he says "your father" to the Pharisees.

> Ye are from beneath; I am from above: ye are of this world; I am not of this world.
> I said therefore unto you, that ye shall die in your sins: for if ye believe not that I am he, ye shall die in your sins. (Jn. 8:23-24)

101

Truth or Consequences

We could go on with quotes of this sort, and for pages more. That is what is saddest about our world's refusal to listen. Christ went to such great lengths to give us a way out of the darkness.

Situationism, whether the situationists want to admit to it or not, has nothing that can rescue us from our increasingly paganized world. Their stress on sexual pleasure as a human right to be indulged at will, rather than as a part of God's plan which must be treated with reverence and self-control, has, in fact, done much to carry us into a Times Square type of world—and certainly has made it difficult to stop the deterioration. What can a situationist say to a young boy—or girl, for that matter; that's progress for you—standing before a Times Square massage parlor or movie house featuring films of bestiality, and the other kinds of fun the cats call "mixed combos?" The same thing as the guy in the box office! "So what's the madda anyway, kid? You ain't gonna hurt nobody. How do you know if you're gonna like it till you give it a try? If it turns you on, who's to criticize?" I do not mean to be disrespectful. The situationists are most often university types who would not like to be compared to the rodents who run porno parlors. But in all sincerity, how does their analysis offer a reason for not ending up as a regular on the Times Square scene?

Perhaps we should not spend too much time on this question of sexual promiscuity. One of the favorite updater ploys is to turn such concerns back on people—to accuse them of a sexual hangup. (Still, if it is a hangup to become enraged at the thought of how hard teenagers are going to find it to remain Christian because of the constant and unforgivable barrage of filth they are forced to live with, I'll wear that hangup proudly.)

But there is something sick festering in America today. Well intentioned liberals and updaters know that. They never thought that freedom of expression would lead to films of people copulating with chickens. They are shocked by the horrors (I presume; I *hope*), but they have been telling people for so long now that free choice for all is the ultimate human goal that they know not where to turn. Certainly there is a difference between what C.S. Lewis used to call "cheery lechery" and people paying to see the latest in Times Square, Al Goldstein-produced extravaganzas. There *is* a disease upon us, and its symptoms are most pronounced in the area of porn. Porn shows us what relativism does when applied to sex, and gives warning of the analogous horrors in store when we allow it to work its way into other areas of our life.

It is a turning point for America. If we cannot work up the resolve to remove the porn outrage from our lives, we might not deserve those lives, and we might even deserve what comes next on the road to full social decay. If the bloodcurdling sight of this Goldstein and his cronies (Goldstein admitted in an interview in the *New York Daily News* in the summer of 1975 that his "stock in trade is raw, flailing sex") gloating over how they have been able to amass small fortunes by putting together consummate attacks on our most cherished values, does not lead an angered citizenry to demand an end to his empire; if we will not stand tall, perhaps we just have lost the will to go on, and really would be better off being made to stand tall by those who will take over the hollow shell of what was once a proud and virtuous social order.

Chapter VI

The Devil

I ADMIT to a temptation to give in here, in the hope of demonstrating sophistication and a willingness to compromise somewhere in the name of Christian unity. Not that I have any doubts about the existence of the devil myself. Christ is quite explicit about his presence and power; and a traditional Catholic accepts papal authority. (The popes have spoken out often in affirmation of the existence of Satan—as recently as 1975, much to the chagrin and embarrassment of Catholic updaters.) Nevertheless, this seemed the ideal spot in which not to press for a fundamentalist reading of the Scripture. I could have agreed that there *might* be something to the argument that Christ *might* have been speaking allegorically; or that, at least, I might be able to see someone taking this tack. I could have conceded that evil is the result of man's failure to respond correctly to God's law and creation, and that such a negative state requires no existent and personal source beyond the human failure itself. I toyed with that idea, in the hope that I might be able to get Christians to take more seriously what Christ says elsewhere.

The refusal to believe in the devil, however, is *often* part of a larger refusal to believe in anything at all that strains the bounds of reason. (I emphasize "often" because there are Christians decidedly orthodox on almost everything else in the Christian dispensation who chafe at this bit. I don't say that this is wise or acceptable; but it is true.) One can refuse to accept the existence of the devil and remain Christian, claim some. But there are dangerous and unacceptable reasons for doing so. For one thing, denial of Satan can betray, or instigate, a prejudice that will take one down the path to rationalist heresy.

Perhaps if I tell you of an experience of mine a few years back I can make the point. It was a brief encounter with an acquaintance who is what is called a fallen-away Catholic. He no longer went to church, and even talked casually of how he recommended an abortion to his sister so that she would be able to enjoy a new camper her husband had purchased one spring without the inconvenience and discomfort of the middle stages of pregnancy. But he did make much of the fact that he was "still a Christian." He and I were members of the faculty in a high school on the East Coast. Often, in the faculty lounge, he would speak harshly of churches and churchmen, always adding the cliched fillip that the churches are not being faithful to Christ—that he liked Christ, but not the institutions that purport to follow him. Everyone has heard the line before. At least I have—and whether it betrays a lack of Christian resolve or not, I seldom try to talk anyone out of it. My experience has been that those who say such things are not open to being talked back into the faith; that most often it is an act of the will that forms their mind, not a lack of information.

So on the afternoon we were returning to the school parking lot from an auto parts store with a set of points I was going to help him install, we were not in the role of debating opponents. He knew that I was a practicing Catholic, I imagine, but not much more than that. It was just about the time that the movie *The Exorcist* was making the rounds. Just to pass the time, I asked him whether he had seen it. He told me that he had not, but that he might that weekend. Without thinking (I was not trying to make a convert) I mentioned that movies of that sort probably are more successful than monster movies because they probe our inner fears with real and possible horrors instead of outlandish creatures.

His eyes turned from the road a moment and squinted at me in disbelief; his mouth pursed slightly.

"Are you kidding?" he asked in a mixture of scorn and incredulity.

We rode on in silence for a moment or two. I wasn't going to respond at first, but I felt a twinge of resentment. After all, I was a "professional educator" too (as they say in teacher union circles).

"Well," I interrupted with as much sophisticated poise as I could work up (which wasn't much), "it isn't a lot more difficult to believe in a personal evil spirit than it is to believe in a personal God."

Our noninstitutional Christian turned, and this time smiled faintly and knowingly. "I know," he said, and then he laughed in a short exhaled spurt. "I know."

I didn't bring up the subject again. I got the message, He did not believe in the

106

Devil, but neither did he believe in a personal God. He didn't pray for the same reason he didn't fear *The Exorcist* (or at least the prospect of seeing it; perhaps the movie suspended his disbelief enough for him to react to the performance). I didn't ask him if he had an alternative image, maybe something like Baum's. It was clear that he no longer accepted the God revealed by Christ. When he called himself a Christian, he meant that certain Christian commands toward brotherly love and social justice corresponded to what he thought were the highpoints of his own secular humanism.

Things That Go Bump in the Night

The point is that many of those who scorn a belief in the devil as something childish and medieval build that case with empiricist blocks. They tell us that it is unreasonable to talk of a devil because modern man knows there are no goatlike creatures with dragon-skin wings living in the bowels of the earth. The danger is obvious. The corollary is that there be no God since modern man has learned there is no white-bearded patriarch sitting on a cloud that can be reached by turning right at the second star on the left and heading straight on until morning.

Christians are forced to believe in neither of these caricatures, as everyone—except perhaps, and only perhaps, some medieval peasant—knows. They have always been understood as artistic representations. Even the best educated of Christians might evoke them when they hear the words "Devil" or "God," but only for lack of something more appropriate. They might even pray to a God who looks like what you would expect to find in a Renaissance chapel. But they are aware—when they think of it—that it is only a device. (Of course, they might pray to Christ and not have to worry about such things.) If you asked them, the well educated and the illiterate alike: "Is God an old man with a beard?" or "Is the devil a horned figure with cloven hoof?" their answer would be reflexive and blunt. "No, of course not. He is a spirit." Perhaps the very least educated would mean by that something like an invisible man with a beard or an invisible satyr. But they *would* mean a spirit, however primitive their understanding of that word, not someone one meets once his space vehicle has passed a certain layer above the clouds, or halfway between New York and China, straight down. (The only one I can remember making such naive statements was the Russian who gloated in self-satisfaction that his country's space mission proved that the God of Christians was a myth.)

What is a spirit? I'll leave the fullness of that problem to the ontologists. I have a hard enough time keeping the black spot off my tomato plants. But, like Christ, and on his testimony, I hold that a spirit is a conscious, individual being with whom we can communicate. At least God is. And if the Marquis de Sade, Gilles de Rais, and Charles Manson (and Christ) can be trusted in this instance, so is Satan.

Certainly mankind has shown no reluctance to believe in an Evil One. A survey of the imagery of primitive and non-Western peoples would lead one, in fact, to conclude that the fear of such a malevolent being has been a more vital presence in the human consciousness than a loving and virtuous Creator. The Buddhist Mara with its serpent-bound limbs, the winged Gorgons of Greece, the menacing Egyptian reptiles, Kali and his frightening belt of human skulls, are all representations of a deep-seated recognition of a source for the evil in the world. And if one were to judge from the witch cults of modern America, the bonechilling refusal of the Black Mass to go the way of other obscene fads, the ugly aberrations of Manson and Hell's Angels-style youth cults, the success of *The Exorcist* and *Rosemary's Baby,* such thoughts are still very much a part of the Western mind as well. In fact, if all the American interest in the diabolical and occult were directed toward some Third World deity instead of a part of the Christian revelation, our updaters would be writing essays telling us that such a deep and personal experience must be reflective of a sincere human effort to find meaning in life, and worthy of ecumenical attention. Too bad this Devil is found in the Bible instead of the Kama Sutra, and is, consequently, unworthy of serious consideration.

The strangely intense attention paid to *The Exorcist* led the American theological community to make revealing admissions. *America,* the proudly progressive, Jesuit owned and edited journal, carried an article at the height of the craze in which an older priest, who had studied and taught in the leading Jesuit universities in America and Europe, argued that the interest in the movie and book was, by and large, healthy. It forced a man-centered and materialistic world to think deeply about things spiritual and eternal. He admitted, quite frankly, that he slept uneasily and with his lights on for nearly a week after seeing the film. He conceded that the story was fanciful and sensationalist, and obscene in parts, but was willing to accept such a vehicle if it shook modern man from his presumptions and smug confidence. He also mentioned several priests he knew (scholarly types, too) who refused to see the movie at all for fear of how troubled they would be by it. They spoke of the danger in treating Satan too lightly, or too graphically.

The reaction was clamorous and shrill. It was as if he had pulled the chair from under Margaret Mead during a CBS broadcast of Tahitian burial rites. Younger priests, updater theologians, seminarians of all denominations (most especially of the Jesuit order, as one would expect in a journal published by the group) wrote letters to the editor that seethed with a mixture of sputtering indignation and pained embarrassment. (I quote from memory.) ''Does not the good Father recall what century he is living in?" "That superstitious drivel is exactly what enlightened Christians have been trying to help their brethren overcome." Doesn't he "realize that statements such as his could drive countless young people out of the Church altogether?" "Belief in a personal and effective Devil went out with the Ptolemaic view of the universe." One writer wondered if the priest thought it wise to burn witches and pat the hunched backs of dwarves for good luck.

I do not want to judge the faith of those who responded in such a manner. (I do, however, think it worthy of our attention that most of the writers were Catholic and presumably aware of the Pope's position.) But we cannot overlook the stated reasons for their anger. It was not just the Devil they found beyond belief; it was anything that could not be squeezed within the Bultmannian scope.

One cannot help but wonder what the response would have been to a priest who took seriously a book or movie which took seriously the story of a man's encounter with God. Hollywood has made movies of that sort but, except for the bombs that no one writes about anyway, not recently. What would happen if Hollywood turned out a new film which expressed movingly the story of Joan of Arc or the Curé of Ars, or perhaps a fictionalized account of a case of the stigmata, especially if hordes of people reacted to it with a piety proportionate to the fear they felt at the thought of the devil in *The Exorcist*? That really might thrust up the air.

But let us turn to Christ and examine the context and tone of his references to Satan. Is it possible to come to the conclusion that he was speaking allegorically without swinging from the hip with such irresponsible abandon that we become updaters ourselves—handling Christ's words so casually that we could end up viewing his description of his Father similarly? (Would it be unfair to say that this is exactly the step the updaters want us to take?)

Catholics, of course, know the answer to this question before we begin —those who are still willing to give more credence to the popes than to the modern theologians, at any rate. For them, looking at Christ's words should make clear why the popes have taught with such assurance in this area.

My Name Is Legion

The obvious place to begin is with the temptations in the desert. It is the first New Testament mention of Satan. First of all, those who think the story farfetched cannot blame it on a hyperimaginative Evangelist overeacting to his experience of Christ. No Evangelist was witness. It was Christ and the Devil, one on one. The Evangelists could not have been affected by their love and awe of Christ and led into either conscious or subconscious hyperbole. They were acting in this instance as mere transcribers of a story that could only have been told to them; by Christ. If there are errors, they are His. (Which would be more important for polemical purposes if the updaters still thought Christ incapable of error—but they no longer do. But more of that later.)

If one compares the story as it appears in Matthew and Luke (Mark just mentions that Christ was tempted in one sentence; John not at all), the extent of their dependence on Christ becomes unmistakable. The two versions are near to identical, down to the choice of wording and sentence structure. (No talk of conspiracy, now, updaters. No such identity can be seen in the rest of their narration, except in the case of Christ's words—which only confirms our point. They go to greater pains to get Christ's words just right than they worry about the rest of the details of their accounts; including what he says about the Devil. The same order of temptations, the same locales: the stones into bread, the pinnacle of the temple, the mountain top. Besides, updaters, you can't have it both ways. When the narratives are identical, you tell us it is a conspiracy; when there are incongruities, you tell us it proves inaccuracy. Which is it, brethren? Whichever makes us doubt the most? Whatever belittles Scripture the most?)

Can we find some hint that Christ wants us to see the story as poetic imagery representative of the human struggle with "personal demons?"

> Then was Jesus led up of the spirit into the wilderness to be tempted of the devil. And when he had fasted forty days and forty nights, he was afterward ahungered. And when the tempter came to him, he said, If thou be the Son of God, command that these stones be made bread.
> But he answered and said, It is written, Man shall not live by bread alone, but by every word that proceedeth out of the mouth of God.
> Then the devil taketh him up into the holy city, and setteth him on a pinnacle of the temple,
> And saith unto him, If thou be the Son of God, cast thyself down: for it is written, He shall give his angels charge concerning thee: and in their hands they shall bear thee up, lest at any time thou dash thy foot against a stone.
> Jesus said unto him, It is written again, Thou shalt not tempt the Lord thy God.
> Again, the devil taketh him up into an exceeding high mountain, and showeth him all the kingdoms of the world, and the glory of them:
> And saith unto Him, All these things will I give thee, if thou wilt fall down and worship me.
> Then saith Jesus unto him, Get thee hence, Satan: for it is written, Thou shalt worship the Lord thy God, and him only shalt thou serve.
> Then the devil leaveth him, and *behold,* angels came and ministered unto him. [You would not have to say ''behold'' if that meant he returned to good spirits— just as an aside.] (Mt. 4:1-11)

To make clear how extensive has been the updater fouling of the air on this issue, permit me to make mention of the coverage of this scene given in *A Catholic Commentary on Sacred Scripture,* the research aid used by the most respected and serious of Catholic Scripture scholars before the revisionist zeal reached full tilt. The book is not a down-home, folksy, message-for-the-day account. It was the most widely respected tool for the most learned Scripture scholars at leading Catholic universities in the English-speaking world. In it, one finds some difference of opinion, perhaps more than Protestant fundamentalists would think proper. But it is starkly different from the kind of outright dismissal we face in our day—the treatment of it as a parable used by Christ to illustrate the need for Christians not to work with the power structure of their time, for example. (This was Bishop Pike's neat piece of work.) The community of scholars who used the book were not faced with the question of whether the temptations actually occurred or not, or whether there was a personal confrontation with Satan, but whether:

a) the Devil appeared in human form,

b) the Devil actually levitated Christ and flew with him hand in hand up to the mountain top,

c) Christ and the Devil would have been visible to someone taking an evening stroll beneath the temple, if he happened to look up.

Because of the updater influence, questions such as these now seem to fall into the same category as angels on the head of a pin. But, in all sincerity, they are not naive or unworthy of serious thought for anyone who takes Christ at his word.

If an enemy of the Faith had been told thirty years ago that there was a chance that some of the most earnest scholarship of the best trained Scripture scholars in Europe could be made objects for ridicule or patronizing silence by the 1970s, he probably would have dismissed the hope out of hand. But it has been done. I ask the most orthodox of my readers: Would you be willing to ask such questions out loud these days with your fellow Christians, and not just because of the fight that you would get?

It is not only a scholarly question. The Devil of which Christ speaks is working to drag us with him into a "furnace of fire" where "there will be weeping and gnashing of teeth." Christ does not speak of a phantasm that exists only in our minds or as a projection of them. We do not "create" the evil force he calls Satan—unless pigs know that trick too.

And when he was come to the other side into the country of the Gergesenes, there met him two possessed with devils, coming out of the tombs, exceeding fierce, so that no man might pass by that way.

And, behold, they cried out, saying, What have we to do with thee, Jesus, thou

Son of God? Art thou come hither to torment us before the time? And there was a good way off from them an herd of many swine feeding.

So the devils besought him, saying, If thou cast us out, suffer us to go away into the herd of swine.

And he said unto them, Go. And when they were come out, they went into the herd of swine; and, behold, the whole herd of swine ran violently down a steep place into the sea, and perished in the waters.

And they that kept them fled, and went their ways into the city, and told everything, and what was befallen to the possessed of the devils.

And, behold, the whole city came out to meet Jesus: and when they saw him, they besought him that he would depart out of their coasts. (Mt. 8:28-34)

The residents of the area saw enough to fear the presence of Christ. They would have to be taught by *what* authority Christ exorcized, but they doubted not that something unworldly had happened. We should not forget, in addition, how foolish it would have been for the Apostles to lie about such an incident, since they were writing the Gospels to gain converts. Why make witnesses of an entire town if you were going to fabricate a story? They *had* to be confident that the Gergesenes would corroborate their claims.

Mark tells the same story, but is more graphic in his description of the symptoms of the possession. His detailed, reportorial account cannot be viewed as parable:

And they came over unto the other side of the sea, into the country of the Gadarenes. [Notice, once again, that there is no attempt by the Apostles to "get their facts straight" the way good con men would. Matthew refers to the inhabitants of the Gadara as Gergesenes, Mark and Luke as Gadarenes. Mark and Luke mention only one demoniac, Matthew two. But they agree on the rest—the part the moderns would have us discount as impossible.]

And when he was come out of the ship, immediately there met him out of the tombs a man with an unclean spirit,

Who had been dwelling among the tombs; and no man could bind him, no, not with chains:

Because that he had been often bound with fetters and chains, and the chains had been plucked asunder by him, and the fetters broken in pieces: neither could any man tame him.

And always, night and day, he was in the mountains, and in the tombs, crying, and cutting himself with stones.

But when he saw Jesus afar off, he ran and worshipped him,

And cried with a loud voice, and said, What have I to do with thee, Jesus, thou Son of the most high God? I adjure thee by God, that thou torment me not.

For he said unto him, Come out of the man, thou unclean spirit.

And he asked him, What is thy name? And he answered, saying, My name is Legion: for we are many. (Mark 5:1-9)

112

Mark goes so far in his reporter's zeal to tell us that about two thousand swine rushed into the sea.

One would think that Christ would have at least left some uncertainty in his words about the existence of these devils, for later generations to reinterpret his position, if you want to take the line that Christ spoke of devils only because such creatures were part of the folklore of his time, and an effective way to get his message across to his contemporaries. Some talk of the "devil within us," or the devil who "lives only with our cooperation," or the evil spirit that "lives in hardened hearts," or something. But not a hint, not a *double entendre* in sight. If he had dropped just one clue of that sort, I could see myself playing updater here, too. But he doesn't.

Think of the marvelous opportunity to do that when the Pharisees charged him with exorcizing devils through the power of Satan. He could have said something, updater fashion, about the very thought of man being able to act under the influence of an Evil One, or accused the Pharisees of a typically thoughtless attempt to foist guilt onto a nonexistent creature. Why did he not say that: "All evil is from your own hearts, not from another. Leave such childish things. We have met the enemy and he is us."

Instead, he treats the devil as a creature real and potent enough to rival his Father:

> Every kingdom divided against itself is brought to desolation; and every city or house divided against itself shall not stand:
> And if Satan cast out Satan, he is divided against himself: how then shall his kingdom stand? (Mt. 12:25-26)

The inconsistency is not in believing in the Devil. It is in believing that the Devil would use his power (a power conceded to be real) against himself.

In Luke we find a comparably straightforward treatment. Remember, as you read Luke's description of an exorcism, that nowhere else does Christ speak of his healing powers as a confrontation with Satan. When he cures the lame or the blind, or raises the dead, there is no mention of evil powers being purged to effect the cure. Revisionists would have us believe that since the Jews of the first century saw physical ailments as the work of an evil spirit, the Evangelists resorted to this imagery when describing Christ's cures. But they do not. They *only* talk of exorcizing devils when the "sickness" in question has all the symptoms we moderns—psychologists and anthropologists included—refer to as demonic possession. There is no mention made of the "devils of blindness" or "the devils of leprosy." Only when the sickness is the one described below does Christ cure with the words used by exorcists. Luke's description could have been taken from a medical manual written yesterday. He is not talking of heartburn:

And it came to pass, that on the next day, when they were come down from the hill, much people met him.

And, behold, a man of the company cried out, saying, Master, I beseech thee, look upon my son: for he is mine only child. And, lo, a spirit taketh him, and he suddenly cried out, and it teareth him that he foameth again, and bruising him hardly departeth from him.

And I besought thy disciples to cast him out; and they could not.

And Jesus said, O faithless and perverse generation, how long shall I be with you, and suffer you? Bring thy son hither. [He upbraids them not for believing in the power of Satan, but for not believing enough in Christ's power over him.]

And as he was yet a coming, the devil threw him down, and tare him. And Jesus rebuked the unclean spirit, and healed the child, and delivered him again to his father. And they were all amazed at the mighty power of God. (Luke 9:37-43)

Luke is no less explicit elsewhere:

Now when the sun was setting, all they that had any sick with divers diseases brought them unto him; and he laid his hands on every one of them, and healed them.

And devils also came out of many, crying out, and saying, Thou art Christ the Son of God. And he, rebuking them, suffered them not to speak; for they knew that he was Christ. (Luke 4:40-41)

If Christ is speaking metaphorically, Luke is not aware of that fact. Whatever attributes you might want to affix to a human weakness, *knowing* that Christ is the Son of God is not one of them. When his disciples returned after a successful mission, on which they exorcized in Christ's name, Christ commends their efforts:

And the seventy returned again with joy, saying, Lord, even the devils are subject unto us through thy name. And he said unto them, I beheld Satan as lightning fall from heaven.

Behold, I give unto you power to tread on serpents and scorpions, and over all the power of the enemy: and nothing shall by any means hurt you.

Notwithstanding in this rejoice not, that the spirits are subject unto you, but rather rejoice, because your names are written in heaven. (Luke 10:17-20)

In a disdainful response to rumors that Herod is about to make a threat on his life, Christ shows the same stress on the unique and revealing nature of his exorcisms:

Go ye, and tell that fox, Behold, I cast out devils, and I do cures today and tomorrow, and the third day I shall be perfected.

114

Nevertheless I must walk today, and tomorrow, and the day following: for it cannot be that a prophet perish out of Jerusalem. (Luke 13:31-33)

Christ is saying, in effect: "Look, men, you've seen what I have been doing around here for the last few days. Do you really think threats from that old coot are going to shake me?" But that is an effective pluck of the royal beard only if he has done something more awe-inspiring and indicative of powers beyond Herod's than helping folks to get their "heads on straight." The most startling of those acts is direct and open combat with Satan.

And Thou Art Tormented

Christ's persistent refusal to treat the Devil as synonymous with our lack of moral resolve was meant to tell us something: that there is an evil tempter who wants us to join him in his eternal "reward."

Christ wants us to fear Satan and all his works and pomps. That much is clear. For some, that leering goat with the pitchfork might help do that; quite well. Philosophers might be able to construct a better metaphor for themselves. But it will still be *metaphor*, and in all likelihood, closer to the truth only to the degree that a third-grader's crayon sketches are closer to a Rembrandt than a first-grader's finger painting. But not if it helps us forget the question of those furnaces of fire, rather than bring them to life. That is the central issue.

There is that place of punishment. Some of us are going to experience it first hand.

And there was a certain rich man, which was clothed in purple and fine linen, and fared sumptuously every day:

And there was a certain beggar named Lazarus, which was laid at his gate full of sores,

And desiring to be fed with the crumbs which fell from the rich man's table: moreover the dogs came and licked his sores.

And it came to pass, that the beggar died, and was carried by the angels into Abraham's bosom: the rich man also died, and was buried.

And in hell he lifted up his eyes, being in torment, and seeth Abraham afar off, and Lazarus in his bosom.

And he cried and said, Father Abraham, have mercy on me, and send Lazarus, that he may dip the tip of his finger in water, and cool my tongue, for I am tormented in this flame.

But Abraham said, Son, remember that thou in thy lifetime receivedst thy good things, and likewise Lazarus evil things: but now he is comforted and thou art tormented. (Luke 16:19-25)

115

After conceding all the parabolic metaphor you want, Christ is saying that after death, we, like Abraham and Lazarus, will be personally aware of a divine reward if we follow Him; or, like the self-centered rich man, a personal punishment apart from God if we don't. What the devil does it matter what the people in that hell look like?

But let us not spend all our time worrying about those who make light of Satan. There are those who are as contemptuous of God, and they talk from pulpits too often to be ignored.

Chapter VII

Hallowed Be Thy Name

UP UNTIL RECENTLY it was difficult for Christians to be certain that the existence of God was being denied by an innovative theologian. We agreed that the knowledge of God in His fullness was beyond human intelligence, and that the very best of human explanations never went beyond a comparative and shadowy metaphorical level. Prime Mover, Omniscient, Omnipotent, Ground of Being, *Ens in re*, the Absolute . . . we do not picture such thoughts. They remain concepts, and never as clear as the more common extensions of held memory we usually call knowledge. The greatest of minds of the classical world never went beyond this level of abstraction; and neither would we—if it had not been for Christ. He gathered the multitudes to his side and gave what their minds would never reach on their own. He spoke of a God who was Aristotle's Prime Mover, but more—a loving Father who numbered every hair on our heads. He taught us to pray to that Father, and confirmed the wildest and most pollyanna speculations of the ancients: that we were made to share an eternity of bliss with our Maker. When modern theologians struggled to extend and refine our understanding of what is meant by God, and insisted upon working without a literal acceptance of Christ's revelation, we understood. It is possible for man to come to certain conclusions about the nature of God from reason alone. Why not allow them to push forward the frontiers of natural

117

theology? After all (and fortunately for us), St. Thomas Aquinas did not agree with Tertullian that Christ's words had made metaphysical inquiry unnecessary. Perhaps there *will* be a *future* theologian to contribute as much to our understanding of the divine. It is possible, even if not probable.

The current crop of updaters, however, do not work within the confines of such a discipline. They are not writing to tell us more about the God taught by Christ. Their scholarship is dedicated to the emancipation of Christians from that thought.

The revisionists of earlier eras often seemed to be working toward that end, too, but their scholarly language was either too complex or too abstruse—or, perhaps, too mystical—for us to be sure. Perhaps, we told ourselves, the Bultmanns and Tillichs, the Bonhoeffers and Teilhards were delineating a deeper understanding of our God, rather than a denial.

I do not applaud this deference we paid to the updaters of a generation or two back. A rereading of Tillich and Bonhoeffer, especially, makes one marvel that anyone could have doubted that their objective was any different from Gregory Baum's—an all-out attempt to keep alive the socially desirable Christian emphasis on brotherly love even though the Christian reason for such a sentiment was dead.

Tillich: "There is no religion as a special spiritual sphere. Everything is secular." And: "We must forget everything traditional we have learned about God, perhaps even that word."[1]

Bonhoeffer: Man must adjust to a new world where the need for God "is being more and more edged out of life, losing more and more ground." "Before God and with God, we live without God."[2]

But I have no interest, nor do I feel a pressing need, to fight these old battles. Whether or not there was a conscious effort in the past to dispel rather than faithfully refine our idea of God, there is one now. It matters little for those of us who are more interested, at present, in living our faith than in outlining its intellectual history, whether the updaters are correct in their belief that they are carrying the work of Tillich and Bonhoeffer *et al.* to the next logical plateau. *They* are denying the existence of God.

It is, however, true that the growing interest in the linguistic analysts has blurred our focus. By maintaining that we cannot even express the thought of God, they deny our ability to condemn heretical denials too. We cannot condemn those who say incorrectly what cannot be said at all. The wall plaque phrases it well: "I know you believe you understand what you think I said, but I am not sure that you realize that what you heard is not what I meant." It is the

[1]Paul Tillich, *The Protestant Era,* p. 175.

[2]Quoted in John Robinson's *Honest to God,* p. 24.

triumph of solipsism, of course. After two thousand years of thinking otherwise, we now know that Socrates lost his battles with the Sophists. What is truth?

Hans Kung, the Swiss theologian, applies the insight these days to papal infallibility. The pope *is* infallible, he tells us, but we don't really know the thought that word expresses. Neither does the pope. Such verbal contortion might not bother Protestants, since Kung is using the ploy to defuse the power of the papacy, but it does not take much imagination to see how the trick can be played on other stages—and with other words. "God," for example.

One would think that theologians would shy away from speculation of this sort, since, necessarily, the linguistic premise signals the death knell for the field in which they toil for their daily bread. Why bother, if we cannot arrive at a degree of knowledge worth our efforts? Especially since we won't even be able to communicate the reasons for our inadequacies to our fellow "futilists" (if I may be so bold as to resort to a neologism). Why have departments of theology at all—or departments of anything other than the applied sciences? (But the linguistic analysts were able to communicate *that* despair to us, weren't they? How did they do that?) If the modern theologians playing with linguistics are right, they will be the last theologians on earth. There are no more courses in alchemy—except maybe at Berkeley and The New School.

Why do they do it then? For the same reasons that liberal intellectuals who are so critical of the United States end up mooning over the brotherhood of Castro and Mao. And college girls who have knowingly debauched themselves to demonstrate their contempt for the moral and social order of our people now yearn for a national decline. ("If this place survives and prospers after all, then, dammit, I'm just a slut.") Linguistic analysis is the death cut. They have been telling us for so long now that our traditional beliefs are mumbo-jumbo that it is quite logical for them to take this last step: to tell us that the whole sorry mess was not worth studying in the first place. They want us to feel that despair. After all, it took a lot of reading and summer seminars for them to develop it. (How about modern theologian is to Christianity as AA is to booze?)

Big Daddy

A quick glance at the updater literature of the last few years indicates how explicit the denials have become. Apparently, the combination of ecclesiastical permissiveness and indecision (and possibly despairing faithlessness) has opened the floodgates.

There are some, it is true, who still walk the tightrope. Michael Novak used to be the best of the daring young men. He would insist that "God is conscious —at least as conscious as I."

After that, you would think that orthodox Christians would give him his head. Maybe he would be the one to come up with something better than St. Thomas. After all, we did concede that God is not Michelangelo's old man made invisible. He wouldn't leave His footprints in the snow. Maybe there are better images, and maybe a man as bright and as learned as Novak can work one up. Maybe an all-persuasive, conscious fog, undulating through the universe like *The Green Ooze That Swallowed Cleveland*—or whatever they called that movie. As long as it is a conscious fog, why not? How about "the infrastructure of the universe?" Too much like pantheism? I agree. But if someone wants to try to refine it somehow . . . they used that theme for *Star Trek*. Probably Novak is as perceptive as they. How about that thinking stone in *2001? Who knows what wisdom lurks in the mind of man? Maybe Michael Novak does.*

But then we hear Novak's variations . . . Can one speculate as he does without displaying a coarse indifference to Christ? Ought one write with scorn for those Christians who "speak of a mythical Big Daddy,"[3] or assert that God is found "within and through the human spirit"; and that sophisticated moderns are becoming increasingly offended by churchmen who continue to "treat God as a vague guarantor of the good order which makes them secure," and "the projection of that superego which keeps them conscientious when no one is looking?" Especially after writing pages of supplicating encomia to Jean-Paul Sartre? Can one state confidently that "God is hidden from the believer and unbeliever alike" without showing utter contempt for Christ? Hidden *alike!* Hidden, maybe; but the words of Christ in description of his Father are supposed to give us a *little* bit of an edge. If you are unwilling to call Christ a liar, at any rate. But perhaps that is possible once you begin to think in enlightened terms. Novak tells us that "no one has seen God."[4] Apparently the leader seen by Mary, Joseph, Peter, James, John, Judas, Herod, Pilate and the multitudes at the sermon on the Mount was not who He said He was.

Nowhere, in fact, in the pages of his *Belief and Unbelief*—the book in which he deals with these topics most directly—does Novak hint that Christ's revelation is special. Apparently we are to forget about that Father and pick up where Plato and Aristotle left off, searching for the answer to these deep questions, along with the existentialists, as if Christianity were a two-thousand-year mistake. Our father is the Big Daddy he finds so contemptible; and our Father is Christ's Father.

But if Novak leaves us uncertain, others burn their denials onto our flesh. We have already made much of Gregory Baum's claims—what he, in fact, calls the "third way" between theism and atheism. At the risk of overemphasizing his

[3]*Belief and Unbelief,* p. 113.
[4]*Ibid.,* p. 23.

importance, let us go on. His candor puts so much else of what we hear in perspective. Baum speaks shamelessly of what others, less brazen, only hint at as they chip away at our belief. He talks of the major concern of the modern theologian: "the God problem." How are Christians to be shown that "God is not an object of which existence may be predicated?" God, after all, "does not exist," he *becomes,* as man moves toward him—"the ever new and gratuitous summons present in life" that "orientates men toward a more perfect future."[5] But don't accuse him of atheism, please. He believes that the cosmic template, that spiritual stencil, really exists. It is "there," waiting for us to realize it in history.

But even after hearing someone dismiss God with verbal gymnastics of this sort, Christians often refrain from condemnation. We may tell ourselves that the learned man in black must be trying to adumbrate for us the *effect* of God on an individual. I used to keep telling myself that story during theology classes where certain Jesuit professors seemed to be talking of a vague God not unlike Baum's. Especially after I saw them saying Mass in the student chapel. How could anyone lift the chalice piously before his eyes (especially in a dark chapel with only a handful of people present, and with six other priests doing the same thing) and say *"Hoc est enim corpus meum"* to an "ever new and gratuitous summons?" (How does *Baum* do it—if he still does?)

Prayer. It seems to me the key. Does a progressive cleric *really* pray? Or does he try to get us all to join in a collective consciousness raising? That is the way to tell those who are working with us from those who are doing a job on us, I would suggest.

No matter how profound the inquiry, or how far beyond the grasp of the rest of us, is the updater telling us of a God who hears us in prayer? Okay—maybe not *hear.* A spirit does not have ears. But *know,* and care. (Christ has ears, anyway. Maybe not like Clark Gable's. The resurrected body is different from ours. But that means perfected, not mixmastered into the Spinozean ooze.)

It was Tillich who wrote of the "paradoxical nature of every prayer, of speaking to somebody to whom you cannot speak because he is not somebody, of asking somebody of whom you cannot ask anything because he gives or gives not before you speak, of saying 'thou' to someone nearer to the I than the I itself . . . a God above the God of theism"—it was then that I stopped giving him the benefit of the doubt. (Do you know that there are religion textbooks used in Catholic high schools in America that speak of Tillich as a master theologian trying to make God relevant and meaningful to modern man?)

As if to dispel our doubts about himself, Baum writes that prayer, like God, is a "problem" since it focuses our attention on a "heavenly Thou whom we seek

[5]*New Horizon: Theological Essays,* p. 69.

through a gesture of turning away from life," and "prevents us from seeing and feeling what really goes on in our world." These difficulties are less evident, though, "in public worship" where "the mystery we call God is present in our midst." Doesn't it sound like a restaurant owner bragging about his new decor's power to evoke *Gemütlichkeit?* This understanding of God, he assures us, is the reason why modern Catholic theologians worked so hard to convince the hierarchy (who tend to be backward in these things) to have priests say the Mass facing the people. No longer will priests face a God "who was situated beyond them." They will, instead, face the "people and make a wide circle with them in a new liturgical formation that signifies that the divine mystery which is worshipped is in the midst of the community; it is present in his people."[6] Prayer is not a "kind of spiritual telephone conversation with man on one side and God on the other." I hope Catholics especially are as infuriated by these words as I am. Traditional Catholics were shouting from the rooftops that just such a ruse was being played *on* the Church by the updaters, and they were called backward fanatics for it. The updater theologians denied that they were working for such a rethinking of the nature of the Mass. "We just want the people to be able to see better," they told us, not scrupling over the barefaced lie. Keep Baum's admission in mind when the next round of proposed changes comes down the pike. He is telling us what it is all about.

In James Hitchcock's study of Catholic updaters, *The Decline and Fall of Radical Catholicism,* a book accurate in everything but its optimism that the updaters have had their hour, there is an inventory of some current revisions of the nature of God. I don't know if I would want to press the case that Hitchcock's catalogue of absurdities is more startling than Baum's, but at the time Hitchcock wrote the book—1971—Baum was being chided by his fellow progressives for not having moved far enough from orthodoxy.

Father Eugene Schallert, for example, tells us that even though some of us have heard that the Word was made Flesh, "the man who says he has found God is a fool"—thus, says Hitchcock, "condemning Jewish patriarchs, Catholic saints, and the great heroes of historic Protestantism, as well as countless numbers of ordinary believers."

Father William Dubay, in turn, proclaims that "Knowledge of God is not only impossible but inhuman," and that "the only trouble with Christian education today is that it attempts to teach people about God." Christian education—and Christ.

Father James Burtchall, a Notre Dame theologian, assures that "There are no direct transactions with the Father; no one has ever spoken to him, no one has

[6]*Ibid.,* pp. 73-4.

ever heard him.'' Which is true if by "transactions" you mean something like buying nails. But "no one has ever spoken to him?" "Whatever you ask the Father in my name . . .''

Hitchcock's best discovery, however, was a more obscure updater—a young theology student. As in so many instances, the less learned are the ones to search out when you want to learn what a movement for change is all about. They usually have not found out how to cover their tracks. They put the new insights into simpler and blunter language. They also indicate the *effect* of a movement or ideology, which in many ways is more important than what the learned scholars at the head of the movement say they *really* mean. If a scholar's words are causing serious ruptures in the Faith, it is no excuse for him to beg off with the disclaimer that he is being misread. He can save his scholarly reputation that way, but he must seek to correct mistaken impressions if those misreadings are taking people into heresy.

The young woman (I won't mention her name. We should not have to live with the scholarly excesses of our younger years. Although I don't know if in this case there has been a a return to wisdom or a further flight into the absurd) suggested in an article in *Commonweal,* not long after Martin Buber's death, that Buber was really a secularist in spite of his now famous treatment of Yahweh as "Thou." She told us such "God-talk" was a mere concession Buber made to the less sophisticated so that he could make his more important points about the need for human reconciliation on earth. She "rescued" Buber from his theism so that he too could make it in the age of Baum and Pike.

Of course, we can always find rare plums in the basket of Daniel Callahan. "I do not believe in, nor have I any interest in the transcendent or immanent God of the Christian tradition. Such a God seems to me rationally implausible, a threat to Christian values and an offense to morality." It is not that "God is dead; he never was in the first place."[7] It should bring a shudder—this man was one of the favorite theologians of many young clergymen in the mid-sixties, the ones that you can't seem to figure out because of the strange and defensive way they treat the question of God and divine law. Perhaps they would clear things up for us if they were on the payroll of a think tank, as Callahan is, instead of dependent upon what we cough up in the collection basket Sundays.

Leslie Dewart has also grown honest enough to make his denials of a personal God the starting point of his theorizing rather than the unspoken conclusion his words are designed to elicit from us; as if we had just started to get such doubts on our own:

[7]*Spectrum of Catholic Attitudes,* pp. 2–3.

123

To say that one believes in God is to assert that one plans or projects as one's free contribution, as it were, to the cosmic process, to the history of the universe of being, in the presence of that which transcends being. Conversely, God is that historical reality to which we not merely pledge our intentions and our will; but for which we make ourselves to be whatever we decide to be, and in the light of which we understand ourselves in whatever way we conceive ourselves to be.[8]

Got that? Perhaps we could read Freud or Herbert Marcuse for a more easily understood expression—and more forthright. But Dewart can get explicit, too: "There is no God behind our belief." There is only that cosmic template luring us on to higher plateaus of human perfection. Christ is God because he envisioned a community of human brotherhood in which the template is scribed accurately and completely. God is "in us"—as the updaters are found of saying—when we too lift our sights, with the Marxists and secular utopians, and aspire to human perfection on earth.

We could continue to quote from updater essays, from Harvey Cox and Bishop Robinson and every press release from the World Council of Churches, to get a more complete picture of the new God of the moderns; but not a clearer one. It is, really, all the same. After two hundred years of standing firm against those who would end the presence and power of the Christian faith, whether Enlightenment *philosophes,* Feuerbach, or Marx, the Christian community is being asked to give in—to admit that *man is God,* or at least that he can become God with the right social reorganization setting the stage.

Some may find this a stupid or a shallow position. Yet today it is the highest hope of the brightest and the best minds of the secular world—the noblest dream of the atheistic professors Michael Novak found so worthy of praise during his tour of duty in American academic circles. It is Sartre, Camus, Marcuse, Heidegger, Einstein, H.G. Wells, Marx, Bertrand Russell, Margaret Mead, *The New York Reveiw of Books,* the major publishing houses, and all those priests and ministers who have cut their academic teeth "in the world" instead of in seminaries set apart from it.

But Christ tells us otherwise. He promises not a classless workers' paradise, or a flowering of the human potential in a world where bigotry and ignorance have been abolished:

> For as the Father hath life in himself; so hath he given to the Son to have life in himself;
> And hath given him authority to execute judgement also, because he is the Son of man. (Jn. 5:26-27)

[8]*Ibid.,* pp. 5–6.

Either Christ is confused; or the updaters are unqualifiedly wrong. Christ does not speak of some future earthly achievement when he speaks of his Father. He speaks of a Being that can be best understood by the human mind exactly the way he deliberately and repeatedly expresses the thought—as a loving, judging, rewarding, and punishing Father of a human family. Why is it so hard to accept the fact that Christ knew what he was doing when he chose his words? We can't rescue him from these words. He uses no other ones we can emphasize instead. Over and over—*Our Father,* deliberately, repeatedly.

> Verily, verily, I say unto you, The Son can do nothing of himself, but what he seeth the Father do: for what things soever he doeth, these also doeth the Son likewise. For the Father loveth the Son, and showeth him all things that himself doeth: and he will show him greater works than these, that ye may marvel. For as the Father raiseth up the dead, and quickeneth them; even so the Son quickeneth whom he will. (Jn. 5:19-21)

The Father "doeth," "loveth," "showeth," "raiseth." Unless the Gospels are so distorted as to be totally fabricated (which we know they are not), Christ himself is history's best example of the childish and superstitious and literal-minded Christian the updaters find so in need of sophistication and enlightenment. He is the Prototype. When you ridicule the rosary-thumbing woman in the Bronx and the Bible-reading farmer in the wheat belt you ridicule Him.

Little wonder that the study of the Scriptures has become part of the field called "comparative Religion," and the Gospels sit on the shelves in the assigned-reading section of the bookstores between the Rev. Moon's pamphlets and Scientology self-help manuals.

> If I bear witness of myself, my witness is not true. There is *another* that beareth witness of me; and I know that the witness which he witnesseth of me is true.
> Ye sent unto John, and he bare witness unto the truth. But I receive not testimony from man: but these things I say, thay ye might be saved.
> He was a burning and a shining light: and ye were willing for a season to rejoice in his light.
> But I have greater witness than that of John; for the works which the Father hath given me to finish, the same works that I do, bear witness of me, that the Father hath sent me. [How would it go? The cosmic template is greater in importance in its relationship to Christ than was John the Baptist? And the cosmic template *sent* him?] And the Father himself, which hath sent me, hath borne witness of me. Ye have neither heard his voice at any time, nor seen his shape.
> And ye have not his word abiding in you: for whom he hath sent, him ye believe not. (Jn.5:31-38)

Christ, then, clearly distinguishes between the Word "abiding" in man (the effect)—which is what the updaters mean by God—and the Word itself (the cause).

This is especially obvious when he teaches his followers how to behave as individuals in their dealings with others. He calls us to imitate the Father who is perfect in this respect. Now, our never-to-be-caught-up-with future might be able to *inspire* us to reach for a better world, but it is *not* capable of love or wrath. Such states require an active consciousness:

> Ye have heard that it hath been said, Thou shalt love they neighbor, and hate thine enemy.
> But I say unto you, Love your enemies, bless them that curse you, do good to them that hate you, and pray for them which despitefully use you, and persecute you.

Why? Because of such is the kingdom of communal consciousness? No: so

> That ye may be the children of your Father which is in heaven: for he maketh His sun to rise on the evil and on the good, and sendeth rain on the just and unjust.
> For if ye love them which love you, what reward have ye?
> And if ye salute your brethren only, what do ye more than others? do not even the publicans so?
> Be ye therefore perfect, even as your Father which is in heaven is perfect. (Mt. 5:43-48)

By the *standards* of political and cultural leftists, however, an open show of admiration for those with a properly formed social conscience is not only desirable, but necessary. We contribute to the popularization of the correct attitudes and dispositions when we "take a stand" and allow ourselves to be "counted." Christian updaters under that influence ask the same of us. Join the picket line, pour blood on the draft files, get the right bumper sticker, wear a peace medallion, grow some hair, write a letter to the editor, sign a letter of protest for next Sunday's *New York Times,* sell your General Motors stock—if you are not part of the solution, you are part of the problem. Private prayer is self-defeating, irrelevant, worthless, childish, Gregory Baum tells us. Everything is secular, says Tillich; spirituality only makes a difference if it contributes to the proper development of the human community. Antiwar protest is prayer of the highest sort.

But Christ says:

> Take heed that ye do not your alms before men, to be seen of them: otherwise ye have no reward of your Father in heaven.

126

> Therefore when thou doest thine alms, do not sound a trumpet before thee, as the hypocrites do in the synagogues and in the streets, that they may have glory of men. Verily, I say unto you, They have their reward.
> But when thou doest alms, let not thy left hand know what thy right hand doeth: That thine alms may be in secret: and thy Father which seeth in secret himself shall reward thee openly.
> And when thou prayest, thou shalt not be as the hypocrites are: for they love to pray standing in the synagogues and in the corners of the streets, that they may be seen of men. [I wonder, did Marlon Brando ever give an Indian a thin dime without a full media team in view?] . . . But thou, *when thou prayest, enter into thy closet* and when thou hast shut thy door, pray to thy Father which is in secret; and thy Father which *seeth* in secret shall reward thee openly. (Mt. 6:1-6)

I hope no one has forgotten Baum's derisive dismissal of the value of private prayer—that ludicrous "telephone line" between God and man. Well, at the risk of playing with Christ's words myself, let me suggest that Christ's "closet" sounds pretty much like a phone booth. Maybe if Christ were preaching on earth in our time he would even speak of a phone booth—except for the fact that his elevated sense of the poetic would not allow for such banal imagery.

> Ask and it shall be given you; seek, and ye shall find; knock, and it shall be opened unto you:
> For every one that asketh receiveth; and he that seeketh findeth; and to him that knocketh it shall be opened. Or what man is there of you, whom if his son ask bread, will give him a stone?
> Or if he ask a fish, will he give him a serpent?
> If ye then, being evil [sorry, situationists], know how to give good gifts unto your children, how much more shall your Father which is in heaven give good things to them that ask him? (Mt. 7:7-11)

"Santa Claus God" . . ."Big Daddy"—immature at Big Sur, but far closer to Christ's description than any of the updater versions.

Polysyllabic and Duller

What is it, in all honesty, that the updaters have discovered that makes the God accepted and prayed to by Thomas Aquinas, Martin Luther, Ignatius Loyola, Thomas More, Richard Hooker, and Hilaire Belloc so unacceptable? Why should they expect us to be more comfortable with their strange God than with the loving Father these great souls of the Christian past had no trouble praying to? How is "really Real" better? But let me lean on C.S. Lewis. The point is an

127

important one, deserving of the treatment of a master. He writes of those who attempt refinements of our understanding of God, especially the Ascension:

> To say that God "enters the natural order" involves just as much spatial imagery as to say that He "comes down"; one has simply substituted horizontal (or undefined) for vertical movement. To say that He is "reabsorbed" into the Noumenal is better than to say He "ascended" into Heaven, only if the picture of something dissolving in warm fluid, or being sucked into a throat, is less misleading than the picture of a bird, or a balloon, going up. All language, except about objects of sense, is metaphorical through and through. To call God a "force" (that is, something like a wind or a dynamo) is as metaphorical as to call Him a Father or a King. On such matters we can make our language more polysyllabic and duller; we cannot make it more literal.[9]

Unless, if I may be so bold as to add to a thought defined by Lewis, the desired end is a God who *is* impersonal and controllable by man, like the wind. A metaphor is an improvement over another metaphor only if it expresses the correct thought more clearly. Updater versions do not do that for Christ's loving Father. Quite the contrary. They express more clearly the gods of Spinoza, Marx, and Levi-Strauss—regardless of whether that is the intention of those who turn the phrase. At least those who really do think of God as a big Daddy or Michelangelo's old man are erring in the right direction. They are working with the words of Christ; which is better than denying them or treating them as childish.

There is no hidden understanding among educated Christians, by the way (nor was there in the past), that God must be called Father only for the sake of the less educated and less secure mass of mankind, while those who have studied the most profound works of Christian theology work out for the themselves something less personal. Sometimes that is the impression the updaters try to give young people especially; as if those who go to college and take courses during the evening have earned the right to enter a tribe of illuminati far wiser than the superstitious oafs out there going to novenas and church picnics: "Now don't tell your parents this—they might need their beliefs—but it has always, etc. etc." Bertolt Brecht, although not a Christian by any stretch of the imagination, knew the pose. Perhaps he had heard it first from some Christian updater trying to ingratiate himself—Novak-like—with him after he became a shining star in the literary firmament. It is a large part of the updater psychosis. Or perhaps he was trying to insert the thought himself into the minds of potential converts, Christians not quite disaffected enough from the Faith to think it on their own. Whatever, in *Galileo,* a young, sincere,

---

[9]C. S. Lewis, *God in the Dock* (Grand Rapids, Mich.: William B. Erdmans, 1970), p. 71.

and intelligent priest apologizes for the censure of Galileo in the name of the faithful who will not be able to live with a confirmation of Copernicus, even though he agrees privately that Galileo had demonstrated the implausibility of geocentrism. He and Galileo and the rest of the broadminded men of *virtus* can stand to have the Bible questioned; but not the people. They need the fairy tales to fill out the empty spaces—just as the mothers and fathers of the blue-jeaned prophets-to-be in Comparative Religion I & II need their Santa Claus God.

But it just isn't so. It's a ruse. There have been, surely, those who lean in that direction. But it wasn't until this century that such a denaturing of God was attempted in any but an openly rebellious and heretical context. At least Bakunin put his cards on the table. And those who played his hand used to remove their collars first.

It has been an updater coup of major proportions. They have succeeded in purging from college curricula the most important theologians of the past, who never allowed us to doubt their belief in a loving and righteous Father. Our young people—including our seminarians and divinity students—more often than not know absolutely nothing about Maritain, say, or Newman. I said *nothing*—not even the names of their major works. It's all *passé*, they tell us. Not only that: they question our right to question them if we have not digested Teilhard, Cox, Dewart, and the like, even though a familiarity with only these moderns makes one familiar with a minor heterodox (and I hope passing) phase in the intellectual history of the Faith. It is a bedeviling and illegitimate demand—on academic and scholarly grounds alone. It is as if a professor of literature had read only Vonnegut and Richard Brautigan, and turned these faddish favorites into experts, and then made a sympathetic reading of them a *rite de passage*. When you dare question or challenge a position learned from these experts by citing Newman or Lewis or Maritain or von Hildebrand—you guessed it, "That stuff is *passé*." I am not being facetious. I can remember going through the proofs of God's existence developed by Thomas Aquinas for a class of high school juniors I was teaching in the late sixties. In the class was one of those bright and (perhaps excessively) sincere young men who are drawn into the orbit of young priests and seminarians, most usually during a time in their lives when they are considering a vocation themselves. This particular young man used to wear beads and bells (it was just becoming the fashionable thing to do) and carried in his back pocket paperback editions of Cox and Bishop Robinson (which was also becoming fashionable). He had learned the lingo fairly well. He could drop an "immanence" or "sacred and secular" into his conversation without batting an eye. But he still prayed—from all that I could tell from watching him in chapel—to an Absolute Other. I worked up my best summary of Maritain's summary of St. Thomas with him in mind. Not disregarding the other students. It was only that he needed it more, and I knew

129

it. The other kids were all wrapped up in whether Bill Bradley was going to cut into the Knicks lineup after his return from Oxford. (So was I, come to think of it.) The boy was dazzled. He really was. Those over thirty might be surprised that these old-hat arguments from motion and causation can still excite anyone. But—believe me—the kids don't hear anything like it these days in a proper academic setting. Hearing it for the first time is still a stunning intellectual experience. After class we talked about it some more. I suggested some books by Chesterton and C.S. Lewis—Lewis's *Mere Christianity* especially (which every Christian owes to himself to read at least once; save it for a rainy afternoon and a warm fire). I thought I had him—or that he had the Church. He returned, however, after the weekend with a sardonic smile on his face, as if I had played a huge and cutting practical joke, and as if I should chuckle too because I knew I had put one over on him. He had been with his Callahan-reading seminarian friends over the weekend. "Nobody reads that stuff anymore," he told me. "That stuff is out." "But" I was about to say, "just because something was written more than ten years ago doesn't mean that it is dull or wrong." I was even going to hit him with the Chesterton quote I always carry around near the front of my cranial cavity: "Democracy demands that we respect a man's opinion even if he happens to be our groom; tradition demands that we respect a man's opinion even if he happens to be our father." But he shook his head and smiled at me out of the corner of his eye before I could—all very good-naturedly—and walked to his seat. He wasn't going to take seriously a wise guy like me any more.

Needless to say, Christian people will be in for rough times if we cannot end this theological blacklist. It is true: Newman and the others can still win in fair and open combat; but we have to get them into the arena. And we have to do it before the updaters have convinced the young that God is, after all, just a projection of man's highest ideals into an imaginary being. When I say that Newman can win, I mean with those who are still believers—not with scornful atheists who are "above" belief. Once a man's heart has been hardened to the thought of God—once he no longer prays—the Newmans will make little impression. They can make the faith coherent, but it is unlikely that they can bring it back to those who have dismissed it with a sneer. The God Christ called Father must be alive in our minds before the great Christian teachers can explain the nature of our relationship to Him. Before a Newman or a Lewis can make sense we have to be open to the idea that Christ was not a blathering idiot when he spoke of the Father as he did:

> Abba, Father, all things are possible unto thee; take away this cup from me: nevertheless not what I will, but what thou wilt. (Mark 14:36)

That Father will be able to hear our prayers. The updaters tell us that we are talking to ourselves when we pray. Christ says otherwise:

> Behold the fowls of the air; for they sow not, neither do they reap, nor gather into barns; yet your heavenly Father feedeth them. Are ye not much better than they? Which of you by taking thought can add one cubit unto his stature?
> And why take ye thought for raiment? Consider the lillies of the field, how they grow; they toil not, neither do they spin.
> And yet I say unto you, That even Solomon in all his glory was not arrayed like one of these.
> Wherefore, if God so clothe the grass of the field, which today is, and tomorrow is cast into the oven, shall he not much more clothe you, O ye of little faith? (Mt. 6:26-30)

Look: we are not alone. You have to call Christ a liar or a fool to press that case.

> For verily I say unto you, That whosoever shall say unto this mountain, Be thou removed, and be thou cast into the sea; and shall not doubt in his heart, but shall believe that those things which he saieth shall come to pass; he shall have whatsoever he saieth.
> Therefore I say unto you, What things soever ye desire, when ye pray, believe that ye receive them, and ye shall have them. [Why does he keep talking about that Santa Claus Father? Send him on a retreat somewhere!]
> And when ye stand praying, forgive, if ye have aught against any: that your Father also *which is in heaven* may forgive you your trespasses.
> But if you do not forgive, neither will your Father *which is in heaven* forgive your trespasses. (Mk. 11:23-26)

The most revealing references to the nature of the Father, however, can be seen in Christ's own moments of prayer. Shortly before his crucifixion, as he lifted his eyes heavenward (eyes *up*—that didn't bother him a bit), John tells us, Christ prayed, not for the crowds, nor in parable. It is a personal, moving and poignant encounter with God in which Christ prays—as He prays. He had already taught us how to pray. Now he shows us that he practiced what he preached, that the Lord's prayer was no Brechtian crutch worked up for the masses. No updater in any church in America should be allowed to talk of his more relevant and meaningful "God" without facing up to these words. We must demand that of them; force them to explain this Christ in the name of their progressive Christianity.

131

Father, the hour is come; glorify *thy* Son, that *thy* Son also may glorify *thee:* As *thou* hast given him power over all flesh, that he should give eternal life to as many as *thou* hast given him. And this is life eternal, that they might know *thee* the only true God, and Jesus Christ, whom *thou* hast sent. I have glorified *thee* on the earth: I have finished the work which *thou gavest* me to do.

And now, O Father, glorify *thou* me with *thine* own *self* with the glory which I had *with thee* before the world was . . . And now I am no more in the world, but these are in the world, and *I come to thee* . . .

I have given them *thy* word; and the world hath hated them, because they are not of the world, even as I am not of the world . . .

As *thou* hast sent me into the world, even so I have sent them into the world . . . Neither pray I for these alone, but for them also which shall believe on me through their word;

That they all may be one; as *thou,* Father, art in me, and I in *thee,* that they also may be one in us: that the world may believe that *thou* hast sent me . . .

Father, I will that they also, whom *thou* hast given me, be with me where I am; that they may behold my glory, which *thou* hast given me: for *thou lovedst* me before the foundation of the world.

O righteous Father, the world hath not known *thee:* but I have known *thee,* and these have known that *thou* hast sent me. (Jn. 17:1-25)

"Thee". . ."thou". . ."thy". . ."Father": how can they pretend he is talking of anything but a personal and conscious God? How is it we let them get away with it?

Real Footsteps in the Hall

It is usually unfair to guess openly at a man's hidden motives, most especially in his scholarly work. For one thing, it implies suspicion of shameful dishonesty. A scholar's case is supposed to be built lovingly and sincerely in an attempt to add to mankind's body of knowledge. It is not supposed to contain cute tricks of the sort that one would expect in a public-relations campaign. A piece of scholarship ought to be easily distinguishable from a political hard sell, or the tub-thumping for a new rock group. So when I argue that much of modern theology is a deliberate con job, a secularist propaganda ploy, I am aware of the magnitude of the charge.

Fortunately, however, we have historical evidence, carefully recorded accounts of what goes on in a man's mind before he starts to say things comparable to what we hear now from our modern theologians. From the intellectual giants of the Enlightenment on, secularists have been filling out for us the reasons why they have turned to rationalism and a secular liberal hope for the future. We know exactly *why* men begin to talk of building a better world without a "waiting, functionary" God in their plans.

Christians have learned how to handle that challenge—or at least our intellectual defenders have, and passed it on to the rest of us. Never before did we think it strange that a Marx and a Newman, a Sartre and a Maritain, a Heidegger and a Lewis, could live in the same era. We were different. There was nothing that the atheist top guns could do to shake our belief. We denied their basic premise; and they, ours. Christ made a difference, and we knew what that meant for a thinking person; Belloc and Chesterton *et al.* showed us. We were different (and happier, I may add). We were not supposed to be searching for a way to converge Christianity with the "isms" of those who denied it. Others were to be concerned with adding Sartrean insights to their life experience; others were to marvel at the profundity of the theater of the absurd and think seriously about adding the experience of polymorphous perversity to their lives. We were different. We were not supposed to feel at home at the cocktail parties of East Coast literati and the Cannes film festival get-togethers. We were supposed to laugh (to ourselves) at the search for meaning in life through all the fads, drugs, Eastern mysticism, gimmicky consciousness raising, and the rest. Our consciousness was raised. We were different, because of Christ.

Our updaters are asking us to forget that, because they have; because they have sold out, and claim to have found a new way. They want the freedom to be part of the things Christians have always rejected. And they want a less demanding God than the Christian God to allow them to do it. It is that simple. C.S. Lewis, again:

> "An impersonal God"—well and good. A subjective God of beauty, truth and goodness, inside our own heads—better still. A formless life-force surging through us, a vast power which we can tap—best of all. But God Himself, alive, pulling at the other end of the cord, perhaps approaching at an infinite speed, the hunter, king, husband—that is quite another matter. There comes a moment when the children who have been playing at burglars hush suddenly: was that a *real* footstep in the hall? There comes a moment when people who have been dabbling in religion ("Man's search for God!") suddenly draw back. Supposing we really found Him? We never meant it to come to *that!* Worse still, supposing He had found us?[10]

[10]C. S. Lewis, *Miracles* (New York: Macmillan, 1947), p. 114.

Chapter VIII

I and the Father Are One

UP TO THIS POINT our argument against the updaters has rested on one version or another of a simple one-line dig: "if you argue in such a manner (whichever revision in question) you argue against the words of Christ." The case has been presented as if such a demonstration would be enough. Why does it fail with the updaters?

Naturally, their demotion of the Gospels' authenticity is central. We can't expect anyone to feel bound by only purported words of Christ. It is what permits the Rorschach-test religion of today that allows some to defend gay liberation, others abortion, and all in the name of Christ.

But there is a crucial and delicate balancing act that must be performed. The updaters can argue that the Bible is not inerrant. But they cannot dismiss it entirely. There's a catch. They have to preserve an aura of respect for those portions which lend support to their favorite secular ideology. Demonstrate that Scripture *contains* the Word of God, is the way they put it, even though it is not *the* Word of God.

Obviously, if the Scriptures cannot be trusted at all, the updaters themselves are stripped of credibility. The Bible is the source of *their* authority. There is no reason to expect Christians to listen to them if they speak on their own, or in the name of the latest social-science concepts. We listen only because we assume they have studied and are able to interpret the Word of God. Without that presumption, there is no more reason to heed their call than that of a favorite bartender. Maybe less. They cannot, in other words, get us to be good Freudians or Marxists, or whatever, without maintaining their role as good—sincere, anyway—Christians.

So the case for rejecting the "backward" portions of the Gospels has to be constructed deftly, and with the full panoply of academic process. They cannot approach the Bible as superstitious drivel, as would their ideological confreres who do not have to work directly with Christians, without causing even the least educated of us to pop off soon or late: "Then why should we listen to your application of 'Love thy neighbor' to illustrate the Christian 'generous response' to busing and food stamps and revolutionary groups in Latin America?" Their pitch requires a convincing demonstration of a parallel between portions of the Gospels and their favorite teacher—DeBray, Marx, Skinner, Marcuse, Sartre, whomever; and that can only be an effective ploy if we are convinced of the divine inspiration of Scripture. Without that conviction, they must sell us their ideology on its own merits; and so far, Christians are Christians precisely because we have proved immune to those "isms."

The updaters have realized, however, that one stout roadblock remains: Christ. He, like God the Father, has become "a problem." As I hope I have been demonstrating, Christ can only be manipulated for ideological purposes when Christians have succumbed to a religious amnesia. You can select a quote out of context here and there to make Christ seem less a Christian, but (and I guess updaters poring over the Gospels in search of a progressive Christ know this as well as anyone) only at the expense of the fullness of his ministry. You have to make the case that he has been misquoted nearly *everywhere* by his overly zealous followers. Once you say that, however, the updaters lose their audience. They have to speak for themselves, and often enough, that testimony comes up wanting. And they know that.

The problem: How to continue to speak of the Gospels as the "Word of God" from which legitimate and constructive norms for reconstructing society can be deduced, when such a prominent portion of the text features the sermons of a Rabbi who stands in the way of a healthy and progressive vision of the religious needs of modern man? How do you explain away the otherworldly excesses of this Christ without calling the Gospels false in their essentials? Especially since he claims to be speaking as the Son of God who offers man the Word of his Father. He repeats the claim too often to treat it as false, an historical accretion. Even by the standards of secular textual criticism, he must have said something like that, and often. To deny that would be crassly anti-intellectual, irrational. The Gospels are not fairy tales. Atheists would concede that Christ had to have made the claim, at the very least (I say this as if I were a non-Christian), that the Spirit of God was present in him in a *very* special, indeed unique way. Even the author of *The Passover Plot* admitted that Christ was making that claim, if only to enhance his political ambitions.

If you want to retain some credibility for the Gospels, then, for your ideological ends, you cannot deny that Christ claimed to be divine. But if he is divine then his talk of heaven, hell, angels, sin, and obedience to God's law must be divine in origin; and correct. But if so, Marx, Margaret Mead, John Dewey, the editors of *The New York Review of Books,* and all the other beautiful souls are—all wet. Whaddya do now?

The answer came—ingenious, disingenuous, and contemptible—but it came. The updaters are admitting now that Christ might have described himself as he did—as the Son of God. But that he didn't *really* know what he meant by that. That he was as shaky on these matters as any other man of the first century A.D.

Messianic Pretenders

It isn't that there are many (still in their clerical collars) who say it just that way. I don't think that anyone has begun to talk openly of the "Christ problem" in terms comparable to the "God problem." The updaters know how to prepare the ground, know that some of us aren't ready for such an assult. But the ground *is* being prepared.

There are some, it is true, who are remarkably explicit. James Pike, for example. Although we should not place too much stress on the late and troubled Bishop. Even updaters are embarrassed by the gung-ho candor with which he relegated Christ to the role of Semitic Che Guevara. But we cannot overlook *The Wilderness Revolt.* It is revealing, and something of a milestone. In his enthusiasm for Biblical revisionism and political activism of a left-wing type, Pike became a zealot with the iconoclastic energy of a first-year divinity student. But he is different from other, more scholarly, revisionists only in his belief that Christians were ready to consider a completely secularized Christ. He did not grasp the importance that Baum places on proceeding cautiously so as not to shock the faithful. He told us, directly, that Christ was one of a long line of Jewish radical nationalists, "Messianic pretenders" who worked in the SDS style to emancipate their homeland from Roman rule. Christ was a member of one of these resistance movements, the Covenanters who operated near Qumran.

These Covenanters believed in exorcism—and Christ, being a product of his environment (as the liberals hold us all to be), should be forgiven for believing in such silliness. They often spoke of a time of upheaval during which the Temple of Jerusalem would be destroyed. That's where Christ got the idea.

They lived communally, often in groups of twelve, and called upon their members to "love one another"—you guessed it.

"The poor at Qumran had a corporate liturgy—a kind of daily Mass. The principal meal each day was eucharistic"—which explains Christ's strange words on Holy Thursday.

The Virgin Birth? "Inventions . . . Matthew was trying to show that Jesus fulfilled all the possible prophecies, and he reached for it." In fact, "If Matthew had a Hebrew Bible to work with, he wouldn't have had to fulfill the prophecy of a virgin birth"—wouldn't have had to fabricate such nonsense in order to build a "larger frame" for his media campaign, Goebbels-like, in preparation for the coming coup.

Was Christ the Son of God? Well, he was "great" and a "real man" because he embodied certain political ideals which, for Pike, were healthy and forward-looking, and because he worked for political liberation from the establishment of his time. He had a "breakthrough of truth, courage and love." He became God existentially by developing a worldview comparable to that of Pike's and Joan Baez's. Christ is God because his "breakthrough" was total.

But it is a difference of degree only. He is God because he meets the highest standards of Pike's political radicalism of the sixties. Pike puts Christ in the dock, and—*voilà*—Christ makes it. Not, remember, that Christ's breakthrough was the "only" such breakthrough, or even the "best." But it was total. "I am finding that I have come to think so much of Jesus that words fail me," Pike says. "He is great," and "worth coming to know." Not exactly in the same league with Peter's awestruck "Truly, Thou are the Son of God." If that be heresy, he asserts blandly, so what—"It's good first-century Christian Judiasm."

Was Christ really celibate? Maybe. Soldiers have been known to abstain from sex before combat, and it is likely that Christ prepared for his planned coup with as much thoroughness.

"Render to Caesar the things that are Caesar's?" It was a call to revolution, in contradistinction to what we have believed for nearly two thousand years. Rome was Caesar's, Judea was not, because there had been no recorded consent of the governed there. Christ as McGovernite.

Would it be healthy if other modern theologians spoke with the effrontery of Pike? It would, it is true, make it easier to isolate them from the Christian dialogue, and thereby lessen their influence. But then again, their reticence might not be just a manifestation of cunning. The Red Sea and Noah's Ark can be dismissed from a man's mind far more easily than Christmas mornings. A sincere love for Christ and an unshakable conviction that he was "different" might be what stays their rebel hands. And that is a good sign.

Nevertheless, there is a dangerous revision of Christ taking place—and it is one that leads down the path towards Pike (and beyond, to Marx), whether or not those who are experimenting with Christ have such a devolution in mind. It will be little consolation—I hope—for those who share in this cumulative discrediting to one day plead to all the ex-Christians, in Eliot-like despair, "That is not what I meant all;/That is not it at all." [1]

Human Like Me, Jesus?

What is this "cumulative discrediting" of which I speak? If you are fortunate enough not to have a son or daughter of college age who hits you over the head with it, go to a parish lecture, maybe something like "Christ in the Modern World," and you will find out. Or sign up for a course in Scripture study; or roam around the shelves in a bookstore which carries a full line of religious titles; or get a Maryknoll or Paulist Press catalogue. You might try the bookstore on a campus run by a religious order; but that will not help as much as you might think. Maybe it is only because colleges of that sort are trying to downplay their religious character (what's left of it) in order to insure the next installment of federal funds, but nevertheless you will find few books of theology at all. Even the updaters are dying in those places these days—which might be poetic justice of a sort. There has to be some orthodoxy to rebel against. (I thought I would roam around my alma mater in the Bronx in search of some of the latest updater titles while researching this book. It is a Catholic college run by the Jesuits and known not too long ago for a serious and well entrenched department of theology. It is in the Fordham Road area, but I won't mention its name since I don't want to detract from its reputation unnecessarily. Maybe they'll come home again. I walked to the long wall that used to hold all the theology titles. It is now the sociology and psychology section. I found the theology titles on a rather small standing set of shelves. If memory serves, it used to be the place where the college beer mugs were stacked. There were books on Transcendental Meditation, Buddism, I Ching, Marxist alienation, Freud on religion, four stacks of a Gregory Baum book, but not much else. Maybe there was a big order on the way, so I won't pass final judgement. But I'll willingly say that that bookstore is no place to find any trace of the intellectual giants who dedicated their lives to defending Christendom. Neither,

[1]T. S. Eliot, *Collected Poems* (New York: Harcourt, Brace and World, 1934), p. 7.

I'm afraid, is the University. I work with a woman who speaks proudly of that fact. She is a liberated type whose son attends the school, and assures me that he doesn't have to take any theology at all.)

Perhaps in your own investigations you will not find an open presentation of a Feuerbachian image of Christ; not even a version of Bishop Pike. But you will find separate studies which probe topics like the following:

a) Was Christ omniscient? From birth? Did the infant Christ, because he was true God, have divine knowledge? In the manger? In the womb? Or did Christ gradually, or in later life, come to realize that he was God? Perhaps at his baptism by John? Did the fact that he was true man limit him to the point that he was *not* omniscient? Did Christ admit to that when he said, speaking of the last days, "of that day and that hour knoweth no man, no, not the angels which are in heaven, neither the Son . . ." (Mark 13:32)

b) Would a TV camera placed outside the tomb on Easter have recorded anything out of the ordinary when Christ arose from the dead? Was the stone at the entrance really blasted back in a shower of light bright enough to frighten the battle-hardened Roman legionnaires stationed there? Or was Christ's Resurrection a strictly spiritual experience of the Apostles? Was Luke exaggerating (hell, lying) for emphasis when he said that the resurrected Christ cooked a fish dinner and ate it with the Apostles after he arose? Does a belief in the resurrected Christ require that the earthly corpse not be in the ground somewhere?

c) What is really meant by the Virgin Birth? Something literal and physical? (Obviously a problem for those who call God our never-to-be-caught-up-with future.) Or is the concept a literary device used to denote the special election and status of Christ, contrived in either ignorance or reverence or deceitfulness? Is the belief a reflection of a sexual maladjustment that warped our forefathers' minds? Is it true that Mary and Joseph never consummated their marriage? Is that another false insertion? Why did Christians feel it necessary to describe Christ's birth in a manner so different from human birth? What was the source of their hangup?

d) When Christ ascended into heaven did he really go *up?* Did his body change in any remarkable or unexplainable way? What would a camera have shown at that moment? Did he fade from the sight of the Apostles? Or is the whole story just the Evangelists' way of explaining their conviction that Christ was with his Father, and since Christ (or the Evangelists who told the story that way) repeatedly talked of a father "above," did the Evangelists invent a story to corroborate his claim? Is it a way of saying that the Apostles realized that Christ was divine and truly different from them—that he ascended in importance in their consciousness to a divine status? And what better way to communicate that thought to those who did not experience him directly than to talk of him rising into the skies?

e) Was Christ true God because he embodied completely the English word from which the word "God" is derived—"good"? Does Christ grow into that state of perfection in an existential encounter with life, by perfecting his social conscience in the way enlightened moderns strive to perfect theirs? Is he God, then, because he is, as Bishop Pike states flatly, the perfect model for future social activists?

Omitted

Certain of these inquiries may not be improper to pursue. The question of what it is exactly (which is beyond our comprehension, of course) that happens to a truly divine nature when it assumes a truly human nature is open to a faithful theological exploration, as long as the probe does not leave open as a possible alternative the assertion that the truly divine can at any time cease to be divine. "Occasionally divine" is an oxymoron, a limitation on the illimitable. These are not new problems. Arianism and Monophysitism are two of the oldest heresies. Only by redefining the word divine in purely human terms can one even begin to talk of Christ in such a novel way; by using the word to mean something like "with it," or "committed," or "aware."

Nevertheless, I have had such questions proposed to me by a young man, a graduate student, I know to be pious and orthodox in other respects. Especially the idea that Christ could not have had the fullness of knowledge of his identity as the Son of God from birth. Updater presumption is contagious. He explained that he found it more compatible with an adult understanding of the faith to hold that Christ only later in life, perhaps just before his public ministry, became aware of his identity and mission. When I asked quizzically, and sincerely, how he could have learned of these things, the answer was direct: miraculously, and through the divine intervention of the Father. "I find it easier to believe," he said, "that God revealed all this to Christ later in life than at birth or before. Being true man limits Christ at least to that extent." When I asked of the potential dangers—the resulting picture of Christ in purely human terms, as a man who becomes God as he perfects his humanity, and *by* that process, his response was unequivocal: "No, I do not mean that at all. I believe in a personal God and that Christ is his Son, sent to save man from sin. But I can't picture, nor do I think it necessary to picture, an omniscient young boy roaming the hills around Nazareth. I don't even know if it is coherent to argue that the adult Christ knew *everything*. He was man as well as God. Do we have to believe that the

141

historical Jesus could have constructed a space vehicle or told his contemporaries how to find America?" he asked. "Or outline coherently Newtonian physics?"

He could have added, as the updaters do when working with this point, that Christ asserted that he did not have knowledge of the exact date of "the last days." But he did not. Perhaps he was aware of, and satisfied by, the long-standing Christian explanation that Christ *chose* not to reveal his knowledge of the last days even though he could have—and of the heretical denial of Christ's divinity, by all heretofore acceptable scholarly standards, explicitly contained in such an admission to a limitation on his foreknowledge.

It should be noted as well that the narratives of the Annunciation and Virgin Birth are denigrated beyond recognition by conceding limitations on Christ such as these. If Christ did not know of his identity, neither could Mary—unless she kept it a secret from him. Although it makes little sense to press this point since the updaters have even less respect for the Christian understanding of Mary's nature and role than they have for the nature of Christ. The issue is raised only to illustrate the contemptuous dismissal of the Christian heritage the updaters are asking us to consider.

Admittedly, it is mind-boggling to try to grasp the idea of an omniscient infant, born to a virgin who remains virgin even after birth. There is no quarrel from anyone on this point. Being true man limited (if that is the word) Christ to the extent that he felt physical pain and emotional sorrow. Christians acknowledge that. What of his intellect?

But, surely, the point is that we are dealing with a mystery of the Faith. Is there anything here more difficult to accept, *for a believer in Christ,* than the story of the loaves and fishes, or Easter morning? We are dealing with the miraculous and the divine, ideas which, by their very nature, are beyond our mind's reach without the aid of revelation.

What is it then that prompts the kinds of questions the modern theologians are determined to force to the center of our consciousness? Why do they push so determinedly and persistently for a revaluation of our understanding of Christ? In the final analysis, it serves no purpose other than a Feuerbachian one. Why?

Let us admit for the moment, for argument's sake, the illogical (and dare I say heretical?) position that Christ was divine, but did not realize it until somewhere around his thirtieth birthday. That he was divine—but limited. How will that improve our understanding of the Christian Faith? Obviously, truth is truth, and we should seek it, and if some theologian can find a way to square that circle, and demonstrate *how* Christ became aware of who he was, we should welcome his contribution to mankind's understanding of the divine mysteries. But the fact of the matter is that there is no way to demonstrate this strange and implausible new view. It is theological speculation at best. It remains mysterious. One view, however, elevates our sense of wonder at the person called Christ; the other works to drain it of mystery. But both require belief. No element of the Faith has been made more accessible to the human intellect.

Then why do it? To make it easier for educated moderns to accept the Faith, they tell us. Okay . . . but how? How by empirical standards will it be any easier to believe that Christ learned of his divinity in a sunburst of understanding later in life? (No updater with a full deck will dare tell us it was at his baptism, from the dove—which would be one alternative.) How can Christ grow into such a thought? Unless—ahem, ahem—you mean he perfected his social conscience when you say "became divine."

And how will the rest of the Christian dispensation be acceptable to one who refuses to believe in an omniscient Christ? I'd rather try to explain the hows and the wherefores of that than the calming of the seas.

I'll be direct—even if in doing so I display my suspicious side. (The updaters will call it paranoia in the reviews—watch.) I'll admit—as if I haven't given enough hints—to a deep and abiding mistrust of those who ask us to make Christ more believable for the sake of the Faith. Whatever the issue—the Resurrection, and the Ascension, most especially. It seems so clearly an attempt—conscious and calculated or not—to make Christ *manageable*—and whatever he is, it is not that. A Christ who *develops* his divinity is manipulable for ideological purposes. He can then be turned into the "God" who arises in our consciences and lives in our hearts—but nowhere else. I predict, if I may be so bold, that we will hear just that claim in explicit language in the near future (from clerics—we have already had it from the *philosophes;* the friendly ones, anyway). I also assert that young Americans in theology classes taught by progressive clerics are being led to just such a conclusion right now, probably in an institution you support in collections on Sundays.

Christ is being reduced from *The Way* to a mere participant in the human dialogue. His words have value now in many circles only to the extent that they are "relevant." And, they tell us, it is up to *us* to decide when that is the case. The Gospels are useful—when they are useful. Marcuse for school, Marx for the job, Christ for fights (to get the fascists to turn the other cheek). What does Jesus mean to me? How do you see Jesus? He's got a lot to offer. Our forefathers liked certain parts—which are right for us? But, no hangups. Religion shouldn't cramp your style, make you uptight. Are you running with me, Jesus? (Never mind the reverse.) Jesus is love. Jesus is freedom. Jesus makes me feel good.

All that is, of course, distortion. Jesus demands that we see him in a manner starkly different from the other contestants for men's minds. He is—the Word, the Son of the Father, the Light, the Life. He leaves no option to snip away at that image in the name of something *au courant*. I am not saying that that demand is attractive. I wouldn't take it from anybody but God. But it is his demand. Christ insists that he is different from the world's great teachers —outrageously different. We must either condemn his arrogant blasphemy; or worship him without reserve.

> Verily, verily, I say unto you, Before Abraham was, I am. (Jn. 8:58)

> My sheep hear my voice, and I know them, and they follow me:
> And I give unto them eternal life; and they shall never perish, neither shall any man pluck them out of my hand.
> My Father, which gave them me, is greater than all; and no man is able to pluck them out of my Father's hand.
> *I and my Father are one.* (Jn. 10:27-30)

> Are there not twelve hours in the day? If any man walk in the day, he stumbleth not, because he seeth the light of this world. (Jn. 11:9)

> *I am the light of the world.* (Jn. 8:12)

Preposterous? *Yes*—by all human standards. The Scribes and Pharisees were perceptive enough to see that. "Art thou the Christ?" they asked.

> And he said unto them, If I tell you, ye will not believe:
> And if I also ask you, ye will not answer me, nor let me go.
> Hereafter shall the Son of man sit on the right hand of the power of God.
> Then said they all, Art thou then the Son of God?
> And he said unto them, *Ye say that I am.* (Luke 22:67-70)

His Father in heaven is as explicit and unyieldingly direct—although (I know, I know) updaters do not admit to the accuracy of the Gospel rendition of his baptism by John. But if no dove appeared in the heavens, if the clouds did not open, if no voice intoned that "This is my beloved son in whom I am well pleased," you have to place another lie at the feet of the Superstar.

Likewise, if we cannot accept the word of Peter, James, John (and Jesus too), we cannot be certain that at the Transfiguration those words were spoken again. (Although I would give odds that if there were some reason to think that peyote was used at the time, we would be reading articles expressing awe and wonder at the vision. Then it would have a spiritual significance. Cactus plants are capable of what Christ is not. That's progress.)

But such doubts about Scripture are older than the form critics and their epigones. Christ had to tell the Jews to:

144

Search the Scriptures; for in them ye think ye have eternal life: and they are they which testify of me. And ye will come not to me, that ye might have life.
I receive not honour from men.
But I know you, that ye have not the love of God in you.
I am come in my Father's name, and ye receive me not: if another shall come in his own name, him ye will receive.
How can ye believe, which receive honour one of another [don't sell your soul, in other words, for a favorable review in the campus newspaper] and seek not the honour that cometh from God only?
Do not think that I will accuse you to the Father: there is one that accuseth you, even Moses, in whom ye trust.
For had ye believed Moses, ye would have believed me: for he wrote of *me*.
But if ye believe not his writings, how shall ye believe my words? (Jn. 5:39-47)

The updaters, of course, have gotten to the point where they believe neither Moses nor Christ—any more than Wittgenstein, anyway. Too harsh a charge? Irresponsible? Dr. William F. Beck, a Protestant theologian, prepared a simple side-by-side comparison of the King James version of the Bible with the *Revised Standard Version,* an updater-prepared translation designed to give modern Christians a more readable account. Judge for yourself. Below are just a few examples drawn from Beck's carefully prepared study.

	King James	RVS
(Mt. 27:54)	1. Jesus is "the son of God"	1. Jesus is "*a* son of God" (My emphasis)
(2 Thess. 1:12)	2. "Our God and Lord Jesus"	2. "Our God and the Lord, Jesus Christ"
(Jn. 1:18)	3. "The only-begotten God"	3. "The only Son"
(Hebrews 1:3)	4. "He who shines with God's glory"	4. "He reflects the glory of God"
(Hebrews 2:10)	5. "The One who gives them salvation"	5. "The pioneer of their salvation"
(Romans 9:5)	6. "Christ, who is God over everything"	6. "Christ. God who is over everything"
(Luke 24:6)	7. "He is not here, but He is risen"	7. *Omitted!*
(Luke 24:51)	8. "And He was taken up to Heaven"	8. *Omitted!*

Would it be unfair to say that there is evidence here that the authors of the RSV are engaged in a calculated attempt to say something (*not* to say something, would be more exact) vastly different from what Christians have believed about Christ for nearly two thousand years? Would it be unfair to say that a similar mentality is at work in the writing of the Catholic *New American Bible?* The latter changes the words of the angel in the tomb on Easter morning from "He has risen! He is not here!" to "He has been raised! He is not here!" Would it be unfair to suggest that Andrew Greeley, even after arguing for over a hundred pages in his *The Jesus Myth* against the modern reinterpretations of Christ's identity, which he says "border on the blasphemous" (he described French priest Louis Evely's *The Gospels Without Myth* in those words), shows an unhealthy reluctance to come down on all fours in favor of anything remotely comparable to an orthodox understanding of Christ? He says of the Resurrection:

> The real issue is the kingdom and not the resurrection . . . Quibbling about the evidence of the resurrection is quite beside the point . . . The Easter phenomenon, the early Christians' experience of Jesus as dead and yet once again alive [is the major concern]. To get bogged down in reality and not to face the greater and more ultimate reality which it represents is to miss the point totally.[2]

Miss the point! Well, someone is. You can't straddle the fence like that. Even Bishop Pike would concede that Christ was "alive" again in the "experience" of the early Christians. Such equivocation is—well, unbecoming. The question is whether he is alive, not whether he lives on like James Dean in the fantasies of middle-aged women. Such intellectual waffling ignores an all too important part of what it means to be a Christian. "Behold my hands and my feet," Christ says to the awestruck Apostles, "that it is I myself: handle me, and see; for a spirit hath not flesh and bones, as ye see me have." (Luke 24:39) "Thomas, because thou hast seen me, thou hast believed: blessed are they that have not seen, and yet have believed." (Jn. 20:29)

Christ does not call to be followed because he has the key to constructing an earthly kingdom amenable to a mind formed in the faculty rooms and rock concerts of modern America: nor because his words transform turning the cheek from cowardice to virtue. We turn the cheek in large measure because he rose from the dead; and certainly not because we are drawn to such self-effacement to begin with and want to institutionalize that preference for those who aren't. Christianity is true because it is true, and because Christ's life and death demonstrated that beyond doubt. "Jesus saves," all right—but not just the

[2]*The Jesus Myth*, pp. 177–8.

weak from the strong. It is, at best, shameful to use Jesus as a shield—to hide behind his words in the hope of creating a world where the vigorous and assertive are tamed. So much of the "peace" and "love" and "brotherhood" of the moderns seems to confirm the *worst* suspicions of Nietzsche. We have no right to turn the Golden Rule into a woman's skirt. Christ is as much Lord to those confident that life would be a splendid—if incomplete—experience if its high point came from sailing in pursuit of adventure in pagan longboats; to those who do not shrink from the prospect of a world where daring and courage weigh more than gentleness. Christianity is not true *because* it shelters the effete. Christian love is sublime—in contradistinction to pagan calculations —because it has been taught by Christ, the Lord who routed from their thrones the pagan gods. But he has routed them by proving them false, most especially by his death and Resurrection, not by making them less attractive. We do not have to like the ways and commandments of this Rabbi to feel bound by them. He is to be followed by those who would rather cross the Rubicon with Caesar, or northern glens with Fionn MacCumhail, than take up a cross. There are no options: he is *not* simply human like us:

> All things are delivered to me of my Father: and no man knoweth who the Son is, but the Father; and who the Father is, but the Son, and he to whom the Son will reveal him. (Luke 10:22)

> Verily, verily, I say unto you, He that heareth my word, and believeth on him that sent me, hath everlasting life, and shall not come into condemnation; but is passed from death unto life.
> Verily, verily, I say unto you, The hour is coming, and now is, when the dead shall hear the voice of the Son of God; and *they that hear shall live . . .*
> *Marvel not at this: for the hour is coming, in which all that are in the graves shall hear his voice,*
> And shall come forth; they that have done good, unto the *resurrection of life;* and they that have done evil, unto the resurrection of *damnation.* (Jn. 5:24-29)

> Labour not for the meat which perisheth, but for that meat which endureth unto everlasting life, which the Son of man shall give unto you: for him hath God the Father sealed . . .
> This is the work of God, that ye believe on him whom he hath sent . . .
> Verily, verily, I say unto you, Moses gave you not that bread from heaven; but my Father giveth you the true bread from heaven.
> For the bread of God is he which cometh down from heaven, and giveth life unto the world . . .
> *I am* the bread of life: he that cometh to me shall never hunger; and he that believeth on me shall never thirst.
> But I said unto you, That ye also have seen me, and believe not . . .
> For I came down from heaven, not to do mine own will but the will of him that sent me.

And this is the Father's will which hath sent me, that of all which he hath given me I should lose nothing, but should raise it up again at the last day.

And this is the will of him that sent me, that *every one which seeth the Son, and believeth on him, may have everlasting life:* and I will raise him up at the last day . . .

No man can come to me, except the Father which hath sent me draw him: and I will raise him up at the last day.

It is written in the prophets, And they shall be all taught of God. Every man therefore that hath heard, and hath learned of the Father, cometh unto me.

Not that any man hath seen the Father, save he which is of God, he hath seen the Father.

Verily, verily, I say unto you, He that believeth on me hath everlasting life. *I am that bread of life.*

Your fathers did eat manna in the wilderness, and are dead . . .

I am the living bread which came down from heaven: if any man eat of this bread, he shall live for ever: and the bread that I will give is my flesh, which I will give for the life of the world . . .

Verily, verily, I say unto you, Except ye eat the flesh of the Son of man, and drink his blood, ye have no life in you.

Whoso eateth my flesh, and drinketh my blood, hath eternal life; and I will raise him up on the last day. (Jn 6:27-54)

I have refrained from quoting Scripture at this length up until now to help the reader overcome the temptation to skip over the text. Not that I think that anyone is going to overlook Christ to rush ahead into my prose. I know from my own experience, however, that a reader will often assume that he is so familiar with the Bible that he does not have to read it all over again—that he knows what Christ says on a particular topic. Don't do that with the above lines unless you have the lines memorized. Christ's words cannot be skirted. There is no room for us to interpret them as merely poetic. He repeats himself, emphasizes the most audacious of the claims, reinforces his assertion with allegory and symbol. He is telling us exactly what our fathers and their fathers before them thought he was telling the world. He doesn't want to rap. It's didactic, emphatic, exhortatory, persistent, hard-and-fast. He is the Son of God in a way no man ever was or could be. We can only share a trace of that sonship through him, and only through him. One can search the world's great religions and never find words comparable. Mahomet knew too much and was too principled to even suggest it. No one—except the wild-eyed fanatics who roam the sleazy thoroughfares of metropolitan bohemias—makes the claim. Just Christ: *"I and my Father are one."* (Jn 10:30)

Therefore doth my Father love me, because I lay down my life, that I might take it again.

No man taketh it from me, but I lay it down of myself.
I have power to lay it down, and *I have power to take it again.* (Jn. 10:17-18)

To ''get bogged down'' in the reality of the Resurrection is ''to miss the point totally?'' How far we have come that Christians can say such things in quiet confidence.

Blessed Are They Who Have Not Seen

When listening to those who would reduce the supernatural majesty of Christ's life, death and Resurrection, it is important to remember the fate of Christ's Apostles. All but John suffered an agonizing martyrdom. Perhaps one or two fanatics in a Passover plot of one sort or another could be believably pictured continuing to preach the Gospels in the hope of bringing their coup to a successful conclusion even though their commandant was gone. That strange girl with the ferret eyes who tried to kill Gerald Ford in pursuit of Charles Manson's dream for America showed us the power of deranged zealotry. But would Squeaky suffer martyrdom for her lord? Would she have pulled the gun if there were a death penalty to consider? Perhaps. But would *all* of Manson's followers? Christ's did. True, there were henchman of Hitler who went to their death in obdurate loyalty to the Reich. (Who was it who went to the scaffold with an undaunted ''Heil Hitler?'') But would they have gone on preaching the wisdom of *Mein Kampf* after Hitler's death if they had not been apprehended, and if such a display of misguided perseverance would be certain to lead to arrest and execution? They didn't. They would have gone to Argentina, too, as did the lesser luminaries who were able to make a getaway.

What the Apostles experienced had to be more than an ''experience,'' in other words. But that is not the conclusion to which we are being led by updater revisions. The events which quickened the Apostles are being Bultmannized into drivel. We are being led to the conclusion that Christ's relationship with his Apostles was no more than an intensely accentuated precedent to the devotion which others in our time have felt for Gandhi, Mao, or Martin Luther King—or the dark wizards of the Jesus-freak movement. Often you get the impression, don't you, that Christ is meant to be the one flattered by such an association, as if the updaters are sincerely trying to elevate our understanding of him by placing him in such select company. Christ is being pictured as a leader in the perennial quest for the highest levels of development of the human community. He is another of the greats who caught a glimpse of man's potential, and committed themselves to the work of carrying our minds and hearts to that rarefied vision. He calls us to share in that divine hope to be one with him in the

149

Father (the perfected future), to develop that breakthrough of understanding. The Christian communion, as a result, becomes at updater-directed services a ceremonial attempt to effect that breakthrough; to evoke the spirit of love *within* a congregation. It is no coincidence, or passing fascination for the new, that the kiss of peace receives far more loving and lavish attention than does the perfunctory distribution of the Host at Catholic updater ceremonies. (Unless, of course, the congregation is small enough for the breaking and eating of the Bread to be performed with the *bonhomie* of an office picnic.) We are being eased into a more mature and worldly expression of what the "breaking of the bread," according to the updaters, was meant to symbolize all along: the extension of the good will of a family meal to the whole of the human community. And when that love is intense enough, "God" is present in our midst. The symbolic sharing of bread brings about the miraculous transformation. But it is the kiss of peace which is most expressive of the "miracle." It cracks the cold and pious faces of the faithful into warm and tender smiles, takes the Christian's eyes off the cross and their minds off a false God beyond, and brings them to their fellow man.

But where updaters can see all that, the rest of us have to be coaxed and chided into opening up. Rome was not destroyed in a day. Some old rubrics are preserved until we, or our children, are ready for full emancipation. If we get spooked, we might rise up in our ignorance and rout the prophets without honor—who are trying to help us, you see—from the temple. We all know what the natives do in the old Jon Hall movies when the sacred jewel is stolen from Mali's eye. If you are ready to grow into a mature understanding of the purpose of Sunday service, though, you can go to a service or Mass at a college campus—where the presence of narrow-minded adults is not an inhibiting factor. There the kiss of peace can last for a half hour, Communion might be received lying on the floor, and it's Boone's Farm wine and garlic bread to the tune of Beatles' music and the kaleidoscope of strobe lights.

Blasphemous? Come on! It is what Jesus is all about. He makes you feel good. Helps you overcome your inhibitions. Gets it all together for you. All you need is love. He said what? Heaven? Hell? Sin? Judgement? Furnace of fire? Well, nobody's perfect. He said a lot of good things too. And I don't know if he said all that stuff anyway, man.

> And shall not God avenge his own elect, which cry day and night unto him, though he bear long with them?
> I tell you that he will avenge them speedily.
> Nevertheless, when the Son of man cometh, shall he find faith on the earth? (Luke 18:7-8)

Chapter IX

"Where There Is No Vision, the People Perish"

IN THE PAGES that follow, I speak consciously as an American, as well as a Christian. I know the difficulty. I understand full well that the Faith will live on whether our country does or not. I know—we have no promise that the gates of hell will not prevail against the gem of the ocean. I wish it were otherwise. But nevertheless, the roots which nourish the way of life, the sense of historical mission, and the spirit of self-sacrifice expressive of the America I love, are Christian. And a revivified Christianity can infuse new life into a faltering America. I don't suggest that we "use" Christianity. Christianity is to be defended and projected for its own sake, not as a nation-sustaining mythology. But it is that, too, so to speak. If I were a patriot and not a Christian, in fact, I would use it the way I would use martial airs the night before battle. The connection is that direct.

Our national experience has been no different from that of the rest of the world's once great powers. We were strong, respected, and imitated—while we acted as if we represented something virtuous and worthy of the highest of human endeavor. We stumble now because we have lost that identity. We know neither who we are nor what we should be willing to discipline ourselves to achieve, and countries do not survive in that disoriented state if history tells us anything. Whether animated by pagan gods, a vision of racial supremacy, or the

151

simple way of life held dear by those who could sing, unaffectedly and without reserve, "Onward Christian Soldiers" on World War II battleships—countries are only healthy as long as that level of aspiration endures. The late English historian, Christopher Dawson, spent a lifetime demonstrating the point. Hardly anyone would have argued with him until the ethos of liberal hedonism became a seriously proposed alternative. Since then, modern America and Europe seem hell bent on proving Dawson right.

Societies just do not live on without a passionate commitment to a reason for life beyond life: religion. Certainly not on a planet with other societies that have such a commitment. Even the liberals know that, darkly. In the mid-seventies, there isn't a social critic breathing who expects us to be able to go on without some dramatic revision of the system. What they mean (some know it, some do not) is surgery of the soul, of course.

So while I accept John Henry Newman's unyielding insistence that the work of the Church is to "do good to souls," I would attach a footnote. Newman says:

> . . . this world, and all that is in it, [is] a mere shadow, as dust and ashes, compared with the value of one single soul. She [the Church] holds that, unless she can, in her own way, do good to souls, it is no use her doing anything; she holds that it were better for sun and moon to drop from heaven, for the earth to fail, and for all the many millions who are upon it to die of starvation in extremest agony, so far as temporal affliction goes, than that one soul, I will not say, should be lost, but should commit one single venial sin, should tell one wilful untruth, though it harmed no one, or steal one poor farthing without excuse. She considers the action of this world and the action of the soul simply incommensurate, viewed in their respective spheres; she would rather save the soul of one single wild bandit of Calabria, or whining beggar of Palermo, than draw a hundred lines of railroad through the length and breadth of Italy, or carry out a sanitary reform, in its fullest details, in every city of Sicily, except so far as these great national works tended to some spiritual good beyond them.[1]

I accept that—taking into account Newman's broad verbal strokes in this instance. But one cannot escape the fact that our nation's fate is entwined with that of the Christian belief. If we Americans are unable to see ourselves as a Christian people, it is difficult to imagine how we will see ourselves as a free people at all. We will deny ourselves the only spiritual resource with the emotive power to offer an alternative to the lures of Marxism at this historical juncture. A new identity will be forged for us by our enemies. It is no

---

[1] *A Newman Treasury*, ed. Harrold (New Rochelle: Arlington House, 1975), pp. 249–250.

coincidence that as Christianity wanes another faith takes its place, and that faith holds as a central tenet the ultimate destruction of Christianity.

It is not only that America needs the Faith. The Faith needs America too—in the short run, anyway. For the foreseeable future the health of Christ's religion is welded flush to the American ship of state. We are on a Crusade, like it or not. Admittedly, it is not for us to know all the twists that Providence has prepared for us. But even if in the fullness of time it is necessary and proper for America to founder and fall, it is *our* obligation—by all we know as Christians—to defend what is left of Christendom against its avowed enemies. It might be presumptuous to assume that America has a God-given mission to hold off the advances of atheistic Communism. But one cannot go from that admission of human fallibility to the blatant presumption that we have somehow discerned the historical need to collaborate in the fall of the Christian West. That is the blasphemy of the liberation theologians, as we shall shortly see.

Perhaps America is unworthy of this ennobling burden. In fact, an honest evaluation of our recent history indicates that we are likely to falter with such a heavy weight on our shoulders. But there just is no other earthly power willing or able to take America's place, and if we fail, the world appears certain to be communized. In which case, America's Christians will have to resign themselves to the prospect that, while the Faith will live on, it will be most vigorous in the minds and hearts of the new Goths and Franks, and that we, like St. Augustine, might not live to see the conversion. There have been Christians before us, you'll remember, who had to live as a beleaguered remnant in a Dark Age.

But it is not yet time for resignation. It is neither noble nor self-effacing (in a Christian way) to welcome a national decline. Not yet, anyway. It is a thought that troubles me deeply, though: Will there be a future moment, perhaps in our children's lifetime, when Christians, in Celine-like contempt, might have to welcome the sound of enemy jackboots in the streets of a *Deep Throat,* abortion-mill America? Should I admit to having such thoughts most vividly as I read the newspaper reports of the Viet Cong boarding up the strip joints and rounding up the dope pushers and sleek hookers of Americanized Saigon, while expressing their contempt for the decadent people who brought such shame to their homeland? I am afraid that Christian missionaries might get further with these hardeyed Spartans with their belt-buckle inscription—"Born in the North to die in the South"—than with the Honda-happy lavender cowboys who buzzed the city before the American retreat. And let us never forget the base and hideous sickness of soul which was openly, if unwittingly, displayed by our liberal intelligentsia and their media lackeys. They, *too,* were impressed by these Asian rednecks brutally enforcing a harsh and primitive piety on the symbols of the American presence. They, too, saw a lofty idealism of sorts—

in an imposed righteousness they would chastize as oppressive narrow-mindedness if used in defense of Christian presumptions. The degenerates at *The Village Voice* in awe of Viet Cong puritanism!

But even the media masters know that a reservoir of affection for the Christian social order remains in America. Why else go to all the effort to subject it to ridicule in the person of Archie Bunker? But the reservoir is drying up. The sun is hot. And when the reservoir goes, we will have nothing left to fight or die for, and we will surrender. But there is still a glimmer of hope—I think. And even if there is not, shouldn't we let the Christians of the future say, when they look back in curiosity at our decline and fall, that we went out with more noise than the Romans?

Let us ignore, in other words, our theologians who tell us that Christ demands from us nothing more than a timid surrender to the forces that beset us in the modern world: the "liberation" theologians.

Theology of Revolution

In an earlier chapter we noted the naturalness of the drift from existentialism to Marxism—of finding release from the meaningless *ennui* of Sartrean existentialism in a commitment to changing the world under Russian, Cuban or Chinese direction.

The point now is that the trip can be made from another port, with existentialism, as such, only a brief stopover. The proponents of the so-called theology of liberation, or the theology of revolution, who have made that voyage themselves, are working to show us how.

It is not a new charge—that Communism is a distortion and perversion of Christian idealism; a heresy, so to speak. But that insight should be weighed in the context of our times. We are being asked to succumb to the heresy in a new and alluring way. We are being offered the prospect of becoming Marxist without having to break openly and formally with our Christian identity—to surrender without calling it that, to effect a peace with an enemy who has compromised not a jot—and without having to fight to effect the accord. We are offered a "Peace with honor" comparable to the surrender in Vietnam that went by that name. "Give in, give in," they whisper. "Peace, peace . . . it can be done without pain . . . it will seem what you wanted all along . . . and peace, peace."

The nexus will bedevil the historians of the future. How? Can anyone imagine Saracen and Christian sharing Jerusalem in peace? Arab and Jew grasping hands in common prayer at the Wailing Wall? Caesar and Vercingenerix co-administering Gaul? Federalism in Bangladesh? All could be ex-

154

plained more easily than Christendom converging with the sons of Marx and Lenin, Mao and Stalin. How did it happen?

I am being disingenuous. I know how it will be explained. Marxist historians have been telling us for years that the noblest impulses of Christians, those achievable at any rate, are contained in the Marxian schema, and that in time we will come around. The Kingdom *is* of this world, and once we see that (and our theologians are helping us along), there will no longer be a reason to resist. We will defect. The Marxist historians of the future will report that process, instead of just predicting it.

In fact, they are reporting it right now, but privately. They understand the need to suppress scholarly enthusiasm in the name of a greater good (something our scholars lack, of course)—the need to tread lightly in the early stages of major defections. Betrayals must be cautiously described, lest the defectors, or those to whom they preach, become startled into an understanding of the full implications of their words and deeds.

Am I saying then that Harvey Cox, Gustavo Gutierrez, and the editors of *Maryknoll* know not what they do? It doesn't matter. I know—they condemn the harsh tyranny of the Soviet dictatorship (although more in the cause of Soviet Jewry than that of Soviet Christians). But that isn't the point. They do not have to be in league with those who will inherit the earth from the enfeebled West to collaborate in their ascendancy. All that is necessary is to drain the West of the will to resist. And *they are doing that,* perhaps in innocence and with highminded intent, by constructing a theology which has entrusted Marxism with the historic task of bringing a Christian politics to life.

Maryknoll, the monthly of the Foreign Mission Society of America, is strikingly explicit. I find it difficult, I must admit, to be critical of the little magazine. With me to this day are fond memories of long rainy afternoons with the *Maryknoll* of old, of paging through the lovingly illustrated stories of missionaries dying for the Faith under the headsman's axe in China, or crossing reptile-infested jungle rivers on flimsy rafts, or piloting jeeps across desert roads to bring Communion to isolated primitive people, or holding the cross high on windswept Andean plateaus that could be reached only over treacherous mountain passes.

Nowadays the magazine is America's most forthright exponent of the theology of liberation. *Maryknoll* speaks proudly of being the American publisher of Gutierrez, and of how their Orbis Books serves as the focal point for the theology of liberation in the United States. One searches in vain to find a way of distinguishing the magazine's message of late from that of, say (to be kind), UNICEF. Not that such a message is ignoble in itself. I repeat: I charge neither malevolence or base-mindedness. But it is not the pursuit of material ends that offends and disappoints—not in itself, anyway. It is the unrelenting and

155

uncritical endorsement of the leftist approach to reaching those ends. They have found a twin villain: the U.S. and capitalism. And not on economic grounds—which might be arguable—but as a moral issue.

There are any number of back issues which could be used to make the point. The editors know that. Invariably, in their letters-to-the-editor section, is an angry letter which complains of the magazine's leftwing stance. Some of the complaints are sophisticated, some not. Either way, the complaint is always followed by a letter or two that speak favorably of the new concern for a Christian redistributing of the planet's wealth in the favor of the underdeveloped nations.

What is so wrong about that, you might ask? Haven't Christians from time immemorial been asked to contribute to missionary efforts? Haven't mite boxes and fund raisings to support Asian, African, and South American orphans become as American as softball for every churchgoer?

But that was different somehow, wasn't it? Indeed it was. It was always a call for an act of Christian charity, a gift from one whose wealth was hardearned and honestly held. At least there was no presumption against that possibility. But the current pitch treats such charity as self-defeating, and with near contempt. The goal, in fact, is political action which will make these acts of mercy unnecessary: a reorganization of the world's political and economic structure to end the capitalist "exploitation" of the Third World. And the governments which take that line—the Marxist dictatorships—are shamelessly forgiven everything else because of the professed identity of interests. "No enemies to the Left"; it could be accurately emblazoned on the magazine's masthead.

Let me give just one, hardly untypical, example. In early 1975, not more than three or four issues apart, were two stories. The first on Mao's China; the second on life in South Korea under the pro-American regime of General Park. (Pro-American as I write, anyway. By the time you read these words, the South Koreans might very well have turned against us too, either because we failed to fulfill our military pledges and the Communists have marched in as in Vietnam, or because they have decided not to depend any longer on the stumbling, contracting American giant and have reached an accord with the Communists, as in Thailand.) The issue devoted to China "regretted" the period of "misunderstanding" which developed between the West and China, and the resulting disruption of friendly relations between Maryknoll and China, and the "historical circumstances" (a nice way of saying that Mao drove them from the mainland or kept them in Chinese jails as he did an older breed of Maryknoller, Bishop James Ford); but spoke with patience and understanding of the determined Chinese attempt to build a just society on the ruins of a corrupt and landlord-dominated past. (Funny how they have to keep guards with machine guns on their barbed-wire borders to keep the Chinese from crossing the shark-infested waters to follow that corrupt regime to Taiwan.) They pleaded for understanding and revaluation ''from both sides'' so that the ''old friendship'' can be resumed. There were pictures of smiling, well fed peasants in their well tended communal fields.

The millions killed? The prisons? The brutal and regular use of naked terror to keep the Cultural Revolution pure? No mention—but everyone knows that you can't make an omelet without breaking some eggs. Their hearts are in the right place, apparently, so all is forgiven.

But South Korea? That is another story. No quarter with evil from Christians. First of all, let me assure you that I have not a fig newton's worth of interest in propping up General Park's regime. Not that I have an animus against it, either. From what I can tell, his government is a typical Asian attempt to hold things together until some kind of political unity and economic modernization takes place. Do I know that he doesn't allow ACLU-observed elections on a regular basis? Yup. Do I know that there is no freedom of the press comparable to America's? Uh huh. Do I know that he has even arrested and deported a handful of priests from his country and has used police force to prevent demonstrations against his government? Yessir. What else do I know? Not much. But I do know—*and so do the editors of Maryknoll*—that Mao and the Communists make him look like Florence Nightingale. To deny it would be either ignorant or dishonest. The experts argue about whether Mao's takeover cost 15 million lives (say Mao's supporters) or 30 million (say his critics).

The article on South Korea, however, ''deplored'' the authoritarian nature of Park's regime and its shortsighted failure to initiate progressive reforms. It fretted over the mistreatment (pushing and shoving) of Catholic priests who had spoken out against Park. (Mao didn't leave anyone around to mistreat.) They mused openly about the improbability of the regime being capable of these reforms. They called for greater frreedom for political dissent—in spite (or because?) of the fact that Communist terrorists would seize such liberties to initiate a period of political upheaval which they would then exploit to bring to power a revolutionary government that would remove *forever* the possibility of democratic freedoms; and in spite of the fact that the Communist tyranny of Mao's, which they were extolling a few issues back, denies such civil liberties openly and *on principle*. They are telling us something, no?

I am not saying that it is necessarily un-Christian to be drawn to certain movements for political change in the Third World countries, South America especially; even if they would have to be designated as leftist. I do not say that missionary groups should necessarily be scolding every peasant guerrilla band organizing in the hills of every South American country. Not only leftists have written in harsh criticism of the dehumanizing extremes of poverty which

157

coexist with jet-set opulence in parts of Latin America, and of the failure of the economic elites to address themselves to reforms which would allow the impoverished to share in the material wealth of their countries. Okay. I have little doubt, in fact, that if I lived in one of those cardboard and tarpaper shanties in the shadow of the Copacabana hotels, and saw my children broken and diseased and without hope, I too would be a leftist revolutionary of sorts. But if that were the case, and I were as educated as a Maryknoller and able to weigh the full implications of my decision, and if I were as concerned about the future of Christianity as a Maryknoll priest should be, I would hold that:

a) My choice was a political choice, not a religious decision: i.e., that I had come to the conclusion that a Castro-type dictatorship offers the only *effective* vehicle for the needed reforms, and that Christians *could* tame its atheism; and

b) I would not be critical of the *religious* convictions of fellow countrymen who preferred a Peronist or openly pro-American junta which would work to achieve a growth of capital investment in the hope that it would generate the material wealth without which poverty cannot be reduced no matter how redistributist that regime. I might call such a choice shortsighted and bound to fail. (Although the record indicates nothing of the sort. And the capitalist countries aren't the ones that put barbed wire on their borders.) But I would have to accept the fact that a man could, *in good conscience,* argue that Brazil has gone further toward solving its problems than Cuba—and without attacking the Christian churches in the process. If such a thought is stupid, it is not immoral. *At worst,* it is bad economics. Not that the Brazilian generals are above criticism. There have been too many reports of torture to deny its existence. But nothing comparable to Fidel's. Sure, you might argue that Fidel's regimentation (to put it mildly) will pay dividends in the long run. But that indicates a faith in totalitarian economics—an economic and political choice about *what works.* Even so, the choice of an economic system which is more than an economic system—Communism—is difficult to defend. Especially if that step is called for on moral grounds. And the liberation theologians are calling for just that.

The Teilhardian Connection

Remember the Frank Sinatra movie, *The Manchurian Candidate,* and its brainwashed POWs who return from Korea to act out the will of their captors, knowing not what they do? Well, I wouldn't be surprised if some Christian who died in the late 1940's or '50's, brought back to life in our time, started an investigation to discover who it was that programmed the modern theologians. Of course, he would be barking up the wrong tree; appearances to the contrary

158

notwithstanding. They're brainwashed, all right. But it was self-inflicted, and proclaimed as a ''maturing in the Faith.'' And it happened not in Manchuria but while their noses were between the covers of books by Harvey Cox and Teilhard de Chardin. Teilhard especially provided the verbal camouflage for those unwilling to tell us, or themselves, that they had accepted a completely secularized Christianity. He baptized the surrender. Or at least the Teilhardians did.

There is no need for me to summarize Teilhard. It has been done often and well, by friend of his and foe, and in ways superior to anything I could work up. My favorite is the treatment by Thomas Molnar in his penetrating *Utopia: The Perennial Heresy*. Our concern, in any event, is not so much with Teilhard as with those who have taken his basic insight and run with it far off into political left field—the Teilhardians. Jacques Maritain, who met and talked at length with Teilhard, insisted that the man was pious and a theist, and that those who have intuited a secular pantheism of sorts from his often poetically expressed scientific and philosophical rummaging have misinterpreted him—that Teilhard would not be a Teilhardian if he were alive today. That's almost enough for me. But I'll reserve judgement for a while. Maritain missed a couple of big plays in an otherwise remarkably surehanded career. Just a couple—but enough for me to hold back on his judgement of Teilhard.

Regardless, Teilhard's ''Christofied'' universe is a notion which has been responsible for incalculable harm to the Faith and the world. It has, among other things, given an aura of respectability to the theology of liberation. If there are still sins of omission, one should be pinned to this French Jesuit for not kicking the coals from under the pot of trouble fired by his words. Although it is true that the boiling point was not reached during his lifetime.

Teilhard's vision of a controlled evolution, proceeding under the direction of men inspired by the universal love of Christ, taking mankind to a point where the Spirit of Christ totally imbues the world, is at the root of our current difficulties. It is what opened the door for the secularizers. It has allowed certain theologians to picture Christ's ultimate promise as one which will be realized on earth and in time, and solely through human effort. It is what had led many to conclude, in spite of Christ's words to the contrary, that the Kingdom is of this world—a world transformed by a combination of love and technical and scientific ingenuity to a new level of awareness. Through that perfected universe, with the very stuff of the planet spiritualized by the message of Christ, Christ will ''come again.'' The Second Coming, the Teilhardians imply, will be a perfected technology and politics, with human governments both shaped by and contributors to the evolution. *That* was what Christ was all about. It just took us two thousand years of evolution for Teilhard and his friends to figure it out.

Inspired by his dream of a Divine Milieu, Teilhardians of various stripes have tried to shift the attention of Christians from Cardinal Newman's expression of the mission of the Church on earth—saving souls for an eternity in a heavenly kingdom which is not of this world. You are not overreacting if you have gotten the impression of late that the good Christian is being defined as the good secular liberal and the Faith as the most ambitious and optimistic social-betterment scheme; if you think that the Love of God sounds like ecology, and Charity the most thoroughgoing leftist redistribution of the world's resources. That is the message.

Certainly it should not be said that an intense interest in organizing our political and economic life along Christian lines is un-Christian—as long as it does not become too intense. Being Christian, it is true, should show, should make a difference. In the Middle Ages, we noted earlier, the Faith was brought into all areas of life. That was not un-Christian. So we should not overreact to Teilhardian pressure. An application of Christian love could make the world a far more pleasant place to live in. It might not tell us how to stop inflation, but it could, for one thing, help create a moral atmosphere more conducive to the preservation of a Christian conscience than Sunset Strip. It might help us save our souls.

But the goal of the Teilhardians is far different. In the medieval Age of Faith, Christians tried to rough out an approximation of the divine order of the City of God; but it was, at best, an imperfect image of a perfection men would only know through Christ in heaven. For the Teilhardians, however, the mirror image is the only reality. To refuse that thought is to tolerate a primitive Platonic dualism. The shadows on the wall are real, and good, and susceptible to a refinement that will make us forget false dreams of a world of ideals beyond them. Christians must immerse themselves totally in making *this* kingdom come, not moon away their lives in anticipation of another. We have matured enough—whereas our fathers had not—to be told that. The Secular City is the only city.

Enter Stage Left

It was this Teilhardian flip-flop that loosened the hitch. It, first of all, lessened interest in Christ's promise of an ultimate vindication for the human experience in a life beyond the present. Now, let us not get bogged down in a debate about exactly *where* that world will be. Christ will come again; we will live again and the world will be transformed through Christ—saved from the existent squalor. We have Christ's assurance of that. Will it be this planet itself with Christ as king in a literal sense? Or a world transformed into a dimension beyond our comprehension? Well, I have no inside information. If it will be this

160

planet it is going to be awfully crowded if those who argue for universal salvation are right. If they are not, and there will be room enough for those who make it through the narrow gate, where will hell be? Manhattan? Maybe . . .

But it is clear that Christ's words are not descriptive of a Teilhardian utopia. He speaks of a world dramatically different from our own, and immeasurably beyond the level of human accomplishment. His Kingdom is not one that can be foreseen or predicted by a linear and mathematically calibrated progression—*as can the Teilhardian.* It is not just the conquest of poverty, disease and human alienation—although these burdens of the human condition will be lifted. It is a world he calls paradise—and its perfection will be experienced personally by those who follow him, not just by the human collectivity, as representative of us, at a future moment in time. It is mystical and divine, and His.

Why is it so important to make this point clear (as we will do, shortly, with Christ's words)? First of all, because it is what Christ *says*, and Christians should know that. But also because it is the Christian failure to insist upon preserving Christ's understanding of the Kingdom that has allowed a liberation theology its flirtation with Marxism. Flirtation? It is a marriage close to consummation.

Think of the consequences of the Christian reluctance to stand firm on this point. If Christ will not come again to right the wrongs and fulfill the world's potential, the human drama is as unbearable and absurd as the existentialists say. Social tribulations, physical imperfections, and economic inequalities become harsh and oppressive and final: shameful blots on the human escutcheon. They *cannot* be endured nobly. They are gross and unnatural burdens which must be attacked with passion by all men of good conscience. Anything less is a disgraceful apathy. If Christ will not save us, *we* must do it.

In the older Judeo-Christian framework these human imperfections were not seen as desirable, certainly, but were understood to be inevitable, the consequences of the scars of original sin. We were not to anticipate, and certainly not pledge our lives to, an impossible societal or scientific remedy. Life is a vale of tears, as they used to say. Eternal bliss would be ours only in the Kingdom that was not of this world.

If, however, as the secularists insist in contrast, the best of all possible worlds is the one we create in time, then the Communists could inherit the earth. They have a plan. At least they are trying. In Marx's projection, remember, the Communist state in its final stages will not only solve the problem of poverty, crime and war, but will also end the psychic alienation that leads to spiritual and emotional distress. We will not only be well fed and clothed, but happy. With the devil of private property exorcized, we will not only have no reason to steal or wage wars—since we will also be joined with our comrades in the consummate social adventure. We will know our identity, for the first time, and our role and its importance in the collective effort. We will be saved. We will use the human skills which best express our true selves in the quest for a perfected world, totally committed and whole within the human family.

It is, of course, a version of the Christian view of heaven—constructed on earth and in history by men who, under the tutelage of the great teachers, Marx and Feuerbach, have taken their eyes off the illusory heaven of the ancients to begin its construction on earth, to "change the world instead of merely explaining it," in Marx's words. Just like the Teilhardians . . .

Just like the Teilhardians, and Harvey Cox in his Secular City moods, and the World Council of Churches, and the liberation theologians. But to accuse an updater of having Marxist allies could get you called a McCarthyite. Or might have, a few years ago; now the updaters might relish the charge. They might protest, correctly, that they deplore militarist dictatorships, Soviet domination of the Eastern European satellites, concentration camps, the lack of freedom of expression, the persecution of Soviet Jewry, etc. Which is true. They do. But the point is that the Teilhardian updaters are in basic agreement with the *ultimate aspirations* of the Marxist world; that if the Marxists have erred, at least they are trying. Their hearts are in the right place—at least their Founding Father's was; and if the Soviet commissars have strayed from the straight and narrow, the updater theologians can bring them back. The harshest words of the updater will only be a plaintive exhortation for the Communists to live up to their highest ideals; and if *they* do, the difference between progressive Christian and Communist can easily be mended, promise the updaters.

The Western democracies—on the other hand—doubting the Marxist optimism and proceeding under their traditional Christian presumption that perfection is not to be achieved, or even attempted, become *the* problem for the Teilhardians. We do *not* have our hearts in the right place, have given up, have jumped off history's train. At least the Marxists offer hope. They have been liberated from their complacency. (Of course, it could be argued that, to the extent that the Western democracies have adopted secular humanism as their social premise, they offer the same utopian future as the Marxists, but through a different historical process; education instead of violent revolution. In that event, the feud between the Teilhardian updaters and the Western democracies centers only on whether the dictatorship of the proletariat is more likely to achieve the necessary intensity of human collective effort than parliamentary democracy, than the Fleet Street-Greenwich Village Axis.)

In contrast, say the Teilhardians, America has *nothing* truly elevated to offer the world. We offer no more than an orderly perpetuation of the lower level of human expectations. And as this thought grows in intensity and spreads through the efforts of the media and academic preachers, it destroys us. America stands for nothing in updater eyes while the Marxists have an earthly version to take the place of the lost dream of Christ's paradise beyond. They offer a variation on Teilhard and Cox. (Actually, it is the other way round.) And if the Communists have yet to show signs of reaching the Teilhardian goal, at least they are trying, unlike those under the spell of the Christian curse that accepts human degradation. Of all the active social and cultural forces, in fact, the traditional Christian is the most obstructive to the race's development. *We are the enemy.*

America Last

When you allow that thought to register—that America is the problem—it lifts the mind in a flash to a new level of understanding. *Metanoia,* I think, is what the Greeks called it. It is an invigorating, albeit distressing, intellectual experience. So much of the *apparent* inconsistency of our recent history begins to fall into recognizable categories. Instead of shaking our heads in bewilderment at what we think is the senseless Left-liberal preference for the Communist world, and taking pride in our ability to demonstrate that inconsistency, as if American leftists would be embarrassed if they knew that their track record was unmistakably pro-Communist. (''If you guys are such good Americans, how come you push for things that keep helping the Reds? Huh? Gotcha there!''), we come to understand that *there is no inconsistency.* That when the Communists fail it is in spite of their intentions; that their heart is in the right place. While when America succeeds, beyond all expectations, it is due only to geographical and historical circumstance, mere coincidence; and is only a short-run success. We have no dream that inspires. Don't forget the motto the college kids wore on their sweatshirts a few years back. The kids might have adopted the phrase themselves and popularized it, but it was only a logical choice based on all they had learned about the nature of American society and its institutions from their professors and religious teachers. ''We have met the enemy, and he is us.'' If your kids wore the sweatshirt, it was a good sign, in a way. It showed that they had paid attention and done their homework while in college. No blue-collar workers in their early twenties wore that beauty, except those who boogied on the weekends with the college crowd.

Once we understand this devolution, we no longer are puzzled by what has happened to the world since World War II. We finally know why ''we won the war, but lost the peace.'' We are able to see the *trahison des clercs* under bright lights at center stage. Why our historical identity and sense of mission were openly subjected to the withering critiques of an alien-minded intelligentsia (who had already rejected the Christian vision of man, or who never held it to begin with); who, and at the same time, were extolling the merits of the Marxist biases, if not the actual policies, of our enemies.

And now, why our secularized clerics join that chorus.

No longer are we puzzled about why bridges should be built to Castro and Mao, while trade is outlawed with Rhodesia; why Europe explodes with violent protest "in horror" after the Franco government executes the killers of Spanish policemen, while South American terrorists who machete kidnapped Americans are lionized as freedom fighters, and the Viet Cong's reign of terror is not mentioned at all; why Soviet ballet dancers are wined and dined through the glass canyons of Manhattan, but South African athletes are barred from international competition; why Angela Davis is escorted to the college gymnasium by the university president, but George Gilder, whose defense of the traditional role of women in society can only be called moderate and commonsensical, is hooted off the stage; why the use of American military force is cruel and barbarous and immoral, but leftist revolutionaries from Algeria to Vietnam to Harlem are engaged in mankind's great struggle for human dignity (they have something to fight for, you see); why kings, knights, medieval monks, American generals and John Wayne are all fit objects of cutting and dishonest media satire, while the truly ludicrous, posturing leftwing tyrants of the globe are not.

We understand why the media masters never let us catch our breath, why they chastise us mercilessly with every isolated instance they can find of failure in America, no matter how unrepresentative of our society. Why we are made to pity heartless drug fiends whose habit is only one, often *comparatively* harmless, manifestation of a self-centered life, as if we somehow had shoved the needle into their struggling arms; to sympathize with the plight of merciless urban punks, dissolute and aimless welfare cheats, irresponsible mothers of countless illegitimate children, vicious prison sodomizers; to feel guilt for every underfed soul on the planet, as if our economic development was what held back their own, and intentionally. It is all our fault. Our system fails to aspire to the secular utopia in which all these problems will vanish. Never mind that only a fool could say the Marxists have offered the key to the solution. *At least they are trying*. If the welfare payments are high, we fail because we do not instruct the mothers in the wisdom of buying protein-rich vegetables rather than TV dinners; if we attempt to monitor and regulate their spending, it is bourgeois meddling. If we allow minority students an individualized approach to their schooling in which lower levels of skills are tolerated, we deny them the "tools" needed to learn a livelihood; if we demand that they meet the standards of the majority, we rob them of their "cultural heritage."

They never let us look up. Forget the charitable associations and civic groups, the church picnics, the blood banks, the cancer research; look at the slums, the spaced-out denizens of Haight-Ashbury (where square America reigns no more, if you want to see the liberated future), the fags, the Louds —that "typical American family." That's America. Dig beneath the surface, newsmen. Find the truth. That's what they're doing. (The same guys who keep their tails between their legs and sheepishly film and report to us on national TV exactly what some Red Chinese party hack tells them is suitable for the American audience. Truth seekers? Rot!) Those neat little homes in the sub-urbs, that one little step up for which so many Americans struggle and save and lavish elbow grease? Materialism, cardboard boxes of conformity, the residents of Manhattan brownstones let us know. Bloated and bored housewives, empti-ness. Go back to the inner city? A garbage-strewn hell. You can't escape—not in this country, man. Cuba? Maybe. We have no right to be happy, content or proud. We must be shown why America doesn't work—or shouldn't work. We might never guess it on our own, you see. Especially if our judgement about these things is clouded by the opiate of the people. We must be *made* miserable along with our existentialist intelligentsia and our liberal elites—be made to shed the ancient and august heritage that keeps us whole. And now we get that message from our own priests and ministers who have crossed over into the enemy camp. Liberation theology.

The distracting and perplexing Christian pacifism that surfaced during the Vietnam war was part of the scenario. The secular liberals, as always, set the stage. Their teach-ins and sit-ins and rock-music sermons established in the minds of barely literate high school students a complex, if erroneous, under-standing of the difference between Munich-like surrenders and compromise with legitimate revolutionary movements of national liberation—a distinction which classroom teachers could never have communicated for solely academic purposes. We were told of voting irregularities in Thieu's government, as if Mao and Ho Chi Minh were honorary members of the League of Women Voters. But, of course, they had a reason for their authoritarian measures. Thieu could not—*because* he was America's ally. He had to be as purposeless as we. Then the tiger cages—although no one asked what the North Vietnamese did to their political malcontents. (Or could even mass executions be performed in the name of the secular utopia of the Left?) Then the black-market profiteers, the drug-dealing generals—the kinds of abuses which can only be purged in a well disciplined regime. But they *screamed* in wild-eyed indignation at any sign that Thieu was resorting to the remedies of a "tin-horn dictator." (How do you tell, Senator McGovern, when a dictator is "tin-horn?" When he is not a Communist?) The South Vietnamese had no vision of a society-to-come to warrant such stern measures. Neither do we.

Except some Christians still think we do. How to defuse them? They still hold that the Kingdom is not of this world; that dictatorships that try to remake man, to abolish original sin, are doomed to failure; that it cannot be done, and that revolutionary movements that attempt to justify their totalitarianism with such a promise offer no justification at all. Whether the Marxist utopia is worth enslavement to the Stalins and the Maos is another question. For Christians they are tyrannies that will not wither away. They enslave for a goal which cannot be reached, and through their unrelenting anti-Christian premises work against the source of true liberation and salvation. They are evils which can and should be fought with enthusiasm and in good conscience.

Enter the Berrigans and Sloane Coffins—the knockout punch. A false and shamelessly selective pacifism is employed to pin Christian vigor to the wall. Pictures of the horrors of war are thrust upon us, as if we were the only combatants, merciless Huns sweeping through innocent villages for plunder. The words of Christ—mercy, kindness, forgiveness—are used to haunt us, while an enemy rampages through the streets of Hue, raping and killing indiscriminately. But we are to blame.

At first we pause, confused, uncertain. Why? Why are America's wars the only unjust ones on the planet? Why is it reasonable and excusable for the Communists to move massively against South Vietnam, and barbarous for America to try to stop them? Why was this war fought with no order to win, with none of the fanfare, the banners and bugles and piping, the parades and war songs needed to help men forget the terrible things they had to do to secure victory? All of that is reserved for heroes, and America was allowed none. Heroes are for those who fight and die in the name of the noble dream, and we had none.

The words of Whittaker Chambers float back to haunt us. The tormented and ridiculed, and then forgotten, Jeremiah was right:

> An educated man, peering from the Harvard Yard, or any college campus, upon a world in chaos, finds in the vision [Communism] the two certainties for which the mind of man tirelessly seeks: a reason to live and a reason to die. No other faith of our time presents them with the same practical intensity. That is why Communism is the central experience of the first half of the 20th century, and may be its final experience—will be, unless the free world, in the agony of its struggle with Communism, overcomes its crisis by discovering, in suffering and pain, a power of faith which will provide man's mind, at the same intensity, with the two certainties: a reason to live and a reason to die. If it fails, this will be the century of the great social wars. If it succeeds, this will be the century of the great wars of faith.[2] ·

It took the genius of our modern theologians to add a new twist. They are trying to take the drama from Chambers' words; to show us how those wars can be avoided; to convince us that the enemy's plans were what we wanted all along. That we can have our surrender with honor. That the enemy's promise is noble, and ours.

[2]Whittaker Chambers, *Witness* (New York: Random House, 1952), pp. 11–12.

166

Chapter X

Burning the Chapel

''THAT THE ENEMY'S promise is noble, and ours''—precisely and in detail. It is the theology of liberation. Those who have read Gutierrez and Cox know I do not exaggerate. For those who have not, a short review is in order. And then, a comparison with the words of Christ to demonstrate the enormity of their revision, and the explicitness of their preference for Marx.

Most readers know of Gutierrez, certainly of Harvey Cox. But it's likely that many have not taken the time to actually study their recent writings. I know from my own experience that the tendency is to reserve those few precious hours we can set aside, in a day taken up with the responsibility of earning a living, for books and authors that reinforce and assuage our own convictions, rather than question them. This is especially true of sincere Christians who have come to a point in their lives when the Faith is no longer an open question; who no longer want to discover whether the Faith is true or not as much as to have it refined and projected. It is not easy (I know, I know), when you have only a few hours on a few evenings a week to indulge a love for quality in writing, to pick up Gutierrez or Cox, when still unread volumes of Chesterton, Lewis, and Newman sit beckoning from the shelves. It seems such an abysmal waste of time.

For that reason, and because my charge against the liberation theologians is so serious, permit me to verify (Scripture and verse, so to speak) my interpretation of this new ecumenism—the convergence of Christ and Marx.

I propose to examine the case of the liberation theologians as fairly and objectively as my anger will permit—to the point that I would hope the liberation theologians and their followers would say that this Mick is really thick; i.e., he sees *exactly* what we are saying, and is still obstinately medieval (which makes the failing a far greater one). And then let Christ speak for himself to show that he too was "medieval" on this point; that, as in the other updater revisions, you can only update in opposition to him.

Salvation as Convocation

My first reading of Gutierrez came as a disappointment and a shock. And I was not programmed for that reaction. Quite the opposite. I had hoped for an impassioned plea by a South American man of the people for the Christians of the world to understand that, while those who were known as Socialists in the days of Pius XI were unabashed enemies of the Faith and doctrinaire Marxists, the new breed of Latin American revolutionary was not a lost cause; that his radicalism was prompted more by despair and a hope for Christian justice —perhaps even a modern version of the call for subsidiarity, widespread property ownership and economic opportunity long a part of Catholic economic principles; or at least that their priests could lead their struggle in that direction and away from Marx and Marcuse. I had hoped that he would defend his people's cause because their degradation was real, because he was resolved to offer Christian guidance rather than Marxist guns to their anger; determined that the Marxists would not win the leadership by default.

What I found was quite different. I found that the struggle of the South American rural and urban guerrillas was worthy of support *because* it was under Marxist direction, and that without that Marxist superstructure their cause would be *less* worthy of praise. Marxism is what rescues it from the kind of irrational and senseless violence that an enlightened and progressive modern would have to condemn.

In all fairness, it can be said that Gutierrez simply summarizes, competently, what the New Left ideologues have been saying since the early sixties about capitalism and the Third World countries. I said *summarize*—not rework, or revise, or reconstruct along Christian lines. *Summarize*—and then call the bloody mess the finest expression of Christianity in the modern world; the response that Christ would want from his followers in our moment in history. He baptizes Marx—as refined by Herbert Marcuse.

168

He starts his case in *The Theology of Liberation*, as you might expect, by confidently proclaiming the error of errors in traditional Christian theology: the belief in a separate secular and sacral sphere, what he calls the "Platonic and neo-Platonic categories" and the "metaphysics which stressed the existence of a higher world and the transcendence of an Absolute from which everything came and to which everything returned." (Yes, they all do start here.) We are called from that otherworldliness in our age, and to our advantage, by "the influence of Marxist thought." A vehicle has finally been found in time and history and by man, through which the "Word of God gathers and is incarnated in the community of faith." "Many agree with Sartre that 'Marxism, as the formal framework of all contemporary philosophical thought, cannot be superseded.'" At least Gutierrez does: "Contemporary theology does in fact find itself in direct and fruitful confrontation with Marxism, and it is to a large extent due to Marxism's influence that theological thought, searching for its own sources, has begun to reflect on the meaning of the transformation of this world [which for Gutierrez is what Christ meant—or should have meant—by the Kingdom] and the action of man in history."

In other words, what Marx calls a materialist experience—the communal perfecting of the human race—is what Christ called spiritual—a world filled with the spirit of his love. But there is no actual difference beyond this semantic one, thinks Gutierrez. Marx is the prophet who best expresses the message Christ not as perceptively (he was limited by the Platonism of his time) tried to give to the world. Of course, you could say that the error is more Marx's, that he incorrectly labelled the sublime human achievement he prophesized as materialist. Then we are not really surrendering, you see. Like two boys arguing over whether to play hockey or football, and one agreeing to smack that little black disc of a football into the goalie's net.

A favorite theologian of Gutierrez, Edward Schillebeeckx, phrases it perceptively: "The hermeneutics of the Kingdom of God consists especially in making the world a better place. Only in this way will I be able to discover what the Kingdom of God means."

How, you might ask, did Christians finally learn that they were in neo-Platonic error all these years, and that the Marxists were right after all? From a divine apparition? Papal pronouncement? (Hardly. Gutierrez thinks that the Pope is coming along, especially in *Populorum Progressio*, but still has a long way to go.) From an enlightened reading of Scripture? Not exactly.

"From Descartes" we learned that "the Platonic and neo-Platonic theology" taught by the churches could be dismissed. Descartes "highlighted the creative aspects of human subjectivity." Then Kant's moral Copernican re-

169

volution "strengthened and systematized this point of view." He brought us to the understanding that "the world we live in must conform to our conceptions of it," not to an "*a priori*" Divine Will, and to a knowledge which leads us out of our religious "naivete" and into "an adult stage."

Hegel then taught us of "the right of every man to participate in the direction of the society to which he belongs" and to work for a future and earthly "society in which [we] will be free of all alienation and servitude."

Of course, as Marxists know (and, to a large degree, *any* Marxist; it is what makes you a Marxist), Hegel had to be set on his feet, to be despiritualized. "Marx deepened and renewed this line of thought in his unique way." He saw the need for "an epistemological break" which he expressed most capably, Gutierrez tells us, "in the famous *Theses on Feuerbach*." "Marx situated himself equidistant between the old materialism and idealism." He opened man's horizons "to the transformation of the world through work," thereby "pointing the way towards an era in history when man can live humanly," when man "will have controlled nature, created the conditions for a socialized production of wealth, done away with private acquisition of excessive wealth and established socialism."

Well, okay, you might say, all of this is the best of Marx. There is an idealism and an altruism in such hopes analogous to the Christian projection. Could not an infusion of Christian love and Christian realism tame the excesses of an untutored and intuitive Marxism, such as one is likely to find in the mind and heart of a South American guerrilla? Is Father Gutierrez manipulating the Marxist thrust to bend it toward Christ the way a missionary would work with the heathen; to make Christ instead of Mao the interior fire which inspires a willingness to work for brotherhood? Nope. There is a new truth that sets you free. "Freud highlighted the unconscious determinants of human behavior," and Herbert Marcuse took it from there. Marcuse recognized the "over-repressive character of the affluent society and envisions the possibility of a non-repressive society, a possibility skeptically denied by Freud. Marcuse's analysis of an advanced industrial society, capitalistic or socialistic, led him to denounce the emergence of a one-dimensional and oppressive society. In order to achieve this non-repressive society, however, it will be necessary to challenge the values espoused by the society which denies man the possibility of living freely. Marcuse labels this the Great Refusal." Abbie Hoffman, as we know, understood the thought when he called for bringing the system to a halt through public fornication and drug use.

This analysis is indistinguishable from the outline of the world's history that could in varying degrees of proficiency, and would, be made by any and every half-literate member of the SDS or the Weathermen. It is, says Gutierrez, the response demanded of Christians in the modern world, in spite of the fact that

170

the Christian churches have been struggling against this secular challenge in all its stages of development for the last two hundred years. Gutierrez summarizes it, and calls it Christian. *Mea culpa*, fellas, now we see what you mean.

Now we can see that true spiritualization awaits those who fulfill the dreams of "all the great social revolutions—the French and the Russian for example" which "wrested—or at least began to—political decisions from the hands of an elite" (*from* an elite—Robespierre and Lenin, the decentralizers). We must learn to appreciate the "secularization" initiated by these great revolutions for "the Christian Community in the future will have to live and celebrate its faith in a *nonreligious* [Gutierrez's emphasis] world, *which the faith itself has helped to create*" [my emphasis].

Archbishop Robert Dwyer shocked many readers when he told of a symposium he attended at a Catholic seminary in which Catholic theologians discussed their conviction that "our aim is to destroy traditional religion." Some tended to doubt that Dwyer had heard exactly those words—the Archbishop must be getting old—or that he was being objective when he reported that the group proceeded to argue for replacing the Faith with "a type of Marxist humanism" and that they "were totally unconscious of their betrayal." But I'm afraid that Archbishop Dwyer was as right as rain. Gutierrez is one of the most read of modern theologians, and that is exactly what he calls for, with the endorsement and encouragement of his publisher, Maryknoll's Orbis Books.

He doesn't even try to be cute (although his followers will when they preach his message in American parishes). He tells us that the mission of modern Christians is to create "a new man" clearly distinct from the Christian of old. And guess who knows what that new man should look like?

> Ernesto Che Guevara wrote: "We revolutionaries often lack the knowledge and the intellectual audacity to face the lack of the development of a new human being by methods different from the conventional ones, and the conventional methods suffer from the influence of the society that created them." This vision is what in the last instance sustains the liberation efforts of Latin Americans.

And the time is now to make Christians see the wisdom of men like Che, to "break out of a narrow, individualistic viewpoint," to see that Christianity ought not to be "so much of a vocation to salvation as a convocation," to look forward to "an anonymous Christianity, in other words, a Christianity beyond the visible frontiers of the Church," the "advent of a Christendom without the name." (There is another name for what he has in mind.) The task of the theologian, naturally, becomes "active, effective participation in the struggle which the exploited social classes have undertaken against their oppressors" for the *"idea of salvation is an intrahistorical reality"* [my emphasis]. He must

171

communicate that thought even though "contemporary theology has not yet fashioned the categories which would allow us to think through and express adequately this unified approach to history." Only one group has—the Marxists. Gutierrez's mission is to help us to see that as clearly as he does.

In the Light of Fanon

It might be foolhardy to speak of Harvey Cox's slant on the theology of liberation. His political and theological positions seem to change with the seasons—which might be commendable from the viewpoint of the thinker who admits to no God-given moral absolutes. Just before starting to write this section on his approach to the theology of liberation, I happened to come across a review he wrote for *The New York Times Book Review* of two books which take a modern empiricist view of the devil—exactly the approach we would expect from writers influenced by Cox's widely read book, *The Secular City*, by the way. But that book's author sees things in a different light these days:

> Maybe there really are things that go bump in the night, and maybe they are not just inside our heads. I am afraid that unless knowledgeable writers stop hiding behind psychological reductionism and comfortable skepticism about all this, our universe will be enlarged again by people who are in no way skeptical, who are in fact prepared to believe almost anything. [One cannot help but wonder—Cox doesn't say—if traditional Christians are the people he fears will rise in influence once the empiricist prejudices have demonstrated their sterility. His contempt for the structure and dispensation of the traditional churches and the Faith as historically understood leads one to that conclusion. There is one constant in his writing—that.]

In spite of this possibility—that Cox might be saying something very different from what he was saying just two years ago in *The Seduction of the Spirit*—let us examine that work. It offers us an accurate and troubling insight into what makes those attracted to the Marxist-Christian convergence tick.

Cox is, in fact, more disturbing than Gutierrez—for an American audience anyway. (It would be difficult to imagine anyone more disturbing for a Latin American than a priest giving his blessing to the revolutionaries about to strike against his entire way of life.) Cox is a North American, and his excesses cannot be excused by the personal anguish of seeing his people impoverished and degraded—which might explain the worst of Gutierrez. Cox should be able to take a balanced and reasoned view of what Marxism means to the world. He should know its horrors. Yet he speaks of it with as much enthusiasm as Gutierrez:

> We must now read Nietzsche, who coined the phrase "God is dead," in the light of Fanon, Mao and Ho Chi Minh, the diagnosticians of the decline of Western dominance . . . Our nation now looms as one of the main barriers to the birth of the new world, and the religion of America still largely endorses our empire . . . The time has come to change.[1]

Radical theologians must take the lead, says Cox, in introducing the residents of the United States, that main barrier to the birth of the new world of Mao and Ho Chi Minh, to the wisdom of the world to come.

Is he uncritical of the modern Marxist? No, no, not a Harvard professor. Marx was not infallible, Cox assures us:

> Karl Marx, child of the Enlightenment that he was, though right in many things, was wrong in his estimate of religion. He not only undercalculated its durability but he also overlooked its seldom tapped potential for catalyzing political and cultural transformation.[2]

In other words, Marx did not see, as Cox does now but did not in his Secular City days, that the secular, internationalist and communal vision for mankind can more effectively be realized in *collaboration* with religion than in opposition to it, that religion can be used to fire the engines of the class warfare necessary to move the dialectic to its conclusion.

At the risk of sounding sensationalist, I ask: How is all this different from what mankind calls treason? High-minded treason, perhaps, but treason. What more can a man say than that the enemy stands for the best hope for the world, and that his own country is the barrier? What would our reaction have been to an American Nazi who wrote that an Aryan-dominated civilization was the best hope for man, and that the wealthy and powerful multiracial American melting pot was the main barrier to its birth? Certainly it would not have been to put him on the Sunday-morning religious talk shows. The fact that Cox gets such deferential treatment and is one of the most read and studied modern theologians, and a regular reviewer of religious books for *The New York Times* and other centers of media influence in America, shows the extent to which the Marxist biases have become a central part of the American dialogue: the enemy within.

---

[1] *The Seduction of the Spirit*, p. 174.
[2] Ibid., p. 190.

Viva Mao!

As Cox sees it, the strong cultural and emotional attachment of Latin Americans to the symbols of Catholicism has been integrated into their struggle for liberation. But there is no reason for a progressive theologian to attack the lingering affection, even if it is false and a childish superstition, and likely to be a problem in the long run. It can be used now, in the present stage of the dialectic. It is not as if they were North Americans and endeared to the churches of the imperialists—which were seen in proper perspective by the "inmates of Attica who burned the chapel as their first act of rebellion." South American Christianity is different. "Since in Christianity it is always the oppressed and afflicted with whom God is present, and among whom the New Reality is appearing, we cannot do our work without identifying their cause as ours."

Follow that carefully. Cox has said elsewhere that God is "whatever it is within the cosmic evolution which inspires and supports the endless struggle for liberation . . . . that power which despite all setbacks never admits to final defeats." He has also written in praise of Pablo Frei's concept of the "conscientization" of the world and Teilhard's "hominisation of reality." Both are descriptions of the planetary process which "will alter the total consciousness of the Third World, but because of the global culture's interactive nature, of everyone." He admits that "we do not have the theological idiom to understand" this new picture of God, but, nevertheless, since "the liberation of humankind is seen as the purpose of Christianity, and if theology is to serve the purpose of faith, then theology too must be directed toward human liberation."[3]

"God," then, is the idealism which inspires the class struggle of the Marxist dialectic—whether you want to call it something else or not. "God" is present most intensely in those groups actively involved in transforming the world in the direction of the collective consciousness: "conscientization" and "hominisation" (but which Marx calls Communism).

But, a problem. The South American revolutionaries who are the standard bearers of this liberation process in our moment in history have a concept of God and the purpose of religion dramatically different from Cox's cosmic process. God is "present" *in* their struggle, for Cox; but for them He is present as the omnipotent, Absolute Other as well. So while these Latin American revolutionaries push for the divinization (Cox's version) of the social order, they do it without realizing the magnitude of their efforts (although their Marxist leaders have their heads screwed on right). In breaking the concentra-

[3] *Ibid.*, p. 153.

174

tion of political and economic power of the exploiting gringo they are furthering the "cosmic evolution"—bringing God to earth. But they don't know that. They are filled with a medieval otherworldliness that leads them to imagine a spiritual world as well—a Kingdom not of this world. They work for the right objective, but for immature reasons.

> In Latin America, insurgency has often broken out under the banners of people's religion. In the backlands of Brazil mystical prophets have often led uprisings. Glauber Rocha's film *Black God, White Devil* depicts one such movement. In Mexico, Father Hidalgo organized his Independistas under the insignia of Our Lady of Guadalupe. A century later Emiliano Zapata led his machete-wielding rural guerrillas beneath the same sign. More recently the Chicano grape strikers marched from Delano to Sacramento under the identical image.[4]

Talk about dilemmas! The insurrectionists with the greatest potential for realizing Marx's noblest dreams toil under banners not only emblematic of their belief in a personal God but of a personal Virgin Mary too, and in a quite literal sense. "What this means," Cox writes,

> for our urgently needed critical restudy of religious history is that we must ask more cogently where and how religion has been used as Mace (to blind and paralyze the protest) and where it has informed liberation. We must learn how to expose the first [as in the United States] and nourish the second [as in South America].[5]

Some day, Cox is certain, these Latin American revolutionaries will be willing and able to read Bonhoeffer and himself and see that the world needs a "non-religious interpretation of Christianity." After all, many of their leaders reached that point: Castro, Che, Allende, etc. But for the others, who carry their statues of Mary in an open and sincere expression of faith? Well, theologians must learn "to treat the actual manifestations of religion without condescension." *Theologians* must learn that. Rio is worth a Mass.

Not that their religion is true. That is not the point. It is primitive. He treats it with obvious condescension, all his advice to the contrary notwithstanding. He writes of the South American Catholic experience as being just another manifestation of a worldwide phenomenon. He studies it the way an under-graduate anthropology student studies the world:

[4] *Ibid.*, p. 193.

[5] *Ibid.*, p. 193.

175

I have haunted the village churches, saints' day fiestas and pilgrimages of the
Mexican hills. I have swayed and sung at Chilean Pentecostal rallies. I have been
blessed by a dark-skinned holy man in the blackness of Rio favella's lurid
Umbanda ritual.[6]

Can't you just picture this plump, bearded Harvard professor, fresh from
lolling nude in the candlelight at Big Sur with Allen Ginsberg, lifting his eyes
heavenward and swinging and swaying with the natives? I'd give an amount
equal to every cent of the royalties from *The Secular City*—if I had it—to get a
tape of the comments of the Chilean Pentecostals about *this* gringo.

Religion, then, is a phenomenon of man in his adolescence. But it can be
used—especially right now, south of the border. It has fire. Fire enough to
make the author of *The Secular City* eat his earlier words. Cox has seen what the
Bonhoeffers of the world could not, that the fulfillment of the secular world will
be brought about not by Secular City technocrats, but by Latin American
theists! But the desired end is still the same.

Who cares if it is true? Does the religion "contribute to the fuller consciousness, the joy, the maturation and emancipation of man?" That is the question.
After Western dominance has been ended, Cox, or one of his cohorts, can give
these religious illiterates—perhaps with UNESCO funding—the book list he
uses now at Harvard, for the new People's Republic schools that will be set up.
Then they will learn that there is no Virgin, nor a Christ, waiting for them in a
life after death, but that it was good—for them and for the world—for them to
believe all that for a while in order to "catalyze the political and cultural
transformation" which "emancipated mankind." Then they too will be able to
read about the nature of the religious impulse:

> We started out reading Nikos Kazantzakis' *Report to Greco*, Elie Wiesel's
> *Legends for Our Time*, Thomas Merton's *The Seven Storey Mountain* (which on
> rereading . . . I found disgustingly triumphalistic and even arrogant), and Sam
> Keen's *To a Dancing God*. Later on we read Simone Weil's *Waiting for God*,
> Bonhoeffer's *Letters and Papers from Prison*, *The Autobiography of Malcolm X*
> [the Muslim triumphalism of which this enemy of Christendom apparently did not
> find disgusting or arrogant], and a book called *Black Elk Speaks* by a nameless
> Sioux.[7]

Naturally, after taking this course of study those Latinos will never again
fight for a religion—if things work out the way they usually do for Cox in his
classes. They will be as incapable of that as the North Americans who lost the

---

[6] *Ibid.*, p. 171.
[7] *Ibid.*, p. 110.

will to defend their civilization after digesting his vision of Christianity. But it will be okay, since, by then, the Latin American People's Republic will have been established and the world will be all that closer to its final hominisation. Their religious fire was only needed to achieve that goal—as was the religious apathy of the citizens of the West. And Cox pushes both.

But for now, let us feed the flames:

> "A specter is haunting Europe," Karl Marx once wrote. The specter he had in mind was Communism. Today another specter haunts us. It is the grin on the skeletal face of a god we have inherited, worshipped, misused and finally killed. [We in the West once had God. We once were revolutionaries.] But while the leering specter still besets us, a new eon is tearing its way from the womb of history. Should radical theologians be morticians or midwives? We have *nothing* to lose.[8] [My emphasis.]

Remember, "we have *nothing* to lose" the next time your Cox-reading prelate or professor tries to get you to rethink your "medieval" theology for the sake of something more "relevant." If he really has read Cox, if he is not just a naive young man who has been swept along by the intellectual fads of the season, fads from which he would have been rescued by ecclesiastical discipline not that long ago; if he has come to grips with Cox's assertion that the Christian Faith as we know it is standing in the way of mankind's progress, that "we have nothing to lose"—then he deserves to be treated to the biggest horselaugh we can work up, or even the threat of some righteous violence, if he persists in preaching his heresy to the young in our name, and Christ's. Would that lead too many of our young clerics into open rebellion? Deplete the already decreasing number of Christians? If that is the case—*we* have nothing to lose.

Neither Moth Nor Rust

It is fortunate that we do not have to rely on our own ratiocinative powers to answer the challenge of the liberation theologians. The anger, and even contempt, that a Christian might, legitimately, feel toward the work of a Cox or Gutierrez should not spring from a belief that they are mean-spirited or lacking in idealism. They are nothing of the sort. They have done nothing worse than succumb to the greatest of the 20th-century temptations: the sin of Adam, to be as God, to construct a man-centered utopia independent of a personal God. Once they accepted the full implications of their God-is-dead theology it was a

---

[8] *Ibid.*, p. 196.

near-inevitable step; perhaps the only possible step for a man of honor once he dispels from his mind the thought of God. In a real sense, they deserve praise for not succumbing to what might have been an equally attractive alternative: the shallow hedonism of the Playboy philosophy. Probably, the Marxist revolutionaries of the world present a far more serious threat to Christianity than the urban swingers, but it is difficult not to feel a greater respect for, yes, even machete-wielding Tupamaros than the alternately cloying and bombastic shells of men who take their Playboy philosophy seriously (as opposed to those—bear with me, I have someone in mind—who finds those plastic and pseudo-leathery dives a nice place to stop for a drink after a show). As the 20th century works its way to the close, it becomes strikingly clear that only Marxism and religion (Christianity in the West) offer fitting receptacles for human aspirations and idealism; and the people worth thinking about will take one or the other route. The rest will be bystanders. At least the Marxists are trying.

But while it is possible to respect and understand the Marxist enemies (know why we must be willing to steel ourselves to kill them, would be one way of saying it), we must not let that understanding of their motives cause us to forget how incompatible with ours are their plans for the world. Trying to make Christ compatible with them is an impossible task, as those who know Christ, and Marx, are aware; it is a barefaced lie when proposed by a knowledgeable thinker. Whatever one would say about the Marxist promise, it is not Christ's. The liberation theologians know that. It is why they, unlike other updaters, do not try to use out-of-context quotations from Scripture to make their case. One searches in vain for Biblical verification for their Marxist claims. Which is not intended as a derogation. At least they are honest (in that respect). They think that Christ had a problem in seeing how his intuitive grasp of the importance of brotherly love could be applied to the human experience in the most fruitful way. Marx, you'll remember, did not get down to brass tacks on these matters until eighteen hundred or so years later. But if Christ had read *Das Kapital*, of course, and if he were able to rise above the Platonism of his time, then he would have been a liberation theologian too. Then he would not have been so naive as to say all those things about a world beyond that could be taken and distilled by the ruling classes into an opiate of the people. He would never have said:

> · Verily I say unto you, There is no man that hath left house, or brethren, or sisters, or father, or mother, or wife, or children, or lands, for my sake, and the gospel's,
> But he shall receive an hundredfold now in this time, houses, and brethren, and sisters, and mothers, and children, and lands, with persecutions; and *in the world to come eternal life*.
> But many that are first shall be last; and the last first. (Mk. 10:29-31)

178

He would never have stressed such an extrahistorical reward as eternal life, and certainly not the obligation to sacrifice earthly fulfillment—which to the liberation theologians is the highest good—in order to achieve this reward from a Father in heaven.*

Neither would he have stressed the need to be willing to forsake earthly achievement, as he constantly does, up to and including social justice:

> Whosoever will come after me, let him deny himself, and take up his cross, and follow me.
> For whosoever will save his life shall lose it; but whosoever shall lose his life for my sake and the gospel's, the same shall save it.
> For what shall it profit a man, if he shall gain the whole world, and lose his own soul? (Mk. 8:34-37)

Nor would he have instructed his followers to disregard dreams of hominisation and conscientization:

> Lay not up for yourselves treasures upon earth, where moth and rust doth corrupt, and where thieves break through and steal;
> But lay up for yourselves treasures in heaven, where neither moth nor rust doth corrupt [not even Teilhard thought his noosphere would take care of this problem; neither did St. Karl] and where thieves do not break through and steal . . . Therefore I say unto you, Take no thought for your life, what ye shall eat, or what ye shall drink; nor yet for your body, what ye shall put on. (Mt. 6:19-25)

At the risk of letting my Catholicism come on too strong for my Protestant readers, let me take note of the fact that there is so much in the institutional life of the Catholic Church that the updaters have to be willing to tear down to push their case. Monasteries, the Eucharist, novenas, prayers in petition, clerical vows of poverty and chastity, sacrifice in general—all become absurd in the updater scheme. Gutierrez can only rise in influence by walking over the memory of St. Theresa, St. Thomas More, St. Stephen, St. Ignatius, St. Martin de Porres, the Cure of Ars, St. Francis Xavier, the North American Martyrs, etc., etc.

Some day soon, Dr. Cox and Father Gutierrez will have to face up to the inconsistency of their case; although sometimes I think that it will be the orthodox Marxists who will have the resolve to push them to the wall before Christians do. But someone will point out to them that Marx was no fool. He

---

*Naturally, all the words of Christ I list in this chapter have to be considered in the corroborative light of Christ's references to the Father and life with Him in heaven, cited earlier.

179

knew what he was saying. He knew the danger Christ posed to his dreams. Christ deserves Marx's wrath. How can Christ be made acceptable to those seeking to expand and project their human powers until the world becomes communized, to those who seek "fuller consciousness, the joy, the maturation, and emancipation of man?" You cannot serve two masters, and that kind of emancipation is not preached by the Rabbi who wants us to take up a cross, to turn the other cheek, to remember that:

> Ye know that they which are accounted to rule over the Gentiles exercise lordship over them; and their great ones exercise authority upon them.
> But so shall it not be among you; but whosoever will be great among you, shall be your minister:
> And whosoever of you will be the chiefest, shall be servant of all.
> For even the Son of man came not to be ministered unto, but to minister, and to give his life a ransom for many. (Mk. 10:42-45)

And please, updater brothers, that was not a reference to giving one's life for the "cause" *à la* Che. We are not to give our lives for emancipation, or liberation, or the fulfillment of material and psychic needs:

> Blessed be ye poor: for yours is the kingdom of God.
> Blessed are ye that hunger now: for ye shall be filled.
> Blessed are ye that weep now: for ye shall laugh.
> Blessed are ye, when men shall hate you, and when they shall separate you from their company, and shall reproach you, and cast out your name as evil, for the Son of man's sake.
> Rejoice ye in that day, and leap for joy: for behold your reward is great *in heaven*; for in like manner did their fathers unto the prophets.
> But woe unto you that are rich! for ye have received your consolation. [Of course the Marxists like to stress this warning to the ruling classes. But the point is that Christ's words are as condemnatory of their earthly paradise as they are of the rich man's. The Marxists only offer to make us all as out of kilter as the self-centered rich.]
> Woe unto you that are full! for ye shall hunger. Woe unto you that laugh now! for ye shall mourn and weep.
> Woe unto you, when all men shall speak well of you! for so did their fathers to the false prophets.
> But I say unto you which hear, Love your enemies, do good to them which hate you.
> Bless them that curse you, and pray for them which despitefully use you. [Now does that sound like the revolution of the proletariat?]
> And unto him that smiteth thee on the one cheek offer also the other; and him that taketh away thy cloak forbid not to take thy coat also. (Luke 6:20-29)

It is so obvious—need it be said? Christ is recommending what Christians for centuries have told us he meant—what our fathers knew all along. That we were not made for this world; that we must be ready to be the fools of God—by the standards of this world—in anticipation of the rewards of a kingdom beyond. To talk of a man-created and perfected "intrahistorical" kingdom is to shamelessly distort his words.

That was why our Lord made a point of telling his Apostles of his refusal to accept the kingdoms of the world offered to Him by their master—Satan.

That was why he warned Peter about the impropriety of taking up arms against the soldiers sent to arrest him; why he showed his willingness to die to this world rather than struggle to save, emancipate and liberate himself with the aid of the legions of angels his Father could have sent to defend him; and would have sent, if his Kingdom were of this world.

That was why we were to reject worldly wisdom and sacrifice all the material comforts the Marxists offer. That was why we should turn the cheek and give away cloak and coat rather than rise up in wrath to gain them for all. Those things, well, just don't matter in comparison to the bigger things: "Rejoice, because your names are written in heaven." (Luke 10:20)

The greatest of earthly tribulations can be endured with that promise in mind: they do not last forever, whereas the flames of hell do.

That was why we should prefer to lose an arm or pluck out an eye than sin and risk an eternity of damnation. Why we should not fear those who can kill only the body, as much as the sins that destroy "both body and soul in hell."

The Sadducees scoffed a bit. They found such talk as unassuring as our updaters do. But that led them to ask the question that forced Christ to make almost kindergarten-simple his insistence that he was talking about a life after death and not a perfected intrahistorical human achievement; for which we should be thankful.

> Then came unto him the Sadducees, which say there is no resurrection; and they asked him, saying,
> Master, Moses wrote unto us, If a man's brother die, and leave his wife behind him, and leave no children, that his brother should take his wife, and raise up seed unto his brother.
> Now there were seven brethren: and the first took a wife, and dying left no seed.
> And the second took her, and died, neither left he any seed: and the third likewise.
> And the seven had her, and left no seed: last of all the woman died also.
> In the resurrection therefore, when they shall rise, whose wife shall she be of them? for the seven had her to wife.
> And Jesus answering said unto them, Do ye not therefore err, because ye know not the Scriptures, neither the power of God?

For when they shall rise from the dead, they neither marry, nor are given in marriage; but are as the angels which are in heaven.

And as touching the dead, that they rise: have ye not read in the book of Moses, how in the bush God spake unto him, saying, I *am* the God of Abraham, and the God of Isaac, and the God of Jacob?

He is not the God of the dead, but the God of the living: ye therefore do greatly err. (Mk. 12:18-27)

Can we ask our Lord to be any more specific? His words give the lie to the best of the liberation theologians. We will personally be resurrected from the dead to live again, "as the angels do," this time in an eternal life with the Father, as will Abraham, Isaac, and Jacob. Our lives will be transformed miraculously in a way beyond the powers of man. Marriage itself will take on meaning beyond the comprehension of our earthly minds. The human brotherhood will be perfected through a divine transformation to a level we cannot imagine.

The liberation theologians want us to exchange that for the pipe dreams of some hopped-up cigar-smoking dictator. Some liberation.

Chapter XI

This Is America

IT MIGHT SEEM disoriented to say it, but nevertheless, the greatest danger in refusing to accept the time-hallowed Christian understanding of man and his eternal destiny is *not* the likelihood that the Marxists will dominate the world —although that certainly will be bad enough. The far greater danger is that we will not share in that eternal destiny with Christ; that we will allow Modernist reservations to so fill our hearts that we will withdraw from our responsibility to construct a social order sufficiently healthy to help us overcome our lusts: to save our souls. We appear to be on the border of bowing to the *Deep Throat*, abortion-mill America that will drag us—certainly our children —to the depths of decadence. Perhaps we are there now. But we must face up to what we are doing to ourselves when we refuse to accept Christ, and because we act out that refusal.

Not only that—we must also understand that this heartless refusal is likely to drive our children mad, in a quite literal sense, during their stay on earth. The jarring clash between a young mind reared in a Christian home and the dominant pagan ethos will wreck all but the hardiest of them. Living on as a Christian remnant is a pipe dream, if that dream includes our loved ones joining us in the ranks of the sturdy Christian outcasts. As a matter of fact, if we haven't developed a remarkable inner resolve ourselves, thanks to the "unbought grace" of having been raised in a society still touched by Christian love, we just might not end up a part of that remnant either.

The liberal-relativist drive to lead us into a social order without a clear vision of its own purpose and direction beyond that of the free exchange of ideas—the open society—has been such a prominent part of America's social and political development in our lifetimes that we tend to forget how novel and truly untested is the idea. The thought has been with us since the Enlightenment—since the Sophists tried to raise Socrates' consciousness, as a matter of fact. But the *philosophes* did not have to face up to the consequences of their ideas. It was easier to be willing to defend to the death the right of one man to voice his disagreement with another (and nothing else) in a world thoroughly shaped and formed by over a thousand years of Christendom than it is in ours. How would Voltaire react to the so-called "snuff" movies, the ultimate porn films in which the heroine, after a bout of sado-masochism, is executed and dismembered for the titillation of the audience? The word is that for $300 a throw one can see such a spectacle in certain New York circles. Perhaps the *philosophes* can be forgiven their error in pushing the anti-Christian idea of the "naturally good man." They lived in a world where Christianity, after centuries of self-application, had worked its way into the recesses of men's minds. Men imbued with those "unbought graces" of Burke's probably did give the impression that they could be trusted to do their thing. It might really have appeared that it would be gentle and kind and pious and far, far, better things they would do once the priests and nobles were put in their place.

We know better now. All but the most frivolous of modern thinkers tell us it just isn't so. Even the liberal descendants of the *philosophes*. They no longer pretend that liberally educated minds will construct a civilized consensus on the beautiful and virtuous in life. I have the feeling they finally conceded that —quietly, it is true—after their liberally educated offspring dumped a fresh bucket of human feces on the head of James Reston of *The New York Times* during a seminar on the war in Vietnam at New York University. They don't even make a healthy pass at the idea anymore. Not that they are turning to Christ. The new consensus is that there should be no consensus. Do your thing, even if it is watching films of bestiality in Times Square, sniffing cocaine, or clapping your hands in time with Mick Jagger's ministrations to a twenty-foot rubber phallus. What is truth? The liberals know: mere opinion, a social convenience. And now our clerical updaters are working to remove the last vestige of reasoned opposition to that fetid nihilism. They are chipping away at the Nazarene colossus whose words once hung menacingly over the self-inflicted social disarray: "I am the Way, the Truth, and the Life." No more. Now, we are told, he has to be taken in context.

But imagine what a citizenry convinced that Christ was who He said He was could do in a country like ours. Imagine how we would approach the squalor if we still had faith in our hearts, instead of the Modernist doubts which cause us to tremble and flinch at the trigger every time we get the passing urge to stand up and shout No to our "evolving consciousness." Imagine. "No, you can't show that filth in our neighborhood." "No, you can't kill another infant in our hospitals." Why? Because such things are evil and unworthy of our country. How do we know? "Easy, pal. God told us." If only we believed we could take Him at His word when he warned that "evil thoughts, adulteries, fornications, theft, covetousness, wickedness, deceits, lasciviousness, evil eye, blasphemy, pride" are the things that corrupt a man. If only we still feared His judgement.

Plato told us that the well ordered state should mirror the well ordered man. Just as reason ought to rule the base instincts in an individual, a well constructed government ought to enforce and maintain the highest standards of justice of its wisest and most virtuous citizens; their understanding of honor and decency institutionalized into law to set the proper level of aspiration and expectation for the rest. America in our time verifies his insight, with a little reverse English. By making the denial of norms for human behavior the most perceptive expression of the best educated minds—liberal open-mindedness—our social order drives men mad. How long will it be before we all receive at birth a therapist on government assignment? This denial of truth from the highest circles of government and academic life has given us a world without purpose, a disoriented, ever more morally centrifugalized, frenetic, pleasure-seeking madhouse. It won't be long before R.D. Laing will be right.

These are not easy things for me to say. I have been called a superpatriot more than once. Yet there are signs that the American social and political premise has come unhinged. Perhaps because of circumstances unforeseen by our Founding Fathers. Perhaps because a "dirty trick" of sorts was played on the system, by perpetrators who knew full well what they were doing. Perhaps because we failed to grasp the premise under which our Founding Fathers worked: that their system would have been able to handle the challenges of modern America if we had understood its unspoken assumptions. Whatever . . . we have come to see that freedom and liberty just aren't enough; that a country cannot be lovable and worthy of our support—all the classroom posters and war slogans to the contrary—simply because it allows for the widest freedom of choice imaginable. We have had those words, quite perceptively I might add, turned against us. "Freedom of choice." "Do your thing, man." Dope, free and kinky sex, homosexuals, abortion, Marxism in junior high—was that what Jefferson was all about? Are those the inalienable rights? Liberty? For that high school teacher in New York who developed a course that featured the latest in porn movies? Why not?

185

It is becoming clear that what Jefferson—Thomas Paine, too?—were talking about, whether they realized it or not, was freedom for the civilized, self-disciplined man of the West who had made the inner checks upon will and appetite a part of his consciousness: the good Christian. We are also beginning to intuit—slowly and darkly—that without that self-control a man cannot be trusted with freedom. As we find ourselves repelled by the coarse and menacing atmosphere of modern life, the thought begins to haunt (I say this carefully) that even life under an American Castro or Mao would be preferable to the Times Squaring of our country. Could there be people hoping to teach us that? The leftwing freaks who carry Mao's *Little Red Book* and march off to Cuba to cut sugar cane under the sweaty and baleful stare of a Marxist overseer are the prophets. They *have* seen and lived the moral disorder of a democracy without purpose. They know its horrors, and have opted for discipline. We have allowed their contemporaries to build a hell, the college campuses filled with drugs and progressive sex (even a rape or two for spice), because of our self-doubts about Christ. "Who are we to tell them how to live their lives?" "How can we act arbitrarily in the name of our bourgeois standards?" No one thought of bringing in Christ. After all, this is America. So they pick Fidel instead.

When this modern permissiveness is considered in perspective, it boggles the mind. Eighteen-year-olds being sent away from home for the first time by their own parents to live in a cluster of buildings filled with booze, drugs and "creative" sex, and New Left professors as dormitory advisors. We *paid* to send them there, and then we brood about their turning away from us. Occasions of sin? We purchased them for our children. Lead us not into temptation?

But perhaps, we might say, God will not be too demanding on an eighteen-year-old who gives in after living for years with all that going on in the room next door. It could be. I've talked to those vacant-eyed, frizzy-haired, drug-aficionado, rock-poetry-spouting cretins. Maybe they are beyond morality. "It's what's happenin', man." "Outta sight." "Outrageous, man." But what of those of us who, at the very least, did nothing to prevent the establishment of *public* places within our societal life for the inculcation and promulgation of their suicidal hedonism? Do they still make millstones?

I include myself. Perhaps that is what feeds the fires of my anger. The relativist surrender has wormed its way around the periphery of my consciousness too—like a borer infecting and rotting away the vitality of the fibers of a tree. Let me give you an example. Just a while back, I was walking to my classroom in the suburban high school where I teach a course the Deweyite nominalists in the New York State Department of Education still, for some reason, allow to be called Western Civilization. I was passing through the tinny clatter of a hall full of students at their lockers (not an unpleasant sound, by the

186

way) to open the room for the first of the morning's classes—7:30 A.M. Outside the door to my room was a young and preciously fresh fifteen-year-old student of mine, draped around one of those moronic hairy gorillas young teenaged girls (why? why?—and don't give me any behaviorist drivel in answer) seem drawn to: the same kind of gas-pumping, toothless oafs they will ridicule heartlessly in only three or so years. Now, I hardly ever go to the movies these days, except for the Walt Disney festival the neighborhood drive-in features in the summer. I don't think I have ever seen an X-rated movie—except for *Midnight Cowboy* (does that count?). So I don't really know how explicit things are these days on the silver screen. But that girl was treating the gorilla to a contorted and graphic embrace the likes of which I have never seen in a movie. I would be more explicit, but what I have been told is an Irish Jansenist streak holds me back. The hall was filled with other students who seemed to notice the scene not at all—I like to think because of embarrassment rather than inurement. At least that was what led me to divert my gaze at first. After all, I had to teach the precious young thing a class on the Middle Ages in about ten minutes, and it is not easy to analyze chivalry for what you think is another Happy Hooker.

In addition, at least four or five teachers had passed them already, and said nothing. I struggled to overcome my embarrassment. Memories floated to mind of the days I worked as a parking-lot attendant in a country club where one of my duties was to shine my flashlight into cars to break up couples who "were making the place look like a cat house," as the manager used to put it. But I paused. I began to think of the fact that in this school, the teachers kid the students in the faculty room about "getting it on with" each other, help students with birth-control information, act as abortion referral agents, and live and dress the counterculture sex life themselves. I know all that, and so do the kids. We must remember that we live in a world where teachers—who mirror the trends in the more liberal segments of our society (the younger teachers, anyway)—are likely to come to their students after constant exposure to the kind of reading and film experience that we Christians were told would lead to an unhealthy lack of moral balance on the question of sex. They are likely to have read one of the explicit sex manuals the night before, or gone to see *The Devil in Miss Jones*, and thoroughly immersed themselves in these images and thoughts (which were available only with great difficulty from the dregs of society just a few years back). And they get these pleasures on a regular basis, not occasionally and secretly from vermin who sell them in the back of a candy store. It is part of a lifestyle, and discussed openly.

What could I say—have you no shame? But why should they? They were not acting out of the ordinary as much as I would be if I made a big deal about their "show of affection"—as they say in health class. And to think that only a few years back they were arguing in the schools about whether to enforce rules about students not holding hands in the halls! They decided to ease up on that rule at about the same time that dress codes were declared illegal. I can remember hearing teachers encourage their students to break the dress codes before the kids had learned of the court's decision. The resulting dissolution into vulgarity in both areas serves as another example of liberalism's naturally good man in operation.

My rage was quieted. Who was I to make the moral judgement that a young girl should not be used by a sullen punk to get his early morning jollies? My anger was turned to a whimper by the lessons of liberal America. How could I force my knowledge of Christ's warning about irresponsible lust onto these young minds? Hell, I know as much about different drummers as anyone. What *right* did I have to tell them about Christ? This is America, isn't it? And aren't they students in a school where they can learn about contraceptive devices "to stay out of trouble" when they "get it on with" each other? But I could not tell them, because of its sectarian origin, to "sin no more."

What did I do? I grumbled my grumbliest "Come on, now. What do you think this is?" It was fortunate that they didn't ask me to tell them. The gorilla smiled tolerantly. He knew me. I had taught him the rudiments of Western Civilization a couple of years back. "Okay, okay," he said calmly. He would amuse me. He patted his lady's bottom, said he would see her later, and then bid me adieu. "Take it easy, Mr. Fitz." Nice boy. He wasn't going to hold it against me.

We have come far, haven't we? How mutually understanding we are of each other's preferences. If that had been my daughter I would have wrung her goon's neck. But the point is, that girl was somebody's daughter. And the public institution that poor soul supports with his hard-earned tax dollars is providing a setting in which she is being turned into a slut. Don't tell me that the school mirrors the society, that he might not be as likely to get angered by such a scene as I. If Charles Manson had a daughter he would not let her be manhandled in public and in broad daylight like that. But this is America. We can't impose our hangups on anyone else—not Christian "hangups," anyway. Freud's and B.F. Skinner's and Bella Abzug's, they're okay.

Now, it is true, teenage sex didn't start in the late sixties. Even Archie Andrews used to leave Veronica's house wild-eyed, smeared in lipstick, and with his tie twisted back to the nape of his neck. But that was only when Veronica's old man was out to the country club. And Archie was aware of the fact that he was being naughty. He knew that the joys of sex came legitimately only to those who had accepted the God-assigned responsibilities for which those pleasures are a reward. Archie was irresponsible enough to want a little of that pleasure before his time, but he, and the reader, were aware of the societal lessons about the nature of sex. It was made clear that his parents, her parents, the dumb local cop, the scatterbrained principal and Miss Grump—civilization—would not approve of their irresponsibility, their misbehavior.

Now our schools and our society help the Archies of the world overcome their hangups about sex while at the same time scolding the Miss Grumps for wanting to perpetuate their Christian narrowness. This is America and not the (Christian) Middle Ages, they tell us. We don't take those things—Christ's things—seriously anymore. We have read Freud and Reich and Levi-Strauss. No more hangups. (Did I call permissiveness the counterculture? Let's be honest. It *is* the culture. Christianity, understood in an orthodox way, is the counterculture now. It is the Christian insight that is considered an illegitimate ingredient in the schools; a violation of our precious separation of Church and state. But the anti-Christian ideas of the secular humanists and Marxists are advanced, enlightened, and *impartial* they tell us—as if we should be thankful for such an institutionalization of unbelief. In this once Christian country, Marcuse can be taught enthusiastically, where Jesus Christ cannot.)

The Decline of the Christian

How did we come to such a state of affairs? Certainly if an intelligent Martian were to study our society like a modern de Tocqueville, he would be unable to accept that the deeply held convictions of a substantial majority of a society could be made taboo in their schools, the institutions set up for the purpose of training the young. How?

We could blame the First Amendment—from which the "wall of separation" of Church and State was deduced. Perhaps it was inevitable that the religious neutrality so cherished by our Founding Fathers (which, as honest students of colonial America admit now, was understood to be freedom *for* whatever version of *Christianity* was practiced by the early American communities) would lead to a gradual deterioration of the Christian consensus, as groups with *no* religion at all demanded the right to enjoy their atheism without the constant irritation of being reminded that their fellow citizens were believers; to be as free from Christian influence as, say, Catholics were from Presbyterian influence, and vice versa. Perhaps that demand was impossible to stop with the no-establishment clause in the Constitution—the demand for equal treatment of non-religion with religion, as well as one Christian religion with another. There probably is something to all that.

But it does, I think, miss the point at least partially. We lived on as a Christian people—even if unofficially—for nearly two hundred years with that clause in our Constitution. It wasn't until we began to waver in the Faith that we allowed the anti-Christians in our midst to tell us that the Constitution meant such a silly thing, so different from what it meant to the Founding Fathers themselves. They weren't selling *The Story of "O"* in Massachusetts in 1790, or any version of it; not openly, at any rate. And nobody at the Constitutional Convention complained of that sectarian censorship. Only after the liberal atheists had gnawed away successfully at our convictions did we allow the absurdity of outlawing prayer in our schools, while at the same time legalizing porn in the movies. A society has to go mad to do that, and Constitutional phraseology neither causes nor arrests that slide into the abyss. It requires a loss of faith.

There are those who gloat over this disintegration of the Christian consciousness. But we shouldn't really complain. From their smug descriptions of how they have turned America around from its "puritanical" bases we learn of the nature of the attack on Christian America. They assure us that it is not paranoia that grips us every time we turn on our televisions, or read the movie reviews, or look at our children's school yearbooks, or listen to the words of the rock music poured into their minds round the clock, tearing down in an afternoon with the verve of Attila the Hun all the disciplines it took the West two thousand years to make its own. It is hardly paranoia. We are under a well coordinated seige led by people who champion the dark temptations, the coarse and sordid pleasures our people through the ages have tried to contain. And the enemy has secured the one weapon missing from his arsenal, traitors at the drawbridge: our updating clergy. But they might not get to us if we can put the traitors to flight. The fortress is old and durable, and has held out the forces of darkness for centuries.

The anti-Christian forces at work in America, it is true, think it too late for us to shore up our defenses. Only that confidence could have led Peter Schrag to write for public consumption a book like *The Decline of the Wasp*, and for the media masters to review it favorably. Although Schrag did have some lingering doubts, like a fighter measuring his opponent for the knockout punch, moving forward slowly, looking for signs of life from the bleeding hulk before him. In his introduction he notes that people are likely to ask, "Who is this guy, anyway. Where did he come from? What's his *schtick*?"

He tells us of the source of his *schtick* in short order, about the kind of WASP that is declining, and why he should be helped on his way.

> The heir of Daniel Boone and Davy Crockett, Honest Abe and General Lee, the builder, tinkerer, woodsman, cowboy, athlete. The muscular Christian (without knowing it); [without *saying* it, would be more accurate; but let us hold off on that. It is an important point which must be treated carefully] the Lone Ranger, Jack Armstrong, Captain Midnight, frank yet cautious, shrewd yet credulous, positive yet skeptical, confident yet shy . . . a mixture of "history," mythology and fact.

Schrag quotes William Dean Howells in a blend of scorn, ridicule, and incredulity. Did these WASPs really imagine themselves to be a country filled with young people who lived by a noble code which

> was everywhere the same, and it was one which mirrored faithfully enough the code of the adult world. Every boy was mischievous, but few were vicious; the bully, the thief, the liar, the sneak were ostracized . . . Everybody had his own high sense of honor and enforced it. He was brave, stood up for himself, fought for his rights and fought fairly, learned to take a dare and a risk, scorned a coward, a tattletale; a sissy, and a skulker. He was gregarious, played in gangs, was loyal to his playmates, and rarely cherished enmities. He was chivalrous toward women, respectful to grownups, indifferent toward girls until adolescence, and then romanticized them.

As you might expect, Schrag scoffs:

> Our boy. It is hard to find a better description of how the official American wanted his kids to grow up, or how he likes to think of his own childhood. The selective memory, part Boy Scout manual, part English boarding school, part fiction.

Schrag goes on to list the writers and magazines that championed the virtues of this Boy Scout image of life, including "*National Geographic*, which made bare teats acceptable in a mainstream magazine by photographing them only on black women."

This is a revealing sentence, a key to what makes Schrag so despise this WASP of his. It is not their physical features or pale skin. He swings from the hip at the "clean cut" self-image of the WASP, it is true; but he has more than physiognomy in mind. What he cannot stand, or understand, is the WASP reverence for themselves and the values they expect to find in each other. He thinks it hypocritical that they would not be scandalized by the sight of a naked jungle woman; sees it as racism. He cannot grasp the understanding Christians have; that they expect something rarefied from each other *because* they are Christian. It isn't race that informs these distinctions. The *National Geographic* readers *would have* been shocked and would have protested if a black singer in a Southern Baptist church had been shown with her white robe pulled from her shoulders—back then, anyway. Now we are not even shocked—at least we do not show it because of our enervated will—that we have to pass *Penthouse*'s scenes of raw porn as we reach for our Sunday paper.

Schrag's wisdom? Why be hypocrites? Why don't we phony Christians ease up and begin to view our women with the lowered expectations we display toward the jungle primitives? Let it all hang out. Stop imposing that Christian sense of decency on ourselves and our national life.

Since we won't stop, at least not fast enough, the Jack Armstrongs and Lone Rangers of the American consciousness earn his derision. Through them, we are scolded for aspiring to a vision of life that is Christian in origin. Schrag will only feel at home in this country when that kind of WASP has been put in his place. We cannot become any less fair-skinned—those who are—or sturdily built (which really bothers him for some reason) to allow him to feel more at home; but we can become less Christian. The Christian temperament can be beaten beyond recognition, smothered with ridicule and shame in the name of liberal open-mindedness, until a new American will rise into view. And, Schrag beams, that new model is finally catching on. America in general has begun to ridicule purity, piety and national honor as much as he does:

> The vacuum left by the old arbiters of the single standard . . . has produced a sort of cultural prison break. And not only among ethnics, blacks or Indians, or among kids, but among a lot of others, including WASPs of all descriptions, who behave as if they have been waiting for this *freedom* [my emphasis] all their lives . . . gurus, cultists, swamis, and T-group trainers hung out their shingles. Look at any issue of *The Village Voice* or the *Berkeley Barb* and you feel as if you're in a carnival where the straightest people are rock musicians . . . liberation schools and free universities, Norman Mailer's ego and Alexander Portnoy's mother, *The Graduate* and *Alice's Restaurant* and *Easy Rider*, the Woodstock Nation and the friends of the Panthers, rebellious nuns and protesting priests, *Rat* and *Screw* and a few hundred other underground papers, mixed-media shows and the Living Theater, bookstores of the occult, tarot cards and freaks and hipsters . . . poster art . . the face of John Lennon, the bodies of John and Yoko, the pregnant Girl Scout over the motto "Be Prepared," the pregnant black woman over the slogan "Nixon's the One," and copulating rhinoceroses with the injunction "Make Love Not War" . . . Sex is no longer that grim act of aggression . . . It is no longer hedged with puritanical restraint [read: chivalry] . . . sometimes the cultural offense is calculated: filth becomes a premeditated reproach against the establishment, and tight-assed sanitation politics is met with anal freedom of expression.

Put that in your pipe, America. Free at last, thank God. Free at last.

Schrag makes much of the rise in power and influence of secularized liberal Jews, the vector of our paganized society from which he comes; which was concurrent with the decline of the WASP. Concurrent with, a result of; and a cause. It must be stressed, however, that he is not talking of Jews *as Jews*—nor do I—except to the extent that it *was* easier and perhaps more likely to develop a liberalized contempt for Christian America if you were never a part of it. The people Schrag talks about rising to the surface in the de-Christianized America (and that includes Schrag) are the agnostic Jews who have rejected the religious convictions of their own people but have refused to be drawn into the Christian ethos of America as an alternative; and who work now to create a God-less America where their norms will become a new orthodoxy of sorts. The American public schools, again, are a good example. The secular humanist, internationalist, and agnostic curriculum of today, the textbooks published in the urban centers especially, are the mirror image of the kinds of lessons the secular liberals would want taught if they had hired a private tutor for their children. The "public" schools are *their* private schools.

The question of anti-Semitism has no place here, and Christians should stand firm against the treacherous and gimmicky ploy which makes us fear that our anger against these inroads is rooted in such a base emotion. Jews serious about the Torah prefer a healthy Christian America, the foundations of which would be in the Torah, to the *Deep Throat,* abortion-mill society being pushed on us by their lost sheep as well as our own. But let Schrag say it:

> If the students did not learn that lesson [the emptiness of the traditional American view of life] from their own experience, they could not have helped learning it from Paul Goodman, David Riesman, Edgar Friedenberg or any number of the other social critics who now form the basis of the intellectual self-definition in American life . . . in the last twenty years a lot of people other than Jews were Semitized [read: made alien-minded secularists at odds with the Christian values of America], became, in one way or another, immigrants to those places and states of mind which Jews had inhabited for centuries. What we learned was that Jewishness [sorry, he means—whether he knows it or not—a refusal to respect Christian America], is in itself a place, a nation more permanent than Abbie Hoffman's Woodstock . . . To become a Jew in America meant growing up with the belief that they were out to screw you. It is, therefore, easy to translate the goys into "the system" or "the establishment" and even easier to transfer your loyalties *from* the nation of Jews [my emphasis] to the nation of Woodstock.
>
> The point is that Jewishness has become fashionable. In New York, which is where the soapboxes are kept, it is the goy and not the Jew (or the Negro) who feels defensive. Half the major book publishers are Jewish and probably more than half the art dealers, the music managers . . . and the senior brass of network television.

Schrag makes a strained attempt to connect the Catholic ethnic minorities, the Irish, Italian, and Slavic experience, to his story; but unsuccessfully. His impatience with WASP America is just not part of their consciousness—at least not in the same way. It was only when the WASP establishment began acting *less* Christian that they chafed at their bits, in contrast to Schrag, who sees his best hope in that devolution. The fact that Victor McLaglen played hard-drinking and dumb sergeants to John Wayne's WASP commanders, for example, bothered Irish Americans not a bit. The ethnic minorities could see themselves as John Wayne and Randolph Scott as well—when they behaved at their best, anyway.

The Duke's values—when Hollywood was healthier, at any rate—were those of the Catholic ethnics. Christian America championed a way of life that made them feel at home. Becoming as brave, truthful, and bold in defense of the innocent—as *clean-cut*—as Alan Ladd's *Shane* was not for the ethnics a sellout to the WASP.

Those clean-cut Hollywood heroes of old posed a problem only to those who felt themselves at odds with the American moral consciousness they represented. Never mind that we didn't live up to the highest of those ideals. Who does? It only bedevils when people who claimed to be good Christians didn't make it—killed Indians, at times, with shameful abandon, or lynched blacks—if you are contemptuous because their faith teaches principles contrary to your own. Can anyone seriously believe that if most Americans were Marxists, or Hindus, or Zoroastrians, or Jews, that Indians would not have been killed or blacks lynched? Why have the Russian Marxists killed and tortured, when they champion the secularist ideals so precious to the Schrags of the world? It is just another con job—but the kind we keep falling for. You know: we bombed Hiroshima because we were Christians, and the only hope for progress and refinement is a loss of our convictions.

Schrag needles us with the rise of Elliot Gould and Dustin Hoffman as substitutes for the John Wayne type of actor; but, he tells us, it is an indication that our young are beginning to see the light—to find admirable the anti-hero who faces a corrupt, hypocritical, narrow-minded and crass America, and prefers an agnostic, existential self-doubt to blustering patriotism and phony Christianity. He is quite right. The fact that Hollywood heroes of this sort are rising in our eyes is an indication of the extent to which we are moving from our Christian moorings. Compare the wheedling, cloying, irreverent Elliot Gould-type hero to the Lochinvars of old, perhaps best portrayed in the scene from the Gary Cooper movie—was it *Mr. Deeds Goes to Town*? Cooper plays a small-town, "clean-cut" American who has come to the big city for some reason which I cannot recall. As he sits uncomfortably in a Manhattan restaurant with a young and perky urbanite woman and a cosmopolitan, pencil-mustachioed dandy, the dude begins to sense the girl's attraction to the simple, honest, unaffected, polite (Christian) manliness of Cooper. He begins to taunt him with the kind of bitchy verbal games the relativists seem to learn before anything else in college. He twists words, drops sly innuendo, and ridicules the small-town pieties of Cooper, then turns on the woman with harsh sarcasm because she is not laughing as uproariously at his cleverness as he thinks she should. Cooper grows silent and tense while our mustachioed friend chuckles with haughty disdain—until Coop sends him sprawling with a neat right cross.

Cooper has reacted shamefully, of course, by all modern standards. He acted

194

too confident, was *too* sure that he was right; refused to open his mind to the possibility that his understanding of what is honorable might not be all that infallible. He does not want to talk it out. Instead, he assumes that a knave must be put in his place; thinks it is not essential that the reasons for punitive and corrective action be demonstrated by the standards of rational discourse set on the isle of Manhattan. He fights with a knight's weapons instead of Oscar Wilde's. He accepts the notion that there are truths which are self-evident, and that men reared in the Christian West (in this case, west of the Mississippi) should be expected to know them; that gallantry and piety are on that list; that indecisiveness in defense of those truths is no virtue. (Of course we are building a straw man. The liberals agree to that. No compromise on busing, detente, women's lib. If you are not part of the solution, you are part of the problem. It is only Christian truths that you may not champion with vigor.)

Mr. Magoo

But that resolve is gone now. And we are paying the price. We cannot close a bordello or discipline a wayward child without fretting at our "rigidity." Interestingly enough, even those who have done so much to push us into indecisiveness are beginning to worry. They are crying out for help; but because we Christians are so timid (faithless), they run aimlessly instead to the Indian fakirs, TM gurus, drugs, sensitivity sessions, and suicide. Listen to the plaintive cry that seeps from between the lines of an article that appeared in *The New York Times* on October 5, 1975. A liberated, freethinking secular humanist, who has taught all those enlightened ideas to her daughter, now ruminates over the casual sex encounters that have become a regular part of the life of children her daughter's age. The article is entitled "Teenage Affairs." She starts, naturally, with the given, the pinnacle of modern worldly wisdom. Freud told us, she recalls, that

> infants have sexual desires and arrangements. Sex is natural in puberty, said clouds of psychiatrists that have rained across this country since World War II. From Holden Caulfield to Portnoy things have gotten wilder and wilder, funnier if not better. Masters and Johnson, the pill, legal abortion, breakdowns of parental authority, the women's movement have reduced the ideal of virginity, male and female, to the size of an appendix, a little organ without much of a future in the institution of human anatomy. But large social currents aside, it's still a difficult thing [but she is going to help us get over it] when your young daughter who leaves rings around the bathtub, her shoes on the couch, and soup on her algebra homework, turns out to be less of an innocent than you (hiding your copy of *Fear of Flying* under a stack of *National Geographics*) had thought.

195

What are we to do, she asks, now that our counterculture heroes have informed our children that the "sweetness of 16 (which was always a con) is gone forever." Now that our children have come to see that "there might be no reason now to say 'no' unless the reason is 'I don't want to,' and just such an assertion is hard for young people who may find themselves undressed and in bed with a stranger when they really wish they were home having milk and cookies with their brothers and sisters."

You see, there is a problem of communication that our culture has created. How can a mother help her daughter in this new age of freedom when "Mothers and daughters do not sit around and discuss what particular sexual positions please them. They each pretend that the other doesn't know anything about it"?

It is a problem, but our liberated author hopes to give the kind of motherly advice her daughter will need in the world of teenage affairs.

> If one of my daughters did tell me that she had begun an affair, I hope I'd be able to ask her if she really wanted to do this, was responding to clues from her own body [the highest truths, right?], not to pressure from her fellow or her friends. I hope I'd be able to tell her of the ways to delay the arrival of my grandchild . . . please, I would ask her, don't forget your work, your mind, your other activities . . . I would hope that, for her, the end of the affair would not be too destructive . . . I'd want her to remember that forever is mostly for fairy tales [and Christians who know that "There Are Such Things"]. I would tell her that sexual excitement and satisfaction grow with experience and that she should not be disappointed if the beginnings don't meet her expectations—that she should be patient with herself and her friend. [*Friend*. Oh for an Italian or a Kentucky father!]

But let's be fair. Our modern Mother Machree speaks of the complexity of the question. She concedes that she is sympathetic with the qualms of conscience that afflict a friend of hers, a headmaster at a private high school. He admits to widespread sexual liaisons on his campus, but prefers "to stumble about and bang my shins rather than see anything I don't know what to do about. I'm a Mr. Magoo on the subject," he says. Not that such a solution is entirely satisfactory. For "the more repressive voices [the Christian prescriptions of our society, to be exact] of his childhood," our liberated mother continues, "clang in his head, saying, 'It is not right, it's not right.' If he asks himself why it is not right, he may retreat into confusion [read: enlightened relativism]. 'I don't know,' he would say. 'Do you?' And I don't know either."

But while we have all been told that such enlightened open-mindedness would lead to happiness, something is wrong, even for our liberated mother. After giving her teenage daughter her mother's counsel—how to stop the babies and to be patient with her fellow—she says she thinks she might "go into my

196

own room, close my door, and weep for the child whose genitals I had once wiped and covered with powder.''

I think those lines are some of the most moving I have ever read. They almost make one forget that the woman who wrote them jokes about the fact that she leaves copies of trash like *Fear of Flying* around the house, and acknowledges that she has taught her child to have the morals of a (choosy) alley cat. Two thousand years of a shared Christian consciousness cry out—whether the woman wanted to be part of that consciousness or not. She lived with us. It rubbed off. She is hearing the Hound of Heaven baying far off in the night. She does know, if vaguely, of the beauty of innocence and purity. The thought that there is a divine order, and that the self-centered groping of *Fear of Flying* is not what she wants for her child, is churning beneath her consciousness. She is trying to fight it off in the name of all that is progressive and modern, but it is making ripples on the surface. She doesn't know it, but she wants a knight for her daughter, not a ''fellow.'' But that happy ending only comes in stories that include fair maidens. And you won't find them in *Fear of Flying*.

What do we Christians offer? Here come our booted and beaded updaters with their newly learned mantras and their junior college-level rehashing of situation ethics, existentialism and Herbert Marcuse. *Herbert Marcuse!* The toad who whipped up the satanic frenzy of Haight-Ashbury and Greenwich Village for us in the first place. Her daughter's fellow probably read a grimy quote from him to convince her that getting in the sack with him was a political act. Do they still make millstones?

Coming of Age in America

Where will it end for us? Is there hope for a revival of our Christian consciousness? Is the darkest night just before the dawn? Maybe. Certainly, if shock tactics work on a still-living body, what we see going on around us might be what it takes to convince us of the need for positive and corrective reinforcement to keep our civilization alive. That is, if we are still alive and still want the responsibility of preserving our civilization. Perhaps the drugs and porn will prove to be just what it takes to demonstrate that we cannot take for granted the unbought graces of Christendom, the legacy which allowed minds as fine as Voltaire's to gush so foolishly about the naturally good man. Perhaps if we seize the moment of cultural disarray we can begin the task of, first, returning the Christian atmosphere to our country, and then teaching our people the beauties and joys of that social reorganization—in contrast to the only other possible reorganization: the Marxist.

But the longer we wait, the more difficult it will be. The work of Walter

197

Bagehot, the 19th-century British economist and historian, sadly ignored of late in America, has much to teach us on this point.

Bagehot demonstrated convincingly what our common sense should have—but didn't, as usual. He argued, especially in his *Physics and Politics*, the uncomfortable (for liberals) conclusion that the social order of Western Europe was not a natural and spontaneously arrived-at condition, but a deliberately and forcibly created political union of peoples who would have preferred to be separate; the work of William the Conqueror, Hugh Capet, Bismarck, Lincoln, Ferdinand and Isabella, Ivan the Terrible, etc. Only after the experience of living together in this forced unity did the association become natural, a felt unity. From that felt unity, and only after it became solidly based, comes the possibility for what the world now calls civil liberties and political rights.* The felt unity generated a confidence. People no longer had to be *subjects*, they could be *citizens*, trusted to say and write pretty much what they pleased, since they could be presumed to have the best interests of the social order uppermost in mind. That was presumed to be true for all but the most unrepresentative of eccentrics, the bohemians of the Western world. Everyone else shared an understanding about what was decent, honorable, and fair. We could be expected to be good Christians since the Christian religion, expressed energetically and confidently, played a major part in forming the consciousness of that felt unity.

In our time, we seem to be hell-bent on demonstrating either that a) the felt unity of the Christian West was neither durable enough nor deep enough to live on without highly visible social and legal corroboration—that we were unable to stay Christian without *saying* it over and over, or that b) no people, because of man's blemished nature (original sin), can live without such reinforcement, and that the Enlightenment was a fit of intellectual presumption at best. Whichever, we are becoming less Christian with each passing day; proving that an America that holds no truths publicly will hold no truths at all.

It is this development that makes our updater's current posture so—ludicrous. Or sinister. Take your choice. The precious freedoms of liberalism depend on the self-disciplined citizen, the good Christian. But the updaters are no longer willing to reinforce the internal convictions and disciplines which will permit us to live free from disciplines from without—even though there is a seriously proposed discipline from without, Marxism, singing a siren's song. Quite a coincidence—the result of amazing naivete or bone-chilling cunning. Take your choice.

The longer Christians wait, then, to assert themselves, the bloodier the forced unity will have to be. Those who fret about the ''un-Christian'' aspects

*I rely heavily here on the work of Dr. Henry Paolucci.

of compelling others to behave in a manner contrary to their beliefs must keep this in mind (unless they see something Christian in making martyrs of us all at the hands of the Marxist reorderers). It will be far more difficult and require far more "intolerance" to bring a more paganized America to its senses than it will to turn things around today—while a still substantial majority of the country considers itself theist and Christian. But it would have been easier in, say, 1951.

If we begin that reordering, it will bring purpose and a mission, and a sane identity, to our troubled countrymen, especially to those in the rag-tag bands of the young who are not beyond hope. They would be freed from searching for an identity in the ephemeral fashions and fads that whirl about in our times. When they intone "Who am I? What's it all about?" someone could give them an answer besides Charles Manson. (Speaking of fashions—it is revealing to note just in passing that fashion design of late has become costume design. The designers give uprooted Americans an identity, a uniform: Army jackets, cowboy boots, farmers' overalls, Emilio Zapata mustaches, Nehru jackets, Mao jackets, the Gatsby look, the Godfather look, the 30's look, the 40's look, the 50's look—but no 60's look, or 70's look. Moderns have no identity!) The young would finally be given real equality of opportunity—to save their souls.

We would also be able to come up with an answer for them on the drug issue; at last. No more of the tortuous presentations of conflicting medical reports about the damage drugs do to our genes, our chromosomes; how they make us bald, impotent (that was the ultimate secular threat: keep smoking that weed, kids, and the rest of the night won't be any fun) and give bad example to our kid sisters who will abuse dope even though big brother might not. We could tell them, simply, that it is wrong to alter your moral consciousness, whether with martinis or a joint; wrong to destroy your ability to act as a moral agent, to discern good from evil with the maximum of your wits about you. It is indicative of our drift from Christianity that such thoughts are only on the outer periphery of the discussion over drug use. We seem never to think of the idea that a drink is *not* an obvious evil because it can be taken in such moderation that it will not alter our moral capacities, while a drug is used precisely to achieve such alteration.

We could also, *finally*, give the young the reason why the rock musicians (the ones who know what they are doing and tell us so) can be forbidden access to our homes. We could take their scrawny guru at his word, accept his declaration of war on our *pietas*—"Mothers and daughters across the land, your sons and your daughters are beyond your command"—and brand the efforts of the enemy for what they are: anti-Christian. We will also be able to see, for our own needs, why the rock stars, like Schrag, have led the attack on the image of the "clean-cut" American.

199

Maybe we could even turn out a television series to teach the message
—maybe a spinoff on the Lefties' assault on us, Archie Bunker. (I'm sure that
all of you have figured out by now what is supposed to be ludicrous about
Bunker. He really *believes* all that tripe about Duty, Honor, Country, God,
family, neighborhood, sexual reserve. What a boor!)

We will have to invent a new character. What should we call him? Your
choice. Maybe on the first show we can have him coming home from his
therapy session to find his daughter spaced out on drugs in the arms of her
"fellow." Our hero's jaw would drop as he sees her tripping across a hassock,
trying to pull up her jeans and stash her nickel bag in her pocket at the same
time. (Audience laughter.) Then our hero would ask them into the den. Where
he would take down his copy of Herbert Marcuse to find out if their evening of
entertainment was genuine—whether it was part of the Great Refusal. (Camera
cut—to an upstairs bedroom where our leftwing Edith would be opening a
bottle of sleeping pills in a room strewn with copies of magazines of nude men.
Canned laughther—hilarious. Cut—back to the den.) The hero's daughter
begins to mumble something about *Eros and Civilization*. Her fellow is rummaging through our hero's jacket pockets for enough money for another fix.

But we really couldn't be that vicious. Maybe let the show run for a week or
so, as a kind of shock treatment for those who would profit from such an expose
of their lives.

Maybe we could even give our leaders a dose of confidence. Make sure that
we don't have any repeats of the Fords, who tried to show their open-
mindedness on the question of their daughter's sex life and their son's drug use
by proudly proclaiming that they would want to talk about such questions. *Are*
they open questions? They might learn from the Christian people of America
that the best and the brightest of Americans no longer have to be moral neuters.

Chapter XII

Adeste Fidelis

OUR TIME in history is no different: the Faith requires faith, and faithful, those willing to believe that the world has experienced an event which sublates the most profound of pagan legend and myth; that there has been a divine intercession in history that serves as fulcrum for time and eternity; that the Word, *really*, was made Flesh, born unto us nearly two thousand years ago in a stable in Bethlehem. It is true. We have Christ's word. Christians are Christians because they are willing to live by the words of that Nazarene carpenter; to accept that He truly was, as the centurion intuited, the Son of God sent to earth to teach all men the Way of His Father, and accept it with bended knee. To winnow Christ is to reject Him. He is "a jealous God," as C.S. Lewis used to say, who will have no strange gods before Him, even those whose praises are sung by pipe-smoking men in tweed. We must make a choice. A hyphenated Christian is no Christian.

We must also face up to the fact that Christianity in America is in a crisis stage. We might have to defend the Faith in a way we will find distasteful: openly and firmly. Not necessarily each and every one of us. It is possible, and perhaps wise, for many to just ignore the constant drumbeat with which the anti-Christian forces in our society taunt and tempt us. It is the wisdom of the world, and it will take a near full-time effort to meet the assault on its own scholarly terms, especially now that all too often we can no longer depend upon the men we used to assume would do that full-time work for us: our clergy.

It is possible, and perhaps wise, to close our eyes and ears to the theological sophistry of the updaters, just as we would to any other base temptation; to refuse to put our faith on the firing line for the clerical debunkers' potshots, as if it were a preference for a brand of beer or a football team we are willing to desert if a better one comes along. There is nothing anti-intellectual in that, for a Christian. Christ is not a cultural thesis. That Dickens might be a better writer than Thackeray can be argued. Whether Freud or Hugh Hefner knows more about the meaning of life than Christ cannot; by Christians. Theologians can, and *ought* to, take it upon themselves to demonstrate *why* that is so. Remember when they used to? That is their job. But when the rest of us are faced with the scheming contrivances of those who seek to spread doubt about Christ, we are acting entirely fittingly if we treat them as did Christ their prototype: ''Begone, Satan.'' We have to, *live by* Christ's words (that is our job) even if we would lose every debate with every sophomore in every junior college in America who asks us why.

The Faith is not a parlor game. We do not *have* to be learned and bright to be Christian; we walk in the shoes of fishermen.

We probably could live out our lives like that, placing the updaters in the same category with the secular intellectuals whose company they seem to find so amenable—and then ignore the lot of them.

Of course if they preach from our pulpits, that will require some effort. But we might be able to do it. I am reminded of my old parish in the Bronx. The parishioners there adjusted to their Teilhardian pastor by making him an innocuous object of polite ridicule: ''Bejabbers, did you hear what he came out with today?'' It was polite because it was never said to his face—which he probably would argue was more of an insult. Why wouldn't they approach him and ''talk out'' his attacks on their beliefs? They came to see ''where his head was at''—as they say at Princeton.

But this kind of resignation is difficult for those who have children in their formative years. For them, the rejection of the updater pitch must be coherent and communicable. How to do that? Well, I would not suggest the obvious —reading the updaters. Unless one is used to these wars, that can do more harm than good. In preparing this book I was forced to immerse myself more than is my wont in the updater ''classics.'' It was not long before a most undesirable reaction set in, one which gives a clue to the defections of so many young priests and ministers. I found myself, despite myself, becoming a spectator to a well wrought (in secular terms) scholarly dispute, open to inadmissible suggestions, even those about the nature of God. I must admit that there were nights when I found it difficult to pray. I began to gravitate toward the thought that for all but the most backward of Christians, theology is a discipline devoted to the selection of the most intelligent angle of disbelief. I overcame it. My library shelves are filled with better company. But what of idealistic young people? When theologian after theologian attacks the Faith, building layer upon layer of doubt, it is difficult *not* to come to the conclusion that the brightest, the best, and the most sincere of Christians in our time are committed to a demythologizing of Christ. The thought begins to haunt: are we witness in our time to a widespread and *healthy* wave of change in the history of Christianity? Cox, Bonhoeffer, Teilhard, Bultmann, Gutierrez, Baum, Callahan, Novak, Rosemary Reuther, Dewart, Coffin, Raymond Brown, *The Common Catechism*—can they all be wrong? Especially if you are a young seminarian who hears nothing else, or an adult who has never received university-caliber assistance in reading the great Christian intellectuals of the past. I'll tell you, I wouldn't want to have picked up Gutierrez before reading Newman and Belloc.

It might be better, then, for those who feel that it will be necessary to answer the Modernists, to undertake a serious reading of the champions of the Faith before entering the enemy camp. Perhaps C.S. Lewis' *Mere Christianity* for starters. It might also be wise to become a regular reader of one or more of the serious (which does not mean "intellectual," necessarily) and still orthodox Christian newspapers or journals in order to pick up the streams of the current discontent: to become aware of the new leaves of the updater challenge as they unfold. As I write, there are new additions. By the time you read these words there will be new and more sophisticated versions. A thinking Christian must be able to catch the new slants as they are thrown at us. "Immanence" . . . "God is Love" . . . "Seeing Christ in our brothers" . . . they all can seem healthy expressions of the Faith (and often enough are, when used in the proper context by still Christian preachers), but are likely to be the wedge used by the Modernists to open the door to our minds.

Far too many adult Christians, especially well educated and successful business and professional types who want to be seen as something more than knee-jerk Christians (which—I repeat—is far better than losing the Faith), fail to develop a mature understanding of their Christian heritage. Let me be blunt. The updaters would not have been able to water down the Faith to the extent they have if Christians had been familiar with the great Christian writers of the past. They didn't win us over; we were duped.

But if we can learn to stand on the shoulders of Lewis, Chesterton, Belloc, Newman, Knox, and their colleagues, we still might be able to hold the Faith as confidently as our fathers, and to state as confidently that: there is a God, the Father Almighty, the maker of heaven and earth, and that Jesus Christ is His only Son and our Lord, who was conceived by the Holy Ghost, born of the Virgin Mary; who suffered, died and was buried, then raised from the dead to sit on the right hand of the Father, from whence he shall come to judge the living and the dead. It's all true. We Christians *start* from here. It is the given. We can go on believing as did all the saints and the finest minds of the Christian West until the secularist assault caused some to stray into error. There is no intelligent reason to desert the company of Paul, Stephen, Augustine, Loyola, Aquinas, the Christian knights, Good King Wenceslas, the Pilgrims, Washington kneeling at prayer at Valley Forge, the American Marines in prayer on lonely Pacific atolls, Douglas MacArthur—everyone in the history of the West who knew that there was more to life than a selfish pursuit of pleasure. All those who knew that the noblest of human behavior develops out of a devotion to God and country. It is the Coxes of this world who have trouble, not us. They are the ones who want to reject "all that" and still stay sane.

And we must make them *say that*: that they stand with Voltaire, Marx, Feuerbach, Freud, and the editors of *Screw* against "all that"—and Christ. They can only go on talking out both sides of their mouths, suggesting that Christ might be one of their coterie, if we allow them to march through our lives as if there is nothing demanded of a man who calls himself a Christian.

There is too much at stake to equivocate. The Faith still needs its defenders, and Christians have a responsibility to do that. We are to teach all nations in the name of Christ, including our own. We are to love our neighbors as ourselves —which we fail to do if we hesitate to help them find their way to Christ. To shy from that responsibility is to assist in bringing our neighbors to Sartre's *La Nausée*.

Jesus Saves—it is that simple. We have His Word. The most spectacular fairy tale of all—the one with the happiest of endings, truly living happily for ever after—is true, once we kill the dragon. We have His Word. We are not alone. The solemnity of quiet chapels, the spectacle of ocean beaches at sunrise, the marvel of watching our children grow, those precious moments when family commitment radiates an almost visible glow of love in a holiday season room: they are all reflections, tantalizing glimpses, of a joy we were meant to share with our Maker in Heaven—once we kill the dragon.

Joy to the World

As I write these last pages the Christmas season draws near. For me that means all of the usual enjoyable hoopla. But it also holds the promise of repeating a private pleasure I experienced for the first time, in a conscious way, just a few years back. It came about on a Christmas morning just a few months after I had taken a new position teaching in a public high school about sixty miles north of Manhattan, an area still semi-rural, but populated by many commuters. I had bought a house in the area myself.

It was my first Christmas out of a structured Christian environment. Until then I had attended Catholic schools, and taught for five years in a Catholic high school. Christmas, even after the updater inroads, was always a special occasion in that atmosphere. The crassest of the modernizers stand in pious silence before the manger—so far, anyway.

But that year there was not a hint that there was a reason for the "holiday break." The school was barren of Christmas decoration. As the kids left the classroom at the bell, after I had wished them all a "Happy Holiday" (yes, I cringed), a few passed by nearly furtively and said quietly, "Merry Christmas, Mr. Fitzpatrick." It was as if we were members of some strange and sinister cult, fearful of being overheard. The snow was piled deep on the ground and heavy on the evergreens in the courtyard. The country air was brisk and clear. It was supposed to be the happiest time of the year, but an empty feeling came over me. I caught a taste of what it must be like to be an atheist.

At home, of course, things were better. The manger was propped near the base of a freshly cut Christmas tree, bathed in an orange glow from the small lights. Carols filled the living room, although they were from my own records. The radio station was still playing the Rolling Stones. The Christmas cards with dozens of different Nativity scenes were draped across a hutch entwined with Christmas holly. If you move in the right circles you can still get "sectarian" Christmas cards.

But those last hours on the job lingered with me. Could a people who really believe in Christ, a Christian people, allow Christ to be driven from their lives? Does America still believe "all that?" Or has Christ been separated from Xmas and our country more than I suspected? Was I like a child learning about Santa Claus? Finally catching on to the great secret of the 20th century now that I was out of the Catholic ghetto?

Christmas morning came just a few days later. I had decided to attend the seven o'clock Mass in a small stone chapel, once the property of a wealthy landowner in the area, that our parish uses for the earliest, sparsely attended Mass. There was not a trace yet of the sun in the East. In the dark, I scraped the frost and the light dusting of early morning snow from my car window. The stars were bright and strong, unchallenged by street lights in the country sky. As I rode down a heavily wooded road toward the chapel, they seemed strangely low. One in particular seemed so bright and clear that I joked to myself that it must be the Christmas star. I flipped the radio to get the scores from the basketball games of the night before; but instead, the simple and haunting strains of "Hark the Herald Angels Sing" came over the air, sung by a boys' choir. I rode on, the stars pressing down overhead and a chill breeze sifting through the opening of my vent window, the words of the hymn coming across in bell-like purity without a trace of static. As the cross atop the fieldstone chapel and the warm light through the stained glass windows came into view up the deserted, snow-ridged road, the hymn came to its conclusion. I am too private a person to try to describe my reaction graphically. Let it be sufficient to say that I exulted. The pieces fell in place. "Christ is born in Bethlehem . . . Glory to the new born King."

You see, it *is* all true. The story that rests at the heart of the Christian West is a *true* story. We have His word for that. They can't take that away from us, no matter how hard they try, and no matter who tells us otherwise. Christ the Saviour *was* born.

Index

208